Why rich people give

Theresa Lloyd
Philanthropy UK

Published by

Supported by

The Esmée Fairbairn Foundation, the Gatsby Charitable Foundation and the Lloyds TSB
Foundation for England & Wales have supported this project by *Philanthropy* UK. The facts
presented and vies expressed, however, are those of the author and not necessarily those
of the Foundations.

Published by Association of Charitable Foundations
5th Floor
Central House
14 Upper Woburn Place
London WC1
Email: acf@acf.org.uk
www.acf.org.uk
Registered charity number 802171

Editing, design and production Laura McCaffrey

Printed and bound by Unwin Brothers

ISBN 1-897916-11-6

Contents

Foreword by Lord Joel Joffe   3

Acknowledgements   5

Introduction   8

Summary of the report and key findings   11

Chapter One   Background and approach to the research   27

Chapter Two   The interviewees – who they are and what they give to   35

Chapter Three   Influences on philanthropy – faith, family and community   51

Chapter Four   Early experiences of giving – developing a philosophy of philanthropy   62

Chapter Five   Motivations, incentives and rewards   77

Chapter Six   Relationships with recipients   111

Chapter Seven   The practice of giving   135

Chapter Eight   Wealth, security and family   175

Chapter Nine   Wealth and responsibility   198

Contents

Chapter Ten   The state, the media and perceptions   221
of wealth and philanthropy

Chapter Eleven   The experience of asking for money   243

Chapter Twelve   The experience of professional advisers   258

Chapter Thirteen   The UK context – estimating the value of   275
private gifts in the UK by Cathy Pharoah

Chapter Fourteen   Major philanthropy – how do we compare   281
with the US?

Chapter Fifteen   Implications and recommendations   303

Appendices

One   Questionnaires   330

Two   Extract from *Wealthy and Wise* by   349
Claude Rosenberg Jr., October 1998

Three   Bibliography   356

Four   Criticism of trusts and foundations   357
Comment from Luke Fitzherbert of the
Directory for Social Change

Foreword

Lord Joel Joffe

As Chair of The Giving Campaign I was delighted to be asked to write the foreword of this important book. The vision which underpinned The Giving Campaign has been the strengthening of a culture of giving in the UK. A particular focus has been the affluent and wealthy, who give a smaller proportion of their income than the poor to charitable causes. However, I am aware that it has been difficult to develop strategies which are appropriate for this group, and I know from my time as Chair of Oxfam and as a donor myself that charities and the larger voluntary sector have been hampered by a lack of in-depth understanding of the attitudes and motivations of higher net worth individuals.

That deficiency has now been addressed. This book is based on the first in-depth research in the UK on the attitudes of people of substantial means to wealth – how they create it, keep it and spend it. Their stance on philanthropy is considered in the context of a range of topics associated with the management and allocation of wealth. The confidential interview process allowed people to express their views freely within a structured framework. This approach adds a richness and colour to a robustly analytical assessment.

The author is Theresa Lloyd who is a consultant in strategic planning, fundraising and governance to the non-profit sector, and Director of Philanthropy UK, set up like The Giving Campaign as a three-year project to promote philanthropy. Following a City career Theresa Lloyd worked with Save the Children, where she established corporate fundraising, and then as UK Director of ActionAid. She has a wealth of knowledge and experience of major donors, and was uniquely placed both to carry out the research on which this book is based and to interpret its significance.

While it was essential that the research and its analysis would be underpinned by rigorous methodology, it is equally important that the interpretation of the information is accessible, and provides useful and practical guidance for a number of groups. These include charities and other organisations who wish to solicit support from those of substantial means, professional advisers to the wealthy such as accountants, bankers and lawyers, employers, the media, regulatory authorities and policy-makers such as the Charity Commission and the Treasury, as well as academic and membership institutions with an interest in fundraising and donor motivation, and complementary research programmes.

I am confident that this window into·the world of the wealthy will intrigue, infuriate and inspire in equal measure. It is my hope and belief that armed with this analysis those who seek partnerships with the wealthy and wish to see a strengthening of their commitment to social engagement will have a firm evidential base for their strategies. Everyone who cares about that commitment, and the improvement to social welfare, education, health, the arts, the environment, overseas aid and development and the whole range of causes which underpin our society which would result from a stronger culture of giving should read this book.

Lord Joel Joffe

Acknowledgements

This book could not have been written without the enthusiastic support of the funders of *Philanthropy* UK: the Esmée Fairbairn Foundation, the Gatsby Charitable Foundation (one of the Sainsbury Family Trusts) and the Lloyds TSB Foundation for England & Wales. Quite apart from their financial contribution, the Directors of these Foundations were unflagging in their commitment and contribution to the development of the project. As members of the Steering Committee, and on an individual basis, they were generous with ideas, contacts and time. The Steering Committee was chaired by Gillian Davies with unfailing good humour, dedication and sensitivity. The other members, who included the Chairman, Executive Committee members and the Chief Executive of the Association of Charitable Foundations were equally involved.

In the early stages of planning the research I was helped by an informal group of senior fundraisers from a range of sectors. They helped me to ascertain and refine the questions which those responsible for seeking donations would like clarified, and in some cases were willing to introduce the research project to one or more major donors.

There were others who were very helpful in identifying and recruiting interviewees for the research; among them were some of the 14 professional advisers who contributed significantly to the research in their own right. Also in this category are the 10 prominent volunteer fundraising leaders who equally pinpointed potential research candidates and presented their own perspective on the research.

Throughout the three years of the *Philanthropy* UK project I have been very encouraged by the generous support and backing of people in the sector. This period has been one of exploration of new models and approaches to philanthropy, and has been characterised by a generous sharing of ideas. I would like in particular to mention Amanda Delew and her colleagues at The Giving Campaign, Bernard Mercer and others at New Philanthropy Capital, Stephen Dawson and others at Impetus and Fiona Halton at Pilotlight. John Kingston and colleagues at the Charities Aid Foundation (CAF) have been equally helpful. I am especially grateful to Cathy Pharoah, who is Director of Research at CAF and very kindly agreed to write the chapter on the UK context. I would also like to acknowledge my appreciation of David Carrington who read the final draft and made very constructive suggestions.

The support was not confined to the UK: I particularly value the generous help of Francie Ostrower and Paul Schervish. Their work in the US was an inspiration for this research, and although we have never met and there is no benefit to them for this work, they were both, through email communication, very helpful with advice about their own approach.

Once the interviews had been completed I was extremely fortunate to be able to involve Jane Ritchie, Founding Director of the Qualitative Research Unit at the National Centre for Social Research. She has been a major support, providing guidance on methodology, enabling me to marshal a mass of complex and sometimes conflicting information, forcing me to cut my initial drafts by as much as half and challenging any conclusions not evident from the data – all in a spirit of constructive progress.

The Framework analysis method, developed by Jane Ritchie and her colleagues, was used as the basis for the report. The challenging task of the management of the accumulation of raw data collected in the interview process was structured and reduced to more manageable proportions by this approach. This could not have been done without the commitment and competence of Ceri Johnson, who was Project Assistant for two years from October 2001. Her support was invaluable throughout her time with *Philanthropy* UK. She left the project on completing her Masters degree and in the last months of the project I have been helped by Mary Wright.

When I was at the point of analysing the data I was lucky enough to receive an offer of help from Susan Mackenzie, an American financial analyst and researcher who had recently moved to London and was looking for experience in the sector concerned with new philanthropy. I am very grateful for her input – the work on which causes are supported, and to what extent, reported in Chapter Two is largely her analysis.

As we considered the various options for the publication of this research we were delighted to be advised by Susan Mitchell, former Chair of the Hamlyn Foundation.

I am also very grateful to Laura McCaffrey, who managed the editorial and production process to an extremely tight timetable with charming efficiency.

Finally, it is no exaggeration to say that there is a group of people without whom this research and report would not have been possible: the 76 interviewees from a range of ages, backgrounds, sources of wealth and approaches to philanthropy who agreed to speak at length about some of their most private concerns, aspirations and attitudes. That they did so was itself a generous contribution to society, and its understanding of those of substantial means. Their willing introspection made the months spent gathering the information among the most rewarding of my professional life. I hope I have respected their willingness to participate by reporting their views accurately and in the spirit with which they were given.

If, in spite of this wealth of advice and interest there are misinterpretations or mistakes, they are entirely my own responsibility.

Introduction

As a fundraiser, the question of why the wealthy give – or do not give – to charitable causes has intrigued me for nearly 20 years. Between 1986 and 1994 one of my roles was to solicit support from higher net worth individuals for Save the Children and ActionAid. By the mid-90s, when the requirement for partnership funding for lottery-funded capital projects was introduced, I had moved into consultancy, and was advising organisations such as the Tate Gallery in its campaign to raise money for Tate Modern.

This encouraged me seriously to consider attitudes of the wealthier members of society in Britain to contributing to public good. I discovered that while there was much useful information available on attitudes of the wealthy in the US, nothing based on systematic individual research had been published in the UK. And while strategies and even policies were being developed on the assumption that what worked in the US would work here in the UK, this seemed unlikely. Our very different histories, traditions and attitudes to central government and the role of the state, particularly in the provision of welfare services, seemed to demand a different approach.

It was clear that research was needed which would mirror US analysis in terms of content and scope, but would be based on interviewees who live and work in the UK.

It was at about that time that *Philanthropy* UK was conceived. This was a three-year project to promote new philanthropy, set up by the Association of Charitable Foundations in April 2001 and funded by three leading grant-makers, the Esmée Fairbairn Foundation, the Gatsby Charitable

Foundation (one of the Sainsbury Family Charitable Trusts) and the Lloyds TSB Foundation for England & Wales.

Philanthropy UK was developed during a period of rapid change in the non-profit sector, with a number of concurrent new initiatives, including The Giving Campaign. A key impetus was to answer some of the current questions such as:

◆ Why does it appear that people in the US are more generous than those in the UK?
◆ Why are younger people who have made money in the City/dot.com business/IT not giving?
◆ What difference will the new tax regime for charitable donations make?
◆ What about some of the ideas and concepts, such as venture philanthropy, which are being developed in the US: will they work in the UK?
◆ What about new models for support of social enterprise; might they attract new funding?
◆ How do we ensure that we are aware of the various ideas and initiatives being developed, that we learn from each other and don't duplicate unnecessarily?

The project brief covered a range of tasks. A core component was the research and documentation of the attitudes and concerns of donors, and of those who do not give. This publication is the report of that research.

The research approach and methodology is described in detail in Chapter One. It has been undertaken with independent scrutiny and full neutrality.

Nevertheless, I bring my own background and understanding to the findings, based on my extensive experience. Information in this report is presented in three ways, with a clear distinction between:

◆ Direct quotes from interviewees (reported in italics).
◆ Explanation, comment and hypothesis, based on the research information.
◆ My own interpretation and analysis. This is provided separately at the end of each section, and underpins the recommendations.

The analysis enables us to consider how best to promote new philanthropy, particularly among the more affluent members of society.

We learn that there is no single route to strengthening a culture of giving among those who have the capacity to give most. Not only is there complex diversity among the wealthy, but a number of factors affect the propensity to give and the experience of philanthropy, each of them determined or at least influenced by different opinion-formers or decision-makers.

At the end of this report we draw together the implications and recommendations for these different groups, in the hope that some at least will be stimulated or provoked to change the way they approach the wealthy, so that more of them will be inspired to become full members of a UK society characterised by major philanthropy.

Summary of the report and key findings

Aims and design of the research

1. This research was undertaken to help promote philanthropy in the UK by developing a shared understanding of the attitudes of people of substantial means to wealth – how they create it, keep it and spend it. On the basis of that understanding, it is hoped that a range of not-for-profit institutions such as charities, education and arts organisations and the health care sector will be more effective in developing and managing their relationships with higher net worth individuals, and society in general will have a better awareness of how to promote philanthropy among this constituency.

2. Because of the nature of the information required, the study was undertaken using small scale qualitative methods. Semi-structured, exploratory interviews were undertaken with 76 people of high net worth (largely between £5m and £100m) currently living in England and Wales. Additional interviews were carried out with 10 volunteer fundraising leaders ("askers" – many also with significant assets) and 14 leading professional advisers to the wealthy, also high earners.

The interviewees and what they support

3. The interviewees ranged in age from 34 to 80 years and four-fifths were male. Three-quarters were born in the UK and a quarter in other countries. Two-thirds currently live in London or the South East although they were often born and brought up elsewhere. Most were currently married (86%) and almost all had children or stepchildren (92%).

4. Reported levels of annual income for three-quarters of the sample who gave this information lies between £100,000 and £2 million. A minority had incomes significantly above this level. The majority (70%) were people whose wealth was self-made. Of these, just over half had made their money professionally (generally through banking, with a few in the law); the rest created their wealth from business or other entrepreneurial efforts. Just over a quarter inherited or married wealth.

5. Estimates of the level of giving were commonly reported as between 5% and 10% of income, although they actually ranged from under 1% to 25%. Some who had made money on flotation of a business had set up a trust with a significant proportion of the proceeds. A small minority were allocating little or nothing from their own income or wealth, but distributing the income from a trust established by a parent or other relative.

6. Charitable giving varied by sector, with arts, culture and social welfare receiving the most funding from the interviewees, followed by health, medical research, and education. Overseas development, environmental and religious organisations received the least support.

Influences: faith, family and community

7. For some, the influences of religion are seen as central to the family values that had been formative in attitudes to giving. Others attribute their early experiences of giving to cultural influences related to their origins, rather than directly to religious tenets. Those from Asian and Jewish backgrounds, even if no longer observant, are linked to strong social networks which reinforce the values and sense of identity underpinning their philanthropy.

8. In addition to, or in place of, religion, many features of family background and upbringing were cited as influential to philanthropic practice. For those who had inherited wealth, there had often been a history of family giving to their local community. A sense of community involvement was also expressed by some self-made entrepreneurs with strong local links, all born outside the South East of England. Others spoke about a parental influence which had brought a sense of responsibility to help "less fortunate" or disadvantaged people within wider society.

9. A third factor, important for some people from Jewish or Asian communities, was that they or their parents had been immigrants to the

UK. People talked explicitly about wanting to contribute to the society which had given refuge to the family.

Early experiences of giving – developing a philosophy of philanthropy

10. Among those who are not members of a family or community with a strong philanthropic tradition, few started serious giving at an early stage. Almost all of the experience of early workplace giving was based in US institutions. Being asked and managed effectively was an important early experience.

11. An individual's process of clarifying philanthropic potential is a blend of self-analysis and external factors. For some the combination of time and the realisation of wealth, linked to existing interests, was sufficient to activate their charitable impulses. Others required an outside stimulus – a dynamic individual, a life-changing experience, a family illness – to point the way.

12. People do not on the whole start as strategic givers. Even those who come from families with a strong philanthropic tradition want to develop their own philosophy.

Motivations, incentives and rewards

13. Although multiple in their origin and variable in their manifestation, the influences that emerge fall under five broad heads:

a) **Belief in the cause** is the strongest motivator, and choice of a cause is often influenced by a wish to change or enhance society's systems or structures in line with a particular interest or belief.

b) **Being a catalyst for change** includes making a real difference – to society, institutions or individual lives – and getting value for money.

c) **Self-actualisation** covers the satisfaction of personal development – applying expertise in a different sector, learning new skills, directing money which might otherwise go to the government, addressing causes with a personal connection and defining a place in history.

d) **Duty and responsibility** is about the satisfaction of conscience, the obligations of the privileged to those less fortunate and the desire to "put something back" into society.

e) **Relationships** encompass the fun, enjoyment and personal fulfilment of involvement with a range of people. These may include the senior staff of the charity, beneficiaries and other donors. Donor networks feature strongly in some sectors and communities. A desire to join such networks may influence some.

14. The factor reported as most likely to increase the individual's overall level of giving is having more money. Finding a new cause about which people care passionately is next most important and a main factor for over half of those who responded. Better tax incentives are said to be important by around a third.

Relationships with recipients

15. After the initial gift, reinforcement comes from donors knowing that they are making a difference, being properly thanked and meeting like-minded people. The way in which the recipient organisation manages the relationship with the donor is a crucial element in the successful development of a sustained commitment to a particular organisation, and by extension to the practice of philanthropy generally.

16. A key aspect of that relationship is that donors want to feel that they are valued and recognised for the interest, concern and passion which motivates them and that they are appreciated for more than their money.

17. The importance of effective and personal communications was constantly stressed. This includes establishing good contact at the outset, maintaining it throughout the relationship, providing regular and appropriate information and giving time and thought to the process.

18. Most people want some kind of appreciation or recognition for their giving from the recipient organisation; wishes range from a private expression of appreciation at one end to public and publicised recognition at the other.

19. In some cases, donors take active steps to avoid publicity or recognition for some or all of their donations. Many have sought

anonymity in certain cases, for a range of reasons, and a few channel their giving through a trust with a name unassociated with their family. Others see public or peer recognition as a bonus, or are persuaded by fundraisers to allow their name to be publicised as an endorsement and an encouragement to others.

20. Some donors said they want to be consulted or "have a say" in how their donations are allocated and spent. This is usually in areas in which they have skills – for example, project or financial management, or IT. People want to pass on expertise as well as money. They look for respect for that expertise, and appreciation for the giving of time which is involved in major philanthropy.

21. Governance was also noted by some as an important aspect of the donor-beneficiary link. For donors who are also board members, the essence of their involvement is related to governance. Certain concerns – about the size of a charity, the quality of leadership or control at head office, or levels of expenditure on fundraising or aspects of administration – had influenced a decision to give in some cases. Many donors make careful checks before they commit to an organisation.

22. There was evidence that the desire for influence and direction is stronger when major gifts are awarded, particularly for capital projects. Where there has been a really major gift to create a new venture – for example a building in a health or educational institution – then the donor may require involvement from the start. For those with family businesses, influence on project design or management is also seen as protecting the family name.

The practice of giving

23. Most interviewees receive a large number of unsolicited requests and well established personal trusts or well known philanthropists can expect up to 1,000 letters a year. A significant minority of those interviewed review all requests. People with established foundations and an administrative infrastructure may have requests filtered on the basis of known criteria. For the majority who do not review all requests, unsolicited applications and "junk mail" are discarded unread. The two most important criteria in responding to a request are the nature of the cause and who asks, closely followed by opportunities to "make a difference".

24. This desire to focus on impact and obtain what is seen as value for money can occasionally deter people from supporting big charities, which were sometimes associated with perceptions of unnecessary bureaucracy. A reluctance to fund core costs, for small as well as large organisations, was mentioned frequently. For many donors the calibre of the individual leaders of the organisation is also crucial.

25. In addition to any major gifts, everyone makes what they regard as small donations, usually in response to requests from people they know, and many recognised an element of reciprocity. A few set aside a pot for gifts to causes or projects where a donation below £1,000 is appropriate – local causes, sponsorships, support of gap years, hardship cases or disaster appeals, for example.

26. Over half the interviewees wished at some time to remain anonymous in their giving. Motives ranged from what might be perceived as selfish – not wanting to be pursued by others – to sensitivity to appearing to be flaunting their wealth or being patronising – whether to individuals or local communities.

27. Many of those interviewed use more than one mechanism for their giving. These include the setting up of charitable trusts, Gift Aid, community foundations and CAF accounts.

28. Half the interviewees have set up a charitable trust and on the whole recognise the benefits of this mechanism, citing tax advantages and the fact that they can involve the whole family. They see it as a strategic commitment to philanthropy, as opposed to the one-off gifts which Gift Aid now allows to be made tax-efficiently. Some of those with their own charitable trusts have serious reservations about one or more aspects of such trusts, including the associated bureaucracy, advice about concentration of shareholdings and monitoring by the Charity Commission, the lack of privacy, inconsistency of government policy to allocation of company shares to trusts, and criticism by the Directory of Social Change.

29. The availability of tax relief for one-off gifts under Gift Aid offers an alternative which does not require a long-term commitment, provides privacy and lack of scrutiny by outsiders and is relatively simple. Of those who had used Gift Aid, the majority spoke positively about the process and the mechanism, because of these factors. A significant minority were strongly critical of the process, largely because of the complexity of the tax relief process, and lack of familiarity by some charities.

30. A group of donors, all based in the North East, had had very positive experiences with a community foundation. Some have their own charitable trust but have also established a fund within the community foundation for local projects.

31. A small minority use a CAF account (always alongside Gift Aid and other mechanisms) and see it as a good mechanism for small gifts.

32. There was limited experience of giving shares. Those who had were positive about the idea in principle. However, there were some concerns about the complexity of the process and the decline in the value of the shares in 2002 between the announcement of the donation and the realisation of the sale proceeds by the charity.

33. Although payroll giving was the most tax-efficient mechanism for regular giving during the period of the research and some interviewees were working for financial institutions and companies which had such a scheme in place, no-one was then using this mechanism, although one had in the past.

34. The vast majority of respondents think that tax incentives encourage giving in principle and take advantage of the benefits for themselves. But while recognising improvements in the tax incentives, particularly with the concept of giving shares, many compared the situation in the UK unfavourably with that in other countries, especially the US. There were two main strands to their suggestions: simplify the administration of the mechanism for one-off gifts (Gift Aid) for higher rate taxpayers; and create opportunities to obtain tax relief on irrevocable pledges of capital gifts made in the lifetime of the donor. A small number of people also referred to the absence of incentives to give works of art and shares in private companies.

Wealth, security and family

35. Interviewees had very different attitudes to money, confidence in their financial position and sense of what is necessary for them to feel secure. Around three-quarters of interviewees said they felt reasonably secure. People running their own family businesses were among those who felt relatively less secure. Younger people expressed concern about the range of unknown expenses and family responsibilities for which they might have to provide – children, parents, health risks. Older people, with least

control over their income, felt less secure. Some were clear that their insecurities about money had complex bases and it is recognised that feelings about such matters are an intensely personal judgment.

36. The question of how much money to transfer to children was a matter of major concern across a range of backgrounds, irrespective of the origin of the wealth. Some were reforming their approach in the light of changing attitudes of society to the traditions of inheritance, their observations of the perceived adverse effect (in some cases) of inheriting major wealth, the different characters and career choices of their children, and understanding that children may not wish to go into the family business. Many were clearly trying to strike a balance between leaving an "appropriate" amount for their children and for other, particularly charitable, purposes. Those with family businesses had least qualms about passing the bulk of their assets to their children.

37. Some people expressed the view that inheritance may be beneficial to society but may be detrimental to the interests of individual children. It was recognised that great houses and estates are a vital part of the national heritage, culture and local community. Not only was it felt inappropriate for them to be a drain on the taxpayer; more importantly, it was believed that the family link ensures greater care.

38. Views about inheritance tax (IHT) and the impact of transferring wealth to children were complex to unravel. Most thought that people should be allowed to decide what happens to their wealth on their death. There was also widespread criticism of current administration of IHT: people see it as a disincentive, inefficient and avoidable. It was commonly viewed as an unjust form of double taxation and an ineffectual mechanism to redistribute wealth. In the context of discussing IHT, there were several references to the benefits of the US approach to planned giving.

Wealth and responsibility

39. Most people are well aware of the choices they enjoy because of their wealth. Several activities and interests were identified, ranging from altruistic initiatives to the creation of collections (themselves a valuable asset) and engagement in a range of enjoyable pursuits, including the arts.

40. There is a range of views about the social obligations of wealth. Reactions are linked to the opportunities that people felt were provided

by wealth – the possibility of allocation or choice between family commitments, individual pleasures and obligations to a wider society. However, many of those who feel it should be seen as an obligation also emphasise that it is a personal choice.

41. The number of people who are positive about the principle of tithing – allocating a percentage of their income to giving – far exceeds the number who actually do so. Nearly all of those who think it is a good idea and practise it, at least to some extent, come from a Muslim, Jewish or strong Christian tradition such as the Quakers. It was suggested that establishing a target expectation could be part of "training" to give, or could help to identify a source of income which could be allocated charitably to ensure compliance with the aspiration to tithe. Those who are less enthusiastic about the idea say they give in relation to the opportunities available rather than having any notion of a fixed quota.

42. There is very little support for the concept of "socially responsible investment" (SRI), and limited understanding of what it can involve. Most feel that their investment strategy should be driven by the highest possible return on capital and any diluting of that benchmark for asset managers would be dangerous. The most negative reactions were from those who equated SRI with political correctness. A few had considered SRI, but for various reasons, including complexity, cost and inertia, had not taken it further. Factors which might influence their asset allocation towards SRI included more competitive investment returns and a positive recommendation from their investment adviser.

43. Plans for leaving money to charity vary widely. Responses ranged from those, particularly without children, who say they will leave all or a significant proportion of their assets to their foundation or to charities they support, through those who have already fully endowed their charitable trust, to those who plan only to give in their lifetime. Some are as yet undecided.

The state, the media and perceptions of wealth and philanthropy

44. There is a range of views about the proper extent of the role of the state, but virtually universal agreement that the state should pay for "basics" including health and education, that the public sector cannot do everything and that private philanthropy should lever rather than substitute for government funding. Some feel that the state is not funding its core responsibilities and that the private donor, via charities, is picking up what

should be state-funded activities. Charities are seen as more likely to be pioneering – creating models of best practice not always taken up by the public sector.

45. Most endorse the idea of some form of partnership between state support and private philanthropy in some cases, and for the majority this is seen as a practical necessity, rather than a political ideology. Others feel that private funding in partnership with government support is less attractive or appropriate in areas they consider the basic responsibility of the state.

46. There is a widespread feeling of unhappiness about the status and respect accorded to philanthropy in the UK. Such perspectives were supported by all with experience in asking for money. For many, the status of philanthropy is linked to the perceived complexity of the attitudes of the English to money and wealth creation, and to class, and the absence of role models or indeed expectations that people in a position to give will do so. An additional facet is the perceived reluctance of the English to talk about money.

47. Several people spoke of the role of the media in generating or perpetuating negative attitudes to wealth and charitable giving. A range of reasons were suggested for this, including envy and resentment of the rich, a lack of understanding of wealth creation, and scepticism about motives, linked, but not confined, to political giving. It was suggested that this led to a desire to give discreetly and more crucially, discouraged a culture of giving.

48. There was also some comment about the apparent ambivalence of the current government to philanthropy. It was seen as wanting the wealthy to give but at the same time sending out messages of "a bias against the rich".

49. The question of how best to recognise outstanding philanthropy and encourage people to be role models was seen as difficult and complex. Some people talked of league tables, such as those being developed by *The Rich List*. Others talked of the importance of giving being seen as the thing to do. It was suggested that one approach is to recognise the need for a range of role models, both as entrepreneurs and as philanthropists. The lack of a tradition or culture of giving among some people with wealth was also identified. The City is a key constituency for this and there was a call for greater focus on the workplace and the role and responsibility of employers.

Asking for money

50. Those with in-depth experience of asking for money suggested a range of factors which create and reinforce a commitment to make a major donation. They highlight the same features which the donor interviewees identified as important influences on their giving.

51. All recognise that a passion for the cause is vital. This may exist already, or might be created through effective introduction to the activities of the organisation, and the particular project. Any approaches must be carefully researched and planned. The level of gift must be identified and the volunteer fundraiser supported by a first class professional team which has high internal status within the recipient organisation. That team must also operate within a corporate culture in which those who deliver the mission see the nurturing of relationships with major donors as part of their role and essential to creating the partnerships which will sustain their organisation.

The experience of professional advisers

52. The experience and perceptions of the advisers reflect the range of attitudes and concerns reported by wealthy people themselves. Advisers are of the view that the factors which make an allocation to charitable giving more likely are being self-made/entrepreneurial, aged at least in their forties or fifties and coming from a strong faith tradition. They felt that some who have inherited wealth and come from a family with a tradition of philanthropy may also give, but this is less likely when there is the responsibility and maintenance cost of an estate and collection being held for the next generation. Other factors which are felt to encourage charitable giving are a desire to avoid tax, a reluctance to pass on too much to the children and a wish for involvement in a cause, with accompanying recognition.

53. Some advisers observed that attitudes to leaving money to children may change; a combination of pressure from the children themselves, a realisation that the children are able to handle wealth and a sense that "blood is thicker than water" may account for this.

54. Advisers reported that feelings of financial insecurity are unrelated to actual levels of wealth, but are linked to a lack of confidence that lost or diminished assets could be replaced. Having such confidence was felt more likely among entrepreneurs. Estimates of the level of wealth needed for financial security varied, but the most common range (reflecting client

actuality) was £30m to £50m. A few advisers were aware of the theories of Claude Rosenberg , and advocated their application as part of a general programme of awareness-raising in the UK.

55. Few advisers saw the active promotion of philanthropy as part of their role, but nearly all see themselves as having a responsibility to advise their clients of the options, mechanisms and benefits, both in terms of tax and for the family. Some observed that a lack of understanding of the real level of wealth combined with the absence of tradition or expectation of giving and, in some cases, perceived complexity, leads to inactivity. This is reinforced by uncertainty as to the appropriate level at which to give and lack of time to devote to the question.

56. There was a range of views among advisers about the minimum level required to set up a charitable trust, from £100,000 to £10m. No-one suggested using a trust as a mechanism through which regular transfers of income could flow. There were comments about the absence of tax incentives to encourage gifts of capital in the lifetime of the donor, such as exist in the US.

The UK context

57. The total current private giving in the UK is in the region of £10.2bn. This comes from three main sources: individuals, charitable trusts and corporations. It represents about 1% of GDP. Participation in giving is decreasing, and the total given has only increased as a result of bigger gifts from those who do give.

58. Accurate data on giving levels by the very wealthy is scarce. Estimates of the top 30 donors in the *Sunday Times Rich List* put the giving figure at around 2.3% of their wealth. This one-year snapshot takes no account of the extent to which this includes the allocation of income from charitable trusts endowed by the donor. However, this compares with the 13% of annual wealth donated by the wealthiest donors in the US. Wealthy donors are four times more likely to give both time and money than poorer people.

Major philanthropy – how do we compare with the US?

59. Philanthropy in the US is a social institution that takes on meaning in a culture of individualism and private initiative and in the absence of a comprehensive welfare state, particularly as it relates to health provision.

It also operates in an environment which is antipathetic to the idea that the state has a very prominent role to play in the provision of welfare and higher education services, cultural facilities and community assets. US philanthropy is not just an option which wealth provides but is a defining characteristic of the elite. In all these respects the US differs markedly from the UK.

60. There are few families in the US who do not claim at least one great-grandparent as an immigrant, and the majority count an immigrant grandparent in their family. A strong theme which emerged from US research was the extent to which people feel gratitude for a society which gave refuge and economic opportunity. That motivation has been strong in the Jewish community in the UK, and as this research has shown, is emerging in some parts of the Asian community.

61. There are fundamental differences between the two tax regimes. In particular, a donor may allocate capital to be given to a charity at some future date, continue to enjoy the income from the capital and get tax relief at the time of the commitment. This addresses feelings of security and encourages people to plan. Such "planned giving" accounts for a significant proportion of major gifts received, particularly for endowments for cultural and educational institutions. US tax relief is available on gifts in kind, including works of art, and this has a major impact on the apparent level of charitable giving. Many who had lived in the US and the UK, and those with experience of asking for money from US and UK citizens, advocated the merits of mechanisms such as these.

62. Approaches to philanthropy also differ between the US and UK in the realm of volunteer activities, particularly board membership.

Implications and recommendations

63. There are many messages for different audiences that arise from the findings of this research. A number of recommendations are made for charities, central government departments (the Treasury in particular), employers, those concerned with donor guidance, professional advisers, the media, the Charity Commission and the wealthy themselves.

64. From the many recommendations those most significant to developing and sustaining philanthropic activity among the wealthy in the UK are listed below.

Charities

Charities interested in developing and maintaining long-term support from major donors should:

◆ **Be prepared to invest in initiating and managing relationships in a way which addresses the interests and concerns of the donor, and involves their partner, if they have one, rather than adopting a standard approach.**

◆ **Consider how to involve high level supporters in a way which demonstrates respect for the expertise which is the source of their wealth, and addresses legitimate concerns about governance and accountability.**

◆ **Involve trustees and senior staff in the cultivation of prospects and donors.**

◆ **Ensure that those likely to solicit support from potential major donors understand and promote tax-effective giving.**

(See Chapter Four on the early influence of being well managed, Chapter Five on motivations and Chapter Six on expectations and rewards of well managed relationships.)

Treasury

The Treasury should promote the development of family strategies for planning giving by:

◆ **Introducing tax relief at the time of a commitment of a gift of capital at some future date, allowing the donor or a nominee to benefit from the income of the capital for the interim period. (Similar to charity remainder trusts in the US).**

◆ **Introducing tax relief for gifts in kind, including works of art.**

◆ **Simplifying the system so that tax relief goes to donors irrespective of their tax rates or method of giving.**

(See Chapter Seven on the practice of giving, Chapter Twelve on the views of professional advisers and Chapter Fourteen on the US experience.)

Major employers in the City and industry

Major employers could promote the expectation and practice that senior staff will contribute financially and in other ways to the communities in which they live and work by:

◆ **Encouraging staff earning above a certain level to pledge a percentage of their income, as well as volunteering time, to charitable causes.**

◆ **Raising awareness internally and externally about these exemplary levels of giving by senior management.**

◆ **Backing such encouragement by making the process easy, for example, by providing advice on establishing a simple charitable trust, and expert guidance on the various tax-efficient mechanisms, including payroll giving, and ensuring that there are timely systems in place at the time of bonus awards.**

(See Chapter Four on early influences on giving, Chapter Ten on encouraging philanthropy, Chapter Twelve on the views of advisers on the need for expectations of levels of giving and Chapter Fourteen on the US experience.)

Professional advisers and others concerned with donor guidance

Those advising donors should encourage the development of family strategies for philanthropy by:

◆ **Raising the question of charitable giving with their clients.**

◆ **Ensuring that that they have the information, training and materials they need to give to their clients, explaining their options for tax-efficient giving, and also the benefits of developing a strategy for philanthropy.**

◆ **Helping clients to understand their actual level of wealth, the amount they want and need to allocate for themselves and heirs, and the amount remaining that they could give to charity should they wish to do so. (The work of Claude Rosenberg in this area is described in Appendix Two.)**

(See Chapter Five on the idea that "having more money" would increase giving, Chapter Eight on financial security, Chapter Nine for the discussion on tithing and Chapter Twelve on the attitudes and experience of professional advisers.)

The media

The media could do far less to discourage philanthropy and far more to promote a giving ethos by:

◆ **The accurate reporting of major gifts and imaginative volunteering.**

◆ **The promotion and celebration of role models from a range of backgrounds.**

◆ **The provision of better information about wealth creation and creators.**

◆ **The development of an informed understanding of the tax regime as it relates to charitable giving.**

(See Chapter Ten on perceptions of philanthropy and Chapter Fourteen on the US experience.)

Many of the proposals will only achieve maximum impact if reinforced by the activities of other people. If each individual constituency were to implement the proposals within their control or influence, there would be some progress. But for a sustained improvement there has to be real changes in the practices, attitudes and values of a range of decision-makers and opinion-formers. If all, or most, of the recommendations were put into practice there would, over the years, be a radical improvement in the exercise of elite philanthropy, and the development of a stronger culture of giving in the UK.

1

Background and approach to the research

What is philanthropy?

The term philanthropy has re-emerged in the UK in recent years. Often used as a synonym for giving, philanthropy is now generally said to cover not only traditional types of charitable giving, but also the range of ways in which people may show their general goodwill to society, including their extended family and communities. It includes giving time and expert advice. There may be a strategic commitment to a set of values as opposed to making one-off or reactive donations. It may also include making investment decisions that take into account the effect of the activities of the company on society, and backing businesses and individuals who are trying to improve the lives of others as well as make money for investors.

Essentially, philanthropy is the mechanism through which people express their humanitarian impulses, and confirm their membership of a wider society.

Purpose of the research

The purpose of the research was to develop a shared understanding of the attitudes of people of substantial means in the UK to wealth – its creation, holding and disposition. Philanthropy was considered in the context of a range of related topics. Issues discussed include influences and motivations to give, focus of and experience of giving, including constraints and barriers, attitudes to philanthropy, wealth, inheritance, financial security and social responsibility, views on mechanisms for charitable giving and tax benefits, and experience in asking others for money.

The analysis is intended to help answer some of the questions which inspired the establishment of *Philanthropy* UK (see Introduction). On the basis of that understanding, we hope that a range of institutions will be more effective in developing and managing their relationships with higher net worth individuals, and that society in general will have a better awareness of how to promote philanthropy among wealthier people.

Why we are focusing on the wealthier

Part of the impetus for the establishment of *Philanthropy* UK was the desire to understand the attitudes of those who had made significant money in the 1990s. It was thought that they were not as inclined to charitable giving as their American counterparts, nor as those from earlier generations in the UK.

In practice, it is difficult to gather accurate statistics about how much people give. As Cathy Pharoah, Head of Research at the Charities Aid Foundation, points out[1], because charities raise funds from the public in a multitude of ways, measuring this diverse set of activities is complex. Data comes from a range of sources, and is not always compatible. Definitions of what is charitable vary and analysts cannot be sure that they are comparing like with like – for example, it is not always clear whether tax relief is included. As Cathy Pharoah notes, it is particularly difficult to capture information on high value donors on the basis of random samples. Because of this, and the fact that legacies are not measured as part of reviews, the main surveys do not capture a representative sample of larger gifts.

Any statistics should therefore be treated as estimates. However, with these caveats, the research evidence indicates that in the UK as a whole throughout the 1990s, a smaller number of donors made larger and more numerous gifts. It may be that wealthier donors have been attracted to tax-effective methods of giving. The trends may be a response to more effective and focused fundraising. The value of estates bequeathed to charities, and inherited by children, appreciated significantly in this period.

[1] *A Lot of Give 2002* Charities Aid Foundation.

What is clear is that in this field, as elsewhere, we see a version of the 80/20 rule: a relatively small proportion of donors by volume accounts for a significant amount of charitable donations by value. Research reported in 2000[2] showed that the 3% of people who give more than £50 a month – £600 a year, or £1,000 grossed up for a 40% taxpayer – contribute more than half the total donations received.

We see similar links in giving by households (as opposed to individuals). Higher levels of education, home ownership, income, wealth, age and spending power are strongly inter-related, and each appears to have a positive influence on giving behaviour. The analysis in Cathy Pharoah's *A Lot of Give* appears to underline the point that while only 10% of gifts are given tax-effectively, gifts made in this way, including legacies, account for at least half of all donations to charities. According to research[3], tax-effective givers are more likely to be from a higher social class, to have a higher level of education, to be a male head of household, to earn more and to give significantly more than those who do not give tax-effectively. Not surprisingly, the evidence shows that although the use of tax-effective giving is still at a relatively low level, rich people make much more use of it than those who are less well-off.

Over the same period, we have also seen increasing affluence (both absolutely and relatively) in the wealthiest 10% to 20% of the population. If this group could be encouraged to give more, and if the number of people giving tax-effectively, and giving more than £1,000 a year could be increased, there would be a disproportionate and significant impact on charitable receipts.

Cathy Pharoah has provided a current perspective on the UK context in Chapter Thirteen.

As the Institute of Fiscal Studies and others have pointed out, in economic terms charitable giving is a luxury good. Certainly for most people it is not an essential item of expenditure. The aim of this study is to provide a guide to the terrain, if not a detailed road map, for those who wish to explore the beliefs and aspirations of the wealthy.

Design and conduct of the research

Coverage and design

As indicated, the intention was not to focus only or even primarily on people's experience of giving, but to place philanthropy and attitudes to it

[2] *The UK Voluntary Sector Almanac 2000* NCVO Passey A, Hems L and Jas P
[3] Conducted by CAF, the Inland Revenue and NCVO in 2000, and quoted in *A Lot of Give.*

within the context of an overall approach to wealth management, family responsibilities, inheritance, taxation and the role of the state.

In considering the range of topics to be covered, I was able to refer to a number of sources of expertise, as described in the acknowledgements. I should repeat here my debt to two US publications: *Why the Wealthy Give*, by Francie Ostrower, published in 1995, and *The Mind of the Millionaire*, which presents findings from a national survey on "*Wealth with Responsibility*", published by Paul Schervish and John Havens in January 2002. In both cases, the authors were generous in allowing me to draw on their source questionnaires. This was not only to borrow from best practice, but to provide the basis for potential trans-Atlantic comparisons.

As the report of the research was to be of practical guidance to those seeking funds, in the early days of designing the questionnaire I also sought advice from an informal reference group of senior fundraisers with responsibility and experience across a range of sectors.

Because of the nature of the information required, the study was undertaken using small-scale qualitative methods. The issues being discussed were complex and much of the terrain covered was unknown at the outset. In addition, the use of flexible and responsive methods of questioning made it possible to explore in depth the factors affecting charitable giving and the influences that underlie donors' decisions.

Design and selection of the sample

The sample contained three groups:

People perceived to have substantial means.
This included those identified as philanthropists, but also people not known to be major givers. While it was not possible to know income and wealth levels before the interviews, the aim was to reach people with annual income levels of £250,000 and above, and net worth, including property and pension funds, of £5m and above. In the event, 11 people claimed a net worth below £5m and 14 reported an income level below £250,000 (see Chapter Two).

The sample was drawn from as wide a constituency as possible in England and Wales. Selection aimed to ensure optimum diversity in terms of age, sources of wealth, gender, ethnic origin and geographical location. A total of 76 people who were perceived to have substantial means were interviewed. Individuals were identified from a number of sources:

a) Those already known to the author, personally or by repute, as major donors to or ambassadors for a range of causes. They were approached either directly, or through someone known to them, with a request for an interview.

b) Major donors to a cross-section of charities in different sectors, and one community foundation, selected to ensure a range of geographical location, gender and ethnic origin. Individuals were approached by the nominating charity or foundation.

c) Those known to one of the project funders.

d) Clients of professional advisers. In this case the adviser (lawyer, accountant or banker) acted as intermediary, selecting against particular criteria – for example, source of wealth. It was unlikely that these intermediaries would have any knowledge of their client's approach to philanthropy or giving.

Given the name of the project and the topics to be covered, it is probable that anyone agreeing to be interviewed on such personal and private matters might be well disposed to the principle of research and the broad aims of the project, even if not at that stage identified as a high level donor. As we have shown, not all the interviewees were approached in the first place by the author, and it is not possible to give exact information on the numbers who declined to be interviewed. As far as we know it is in single figures.

A profile of the socio-demographic and other characteristics of the people interviewed is given in Chapter Two.

Volunteer fundraisers.
A further 10 people were interviewed on the basis of their experience in soliciting support in a wide range of sectors. Most were major givers as well as "askers", and their approach to their own giving was also explored. However, the main intention was to obtain the perspective of those with extensive experience of asking for money, and analyse whether and how their perceptions complemented or contradicted the accounts of the wealthy themselves.

The fundraisers were identified by the author and approached either directly or through someone known to the author who had a personal connection.

Professional advisers.
Fourteen professional advisers – such as lawyers, accountants and private bankers – were also interviewed for the study. Since we were interested in attitudes to inheritance, estate planning, social and other family obligations, it was a useful complement to the views of the wealthy to obtain the perspective of specialist advisers in this field. Again, these advisers are themselves people of means and givers, and their views on the main research questions were also explored.

Initial interviews were conducted with advisers known to the author. Further interviewees in this category were suggested either by these advisers, or, in a few cases, by their clients.

The interviews

The interviews needed to be conducted with great sensitivity. No similar research had been conducted in the UK and we were exploring topics regarded as very private. For that reason, the identity of participants remains confidential to very few people[4]; not even the project funders are aware of the names of those who have been interviewed, although they have made introductions in a few cases. Interviewees were assured of this confidentiality and that their personal information and views would be treated with full discretion. While the level of concern about such confidentiality varied, for some it was undoubtedly very important.

The interviews were semi-structured and all were conducted by the author. They were based on a questionnaire containing largely open questions, but with the opportunity for comments to be added at any stage. There were also a few structured questions, with multiple choice options, designed to mirror some of the US research to allow for later comparison. Verbatim responses were recorded manually – we decided not to tape-record in case this inhibited disclosure. The interview questionnaires are reproduced in Appendix One.

[4] The identity of participants is known to the author, the project assistant and the Chair of the Steering Committee.

Participants were asked to allow for up to two hours for the interview. A few people made it clear that less time could be allocated. In practice, the average time for interviews was one hour and 50 minutes. Some people were willing to have a second meeting, and many completed an email questionnaire to cover any outstanding questions. The location and time of the interview was at the preference of the interviewees. For most people it was either at their office or at their home.

While the focus of the research is about motivation and attitudes, people were asked about their levels of income and wealth (within broad categories) and about their levels of giving, and to which causes. Not everyone was prepared to answer these questions, but the majority did.

Interviews took place between January and November 2002. This period was one of volatility in the financial markets and in international affairs, and some undoubtedly felt less certain in their financial security over that period; indeed, a few interviewees made that point directly.

Analysis

Analysis of the interviews was undertaken using Framework, a method of qualitative data analysis which involves ordering and synthesising verbatim data within a thematic matrix. A series of thematic charts were prepared, each based on a broad substantive area and incorporating a summary of all the evidence relating to the topic concerned.[5]

Because the study was qualitative in design, it has been possible to explore the range and nature of factors and experiences that influence philanthropy. However, it cannot provide any statistical data relating to views or behaviours, nor determine discriminatory variables or the characteristics associated with them. Where any such conclusions are suggested by the data, they are presented only as hypotheses for further research.

Presentation

The approach of interviewees to the discussions varied widely, but a common – if not universal – feature was the appearance of inter-related themes in many of the answers. Matters which had already been explored came up in another context. This report aims to structure the issues into subjects and chapters, but the thought processes do not always lend themselves to rigid logical boundaries. In addition, each chapter is written so that it may stand alone, with cross-referencing where appropriate. In some cases this means that a topic may appear several times under a different section heading.

[5] The process is described in detail in *Qualitative Research Practice – A Guide for Social Science Students and Researchers*, edited by Jane Ritchie and Jane Lewis, Sage 2003.

Audiences for the research

While it is essential that the research and its analysis were underpinned by a rigorous academic methodology, it is equally important that the interpretation of the information is accessible, providing useful and practical guidance for a number of groups. These include:

◆ Organisations who wish to solicit support from those of substantial means.

◆ Those interested in developing new models of investment in social enterprise and the non-profit sector.

◆ Academic institutions with an interest in fundraising and donor motivation, and a complementary research programme.

◆ Membership and other associations with an interest in donor development such as the Association of Charitable Foundations, the Charities Aid Foundation, the Community Foundation Network, the National Council of Voluntary Organisations and the Institute of Fundraising.

◆ Regulatory authorities such as the Charity Commission.

◆ Policy-makers such as the Treasury, and other ministries with links to the voluntary sector, including the Home Office, the Department for Culture, Media and Sport (DCMS) and the Department for Education and Skills (DfES).

◆ Other organisations and projects exploring the field of philanthropy.

◆ Professional advisers to the wealthy such as accountants, asset managers, bankers and lawyers.

◆ Journalists and others who report on the voluntary sector and have an interest in the development of civil society.

2

The interviewees – who they are and what they give to

T his chapter provides a demographic and giving profile of the interviewees as a context for the main chapters of this report. It must be remembered that before the interviews it was impossible to predict key data such as age, origin of wealth, net worth and income. Steps were taken to ensure a reasonable geographic spread and gender balance. Special efforts were made to ensure that members of the Asian community were included. But with so many variables and such a small sample in what was an essentially qualitative study, it was not feasible to plan for any kind of representative pattern among the interviewees.

The sample and the data

There were three main groups in the study sample: people of substantial means, fundraisers ("askers" – many also with significant assets) and leading professional advisers to the wealthy. In total, 100 people were interviewed.

All the data given was taken at face value. Most of the demographic questions came at the end of the interview. This was deliberate, in the hope that the interviewee would be relaxed and confident in the process and more likely to offer the information. Those with only a short time available for the interview did not answer these questions.

Detailed information is given below for the main sample of high net worth individuals. Information about the fundraisers is given in Chapter Eleven, and about professional advisers in Chapter Twelve.

Net worth

The most significant characteristic of the main sample is that all have exceptionally high annual income and net worth compared with the national average.

Of the 76 interviewees, the actual wealth of 14 is unknown, including nine who were not asked and five who declined to answer the question. In general, the interviewees from the Asian community preferred not to give this or other financial information.

Of those who responded to this question, 40% had a net worth of between £5m to £20m, with a further 22% with wealth between £20m and £100m. None had a net worth of less than £1m and two reported a net worth of over £500m.

Net worth

Income bracket £	Number of respondents	% (of those who answered)
Over 500m	2	3
200-500m	4	6
100-200m	2	3
50-100m	8	12
20-50m	7	10
10-20m	13	19
5-10m	15	22
1-5m	11	16
Less than 1m	0	0
Declined to answer	5	7
Not known	9	
Total	76	

From other sources, such as various "Rich Lists", or shareholdings in public companies, it is apparent that those who did not give this information are at the upper end of the scale. At least two appear to have net worth in excess of £500m, and two in excess of £1bn.

Net worth

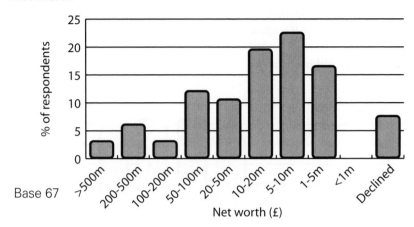

Base 67

Annual household income

Respondents' annual household income was also high. Of the 70% of interviewees who answered the question, 77% reported an annual income of between £100,000 and £2m. Only three respondents claimed an annual household income of less than £100,000.

(According to National Statistics Online, average earnings for full-time workers in 2003 was around £25,000 a year. For women, the figure was just over £20,000 and for men just above £28,000. Less than 1% receive more than £100,000.)

Annual household income (£)

Income bracket £	Number of respondents	% (of those who answered)
Over 20m	1	2
10-20m	0	0
5m-10m	2	4
2m-5m	3	5
1m-2m	9	16
500,000-1m	12	21
250,000-500,000	12	21
100,000-250,000	11	19
Less than 100,000	3	5
Declined to answer	4	7
Not known	19	
Total	76	

As with net worth, some people either were not asked the question, or declined to answer. Again, it is likely that the unreported household income levels were at the upper end of the scale.

Annual household income

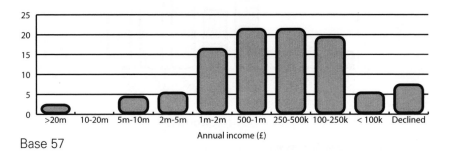

Base 57

The financial information is based entirely on self-reports and assessments. It is extremely unlikely that everyone used the same basis of evaluation, or took a consistent approach to items such as the current value of pension schemes or art collections. The purpose of collecting the data, which is given in broad bands, was to obtain an estimation of the interviewee's income and assets as a context for portraying attitudes to money and its use. It also provided a check that the sample contained a reasonable range of wealth levels.

Age
The age of respondents who answered this question ranged from 34 to 80 years.

Age			
Age	Number of respondents	% (of those who answered)	% (of total respondents)
Under 35	1	1.4	1.3
35-44	13	18.8	17.1
45-54	22	31.9	28.9
55-64	20	29.0	26.3
65 or over	13	18.8	17.1
Not answered	7		9.2
Total	76		

The average age of respondents was 54, with just under half below 55. Almost a third were aged 45 to 54. 60% were between 45 and 64.

Age

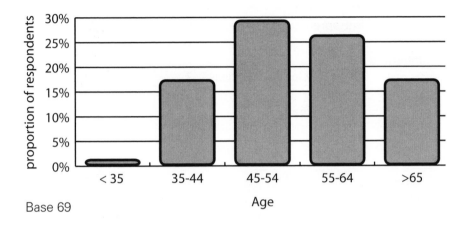

Base 69

Gender
The majority (79%) of respondents were men, and 21% women. In the case of the two couples interviewed, the wealth had been created by the male partner.

Education
The respondents were generally extremely well educated. Almost all were educated to degree level with a significant majority holding postgraduate and professional qualifications.

Marriage and children
Some 86% of respondents were married and 92% had children or step-children. The proportion of those who are married appears significantly higher than the national average, reported as 47% by National Statistics Online.

Source of wealth
The majority of respondents were self-made, with over 70% having derived their wealth from their own efforts. Of these, just over half (38% of the total) made their money professionally, generally through banking, with a few in the law. A third had created their wealth from building up a business or other entrepreneurial efforts. Just over a quarter inherited or married wealth.

Source of wealth

		Number of respondents	% of respondents
Self-made			
	Professional	29	38
	Entrepreneur	25	33
Inherited			
	And grew family business	7	9
	Wealth	6	8
	And self-made	4	5
Married wealth		4	5
Other		1	1
Total		76	

Not all the categories are clear-cut. For example, there are some who inherited small family businesses and built them up to be major companies and others who married into wealthy families. Many who described themselves as self-made were able to borrow crucial start-up capital through their family. Those who are entrepreneurs include people in the creative industries as well as manufacturing and finance. Some in the City generate high income through their professional activities and major wealth through the investment, often as venture capital, of their surplus assets. There is also a very small number who have built up fortunes through creative activities of their own.

Source of wealth

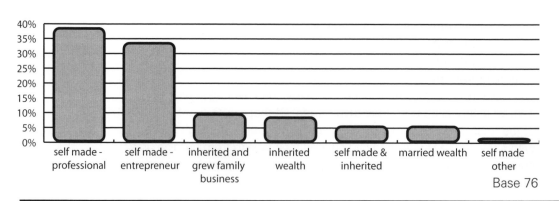

Base 76

Planned giving
Exactly half of the respondents have their own trust. No-one gives through payroll giving.

Geographical origins
Just under half the sample were born in the South East of England, with 10% or less from each of the North West, the North East, and the Midlands and Yorkshire. Around 5% or less were from Wales, Scotland or Northern Ireland. Just under a quarter were born outside the UK, with the majority (almost a quarter of these) coming from East Africa. There were small representations from the US, India and Germany.

Whereas 30 people were born in the South East, 50 people or 66% of all respondents now live in London, with 83% residing in the South East as a whole. At least a quarter of the respondents own at least one second home outside London.

The same numbers as originated in the North East and the North West now live there, but all except one have moved from Wales.

Religious backgrounds
People were not questioned about their ethnic origin, but were asked in some detail about their religious upbringing and source of their values. The broad categories of those who responded (86%) are given below.

Religious backgrounds

	% of those who answered)
Religion never an important factor	22
Christian upbringing and current practice	20
Christian upbringing, now non-practising	19
Jewish upbringing and current practice	17
Jewish upbringing, now non-observant	8
Muslim upbringing and practice	6
Hindu upbringing and practice	2
Hindu upbringing, now non-observant	2
Other	6
(Numbers rounded up)	

As with the net worth and income information, in most cases it was not possible to predict the religious traditions and influences in advance of the interview. The latest Census information for England and Wales (2001) indicates that 72% of the population classify themselves as Christian, 3% Muslim, 1% Hindu and 0.5% Jewish.

Interview times
The average interview time was one hour and 50 minutes. The shortest was about 30 minutes and the longest (in two parts) well over three hours. Some interviews were followed up with telephone calls or emails.

Where they give: philanthropic causes

Charitable giving by the donors in our study reaches a variety of charitable sectors and is motivated by diverse influences.

Individuals were asked which charities they support, and to estimate their annual contribution towards each charity. Data was collected for approximately 75% of those surveyed, and was based on the interviewees' personal estimates as well as reports of their charitable accounts, where available.

Notably, none of the six interviewees of Asian origin was willing to provide detailed data on the charities they support, although they did give information on the focus and general level of their giving. This was consistent with their general reluctance to provide financial background material.

We also compared charitable giving by our surveyed group to overall giving in the UK. The UK context as a whole is covered in Chapter Thirteen, while comparisons with the US are explored in Chapter Fourteen.

Charitable sectors

Charitable giving varied by sector, with arts, culture and social welfare receiving the most funding from the interviewees in our study, followed by health, medical research, and education. In contrast, overseas development, environmental and religious organisations received the least support.

Arts and culture
Arts and culture organisations received the highest amount of funding from the greatest number of people. The performing arts received

funding from more people than other forms of arts activity. Importantly, support reached well beyond large, established institutions such as the Royal Opera House and the National Gallery. Indeed, philanthropy greatly benefited smaller, local organisations as well as individual artists.

Those individuals who focused most of their support (that is, more than half of their total charitable giving) on the arts were more likely to live in and have grown up in London. They were also slightly older, with an average age of 59 versus an average age of 52 for those dedicating less than half of their annual giving to the arts.

An interviewee in his 30s was not giving to the arts "yet". Support for the arts came from those who had inherited wealth as well as from the self-made. However, the majority of interviewees who gave meaningfully to the arts also contributed to other charitable sectors, particularly social welfare, education and medical research.

Motivations for giving to the arts stemmed largely from personal enjoyment and active association. For example, one donor gave to the Royal Opera House because he enjoys opera, respects the institution, and wants London to have a high quality opera house. Moreover, the very nature of arts and culture activities means that they provide frequent occasions for reinforcing the interest in the cause, learning more about it, meeting practitioners and sharing the experience with others.

Importantly, however, such charitable giving is not strictly self-serving. Many donors wish to help individual artists as well as to improve access to the arts for more people (see Chapter Five). Moreover, several of the interviewees who focused all or almost all of their giving on the arts did so largely to support development and training programmes, or for special access, rather than only to enhance facilities for themselves.

It should be added that in the years prior to this research there had been a massive increase in capital projects for the arts, as a result of lottery funding. Many of these were supported by some of the interviewees. This has undoubtedly distorted the figures.[1]

Social welfare

In addition to arts and culture, interviewees also strongly supported social welfare initiatives. Children and youth charities received the greatest funding, followed by those helping the elderly and supporting charities dealing with mental health issues. Furthermore, while donors in the study

[1] For example, the report of the National Audit Office *Income Generated by the Museums and Galleries* in January 2004 showed that fundraising income of the 17 museums sponsored by the Department for Culture, Media and Sport fell from a peak of £90m in 2000-01 to £63m in 2002-03.

supported national charities such as the NSPCC, they gave as or even more generously to local initiatives.

Interviewees based in the North East and North West were more likely than those living elsewhere to focus most of their giving on social welfare issues, and to concentrate their giving geographically, within their local communities.

Gifts to social welfare organisations are typically inspired by the donor's desire to improve social equality generally or to develop the socio-economic base of a specific community.

Those who gave predominantly to social welfare also supported other causes, but typically not arts and culture. Health and medical research was the next most popular area, while education, environment and the arts and culture received 10% or less.

Education
Funding for educational institutions and organisations falls into two main categories: support for a school attended by the donor or the donor's children, and provision of educational opportunities for others via bursaries and other more general programmes. Support for students of the arts is classified under arts and culture charities.

Approximately one-third of the people surveyed contributed to educational charities. Individuals who had lived in or attended school in the US were more likely to fund both their own schools as well as educational opportunities for others. For example, one donor who spent most of his adult life in New York focused his entire giving on educational opportunities for disadvantaged young people.

Motivations for supporting educational advancement are similar to those for social causes, that is, improving social equality for disadvantaged people, especially children.

People who had made their own money were significantly more likely to give to education-related causes than those who inherited wealth, regardless of the age of the donor. This was also true of overseas development.

Health and medical research
Most funding for health and medical research-related causes was directed to children, underscoring the prevalence of support for children's charities

among the interviewees studied. The causes receiving the most financial contributions were dyslexia and other learning difficulties, and hospice care. Similar to those for social welfare organisations, motivations reflect donors' desire to aid disadvantaged children. Other funding for medical research is generally inspired by personal experience, such as having a family member who has suffered from a specific medical condition.

Overseas development

Most people in our survey focused their financial contributions domestically, with roughly 30% of donors sending money abroad. Only a small minority directed more than 10% of their total annual giving to international organisations, and even individuals who had lived abroad were not necessarily more likely to give money to overseas charities. Reasons for reluctance to give overseas include scepticism about effectiveness and impact, as described in Chapter Six.

Donors who gave to overseas charities were motivated by the same issues as those who focused their social welfare support in the UK – that is, to improve social equality and to effect social change. Yet these individuals believe that their money will have more impact abroad than at home. Some of these donors had extensive experience in Africa or Asia, and giving to communities of origin by the Asian interviewees was a significant factor.

Environment

Environmental concerns received very little philanthropic support, with only a small minority of donors contributing to these causes. Moreover, most environmental aid appeared to have come from the donor's efforts to support either their local community or overseas development initiatives. Younger people who had inherited wealth were prominent in this category.

Religion

In complete contrast to the arts sector, religious institutions received the least amount of funding from the least number of people. We have defined this category narrowly as support for a place of worship, such as a church, synagogue, temple or mosque. Organisations associated with a particular religion, such as Jewish care charities, are classified under social welfare or another relevant category.

An overwhelming majority of those surveyed described their religion as "not important" in their daily life, and fewer than 10 individuals in the entire survey gave any money at all to their place of worship[2]. Those people who characterised their religion as "important" or "very important" were more likely to give to their place of worship, but even here the amounts tended to be small compared to overall giving.

Within the Jewish faith, community ties are both religious and cultural, and the feeling of social obligation is very strong. Virtually all of the Jewish donors in our survey supported Jewish causes, giving to social welfare, medical, educational, and arts and culture charities, as well as to organisations based in Israel.

Religious affiliation can also have a direct impact on where an individual focuses their philanthropy. Indeed, religious tenets can inculcate an awareness of social responsibility that extends beyond the immediate religious community to greater society. This sense of social obligation was most apparent among the Muslim and Quaker participants in our survey.

Regional context and local community

As with religious affiliation, locality can also inspire social ties and create community. In the UK, local communities can be defined by town, city, or region, although within Greater London survey participants tended to identify with specific areas, such as Notting Hill or North West London. However, community ties appeared much stronger outside London. A significant majority of those interviewed living in the North East and North West of England consciously focused their giving within their local community, compared to less than half of those living in the South East (but outside London), and a very small minority of those in London. Within the local community, donors spread their giving across all charitable sectors.

How much people give

Although people were asked about their giving, in many cases the answers were estimates. Many of those with charitable trusts provided trust accounts, but no statistical analyses of these were undertaken since the coverage only applied to part of the sample, and not all trusts provided the same level of detail.

[2]It is possible that in reporting their charitable giving interviewees did not include regular but relatively small contributions to collections during a religious service.

Estimates of the level of giving varied. Many reported giving between 5% and 10% of income. But amounts ranged from 25% of income (from someone in the £5m to £10m a year income bracket) to 2% of income (from someone with annual income of about £500,000 with wealth in the £20m to £50m bracket including an inherited estate). Others with inherited estates were giving at comparable levels. There were examples of younger people in the City in the £500,000 to £1m income bracket with much less capital (nearly all in their house) who reported themselves as giving "very little".

Some people who made money on the flotation of a business set up a trust with a significant proportion of the proceeds – "*money they never had*". There were several examples of people who had set up their trust with between 5% and 10% of their wealth; more exceptionally there were cases of allocations of 40% to 50%. When making donations from their trusts, some people were only distributing income, planning to maintain the endowment in perpetuity, and others were, on occasion, allocating a mix of capital and income. Exceptionally, there were plans to spend the entire capital in the lifetime of the donor.

In a small minority of cases, people were allocating little or nothing from their own income or wealth, but distributing the income from a trust established by a parent or other relative.

When it was possible to review the recorded information in detail, it was discovered in several cases that the estimated percentage of income allocated to charitable giving exceeded recorded donations. There are several reasons why this might be the case:

◆ There are people who give through a trust, but also make gifts (usually smaller) in other ways, not always tax-effectively or in a way which is recorded.

◆ Cash gifts are often not counted in the charitable total.

◆ Support of family and friends is not included in charitable giving.

◆ Political contributions are not included.

◆ Gifts in kind are not included.

There are further complications when considering the percentage of wealth or income that people may be publicly reported as giving.

Consider the cases of three people. These examples are based on individuals interviewed in this study, but details have been changed.

A sold the business he had created for £50m and immediately set up a charitable trust with 40% of the proceeds – £20m. He also bought houses for each of his three siblings and supports his retired parents. The trust supports a range of relatively small charities, many of them located in the community where the business was based, some distance from London. **A** continues to live in the same family house and although known locally is not a nationally known donor. The trust distributes about £700,000 a year. **A**'s wealth was estimated at £50m or more in reports such as *The Rich List*, and the giving of £700,000 would be reported as 1.4% of wealth. In fact, he has given 40% of his wealth. The children have become trustees and the trust will continue to support local projects in perpetuity.

B also realised £50m through the flotation of a City institution. He did not set up a charitable trust, but has used Gift Aid to make a one-off major donation of £2.5m (to be paid over five years) to a prestigious project which has significant political and royal support. In the year that the gift was announced it was reported as 5% of his wealth. He is on the board of the recipient organisation and has been publicly honoured.

C is a retired professional woman in her 70s. She established a charitable trust some decades ago with an inheritance of £1m in property, and added to it over the years with "windfalls" and additional fees from irregular publications. As a result of effective asset management it now has about £8m in assets (far exceeding the value of any of her other assets) and distributes about £300,000 a year to a range of projects in different sectors, some of which are well known. In retirement she lives on her pension of about £60,000 a year. She features on no rich lists but her giving is at a level equal to many who do and is about five times her annual income.

Clearly, there may be major differences in how gifts are reported, and how people allocate their charitable giving.

UK

Comparing our study to the 2003 *Charity Trends* report published by the Charities Aid Foundation (CAF) highlights several notable differences. First, the interviewees in this research contributed much more significantly to arts and culture charities. We believe that this is due, to a great degree, to the large contributions to capital projects made prior to the period of the survey, and to the influence of active involvement. This is reinforced by opportunities to enjoy the art forms supported, which may be more accessible to this group in terms of location and affordability.

Second, according to *Charity Trends*, international agencies ranked first in voluntary income received, in sharp contrast to negligible funding by the donors in our survey. Possible reasons for this divergence include potential selection bias in our survey, different fundraising strategies, and a lower likelihood of these individuals to respond to disaster appeals. Finally, compared to our survey, the *Charity Trends* report demonstrates stronger support for animal and medical charities among the general population. This also may be explained by potential selection bias in the survey, as well as fundraising strategies of the charities.

In Chapter Thirteen, Cathy Pharoah of the Charities Aid Foundation explores the complexities of reporting giving by the wealthy in the UK as a whole, and the "patchy" quality of the evidence.

It should be noted that variations in charitable giving by the wealthy people in this study also diverged from those in the US. This is explored in Chapter Fourteen.

Key points

Based on our study, philanthropy by the wealthy in the UK benefits many charitable sectors, with the greatest amount of interest and funding directed toward arts, culture, and social welfare organisations. Overseas development, environmental and religious causes received the least financial support, in contrast to the giving trends among the general population.

The inspirations and triggers which influence this giving are explored in depth in Chapter Five. Motivations for giving to specific charities can be personal – influenced by one's beliefs, active association with an organisation, or a specific personal experience – or can be inspired by a sense of community, religious, cultural, or geographical. Nonetheless, most charitable giving reflects multiple influences. For example, one interviewee gave primarily to three organisations: his church (influenced by personal beliefs and sense of community), a museum of which his wife is a board member (active association), and a cancer charity (personal experience of having a family member die of cancer). Yet, whatever the beneficiary, all the donors in our survey gave because they care, and they want their donations to have an impact.

I believe that a great virtue of charity is that you can support purposes that are good… I give to ABC because I see… its work and can measure what good it is doing. My involvement is regenerative. I become more involved, I get more excited, and I give more. It is enlightened self-interest… Philanthropy is a very binding influence. The day when people are led to feel that charity is not part of their world will be very sad.

(Male, 50s, self-made/professional)

3

Influences on philanthropy – faith, family and community

In this chapter, we explore what people perceive to have been the main influences on or determinants of the values which underpin their approach to life in general, and philanthropy in particular. We have tried to separate these from the impact of early education and work experiences (discussed in the next chapter), although they are closely inter-related. But it is also clear that core values and traditions embedded within the family, or central to people's upbringing, have an initial and powerful influence.

While some people reported no tradition of giving or volunteering in the family or no specific donor interests which could be attributed to upbringing, the majority trace the development of their current approach to philanthropy to some combination of religious, family, or community influence, however latent. Although these factors are inherently inter-linked, they hold different prominence for individuals depending on their family's history and culture.

Faith and religious tradition

The influences of religion were, for many, central to the family values that had formed attitudes to giving. This is mentioned across all backgrounds. Not surprisingly, no distinction is made between community tradition, family and faith, since, in the experience of those for whom religion was important, these are interwoven.

I was brought up in a strong Catholic, Good Samaritan household...those who could help, helped...I started by giving time.

(Male, 40s, self-made/professional)

It's always been something that we've done in our family. One was fortunate to be in the position of having a good life and one should try to help those less fortunate. My early interests were Jewish Care and general Jewish charities. As I got older, I started asking myself questions about how the disadvantaged dealt with life.

(Male, 50s, self-made/professional)

We were always seeing charity at home. Parents and relations gave. Helping the less well off was essential – the temple, priests, families of servants, there was always someone worse off. It was about the community and there was also a spiritual aspect. In my upbringing in East Africa, all had similar attitudes and principles.

(Male, 50s, self-made/entrepreneur)

Each of these shows an element of the importance of a sense of duty or responsibility: to be a Good Samaritan, to help the less fortunate or the disadvantaged. This appears to transcend religious affiliation and the level of wealth in the household. There is a connection between the idea that giving is not just about money, but is a way of life; giving time as well is also linked to the concept of service. The importance of a sense of community, and the shared values and principles which underpin a cohesive society, is echoed by many.

For those who had not been well-off, giving time and helping out appeared to validate their membership of the community defined by their faith. In many cases, the notion of service reached out beyond their local or religious community and included overseas development.

My mother was involved in a small way but my parents were not well-off. They helped with the local orphanage and always put money in the Christian Aid envelope. They were Methodist. The community of the church was important rather than religion itself. They didn't tithe but did help out: church and Sunday School, stamps for missionaries, Oxfam support.

(Female, 50s, married wealth)

The Ismaili Muslim culture is my defining identity. It's a close-knit family. Its essence is giving back to the community through tithing and service. I was brought up knowing that that was part of my duty. One has to

*support one's community. Initially this is the family, then it moves to the
religious and then the national community. The importance of integrating
into the broader community is a fundamental part of faith. The driving
force is the family history and examples in East Africa where they built
schools, mosques and hospitals.*

(Male, 40s, self-made/entrepreneur)

This sense of a widening pool of obligation, from family to employees, to
local place of worship, to community and to a broader society was
mentioned by several interviewees. It is seen as coming with experience,
closely associated with greater capacity (wealth) and, because it is a
process which develops over time, age.

As these passages show, the practical example set by parents, both to
encourage and provide role models, was also a common feature.

*Religion was very important; my parents were Anglican, regular church
goers. I recall it being very clear that there were others in the world less
well off and it was one's duty to help. We were incredibly lucky and
made aware of the issues. My parents' generation saw significant
deprivation, in contrast to our own children.*

(Male, 40s, self-made professional)

Other people attributed their early experiences of giving to cultural
influences related to their faith of origin, rather than directly to
religious tenets.

*My earliest memory was sitting under a raffle table at a Christmas fair.
My mother was Chair of the hospital Friends. My grandfather was
middle-European, there was an ethos of giving back, which was
predominantly Jewish. Doing voluntary work was expected... but the
Jewish background was not admitted at that time.*

(Female, 50s, inherited)

My father [of Jewish origin] *helped several people in life, so it must have
been an influence... I was sent to a Quaker school which must have had
a small influence. We were not a rich family but we did give some money
away. My family would have regarded wealth as having obligations.*

(Male, 70s, self-made/entrepreneur)

Others were almost reluctant to accept that religion, or religious traditions,
were a factor, but instead saw a desire to help others as an innate impulse

related to a sense of being fortunate when so many were not: "*It was natural to try to help*".

Clearly, for those who saw faith and religion as formative, the influence of family and the influence of religion and upbringing cannot be disentangled. Not surprisingly, many of these people were sent to schools where the values of community, responsibility and sharing were strongly inculcated. This is discussed further in Chapter Four. Even those who no longer go to church or participate in organised religion acknowledge the huge importance of this early influence.

> *My mother was a Welsh speaker from North Wales. I came from a successful middle class family. Both my parents came from humble backgrounds. I can remember when my aunt put in a bathroom when I was 14. Religion was very important. My father goes to church daily and kneels to pray every night. My mother was brought up as Chapel but she converted. I was sent to private education at [Catholic private school]. For many, the [religious order] environment of looking after others and taking responsibility for others becomes inbuilt. Community is the central focus: family, school and my company.*
>
> (Male, 40s, self-made/entrepreneur)

Essentially, people who maintain the beliefs and values nurtured and sustained in childhood will choose friends and participate in networks which share the same priorities. Such shared ethics strengthen the sense of cohesion, possibly reinforced by the perception that they are members of a minority. What is noticeable is that on the whole, for those who were brought up in the Christian faith but have now lapsed, there is no alternative framework or community to continue their links with the source of their values and identity. However, it is clear that almost all of those from Asian and Jewish backgrounds, even if they no longer attend a temple, mosque or synagogue, participate in or are linked to strong social networks which reinforce the sense of values and identity. In many cases this underpins their philanthropy.

Other family values and traditions

In addition to, or in place of, religion, many people cited features of their family background and upbringing that they felt influenced their philanthropy. Three factors were dominant, all in one way or another related to the "obligations" or "responsibilities" attached to having wealth.

Contributions to the community

For those who had inherited wealth, there had often been a history of family giving to their local community. For some, this was rooted in a religious tradition within the family, whether or not practised by the respondents themselves:

Church was very important, particularly for my mother. I am now C. of E.; it's a part of life. There's a Christian obligation to give to the less fortunate. I was brought up in an Xshire family with a significant presence. Relationships with the community were very important. As long ago as I can remember I have been invited to join things, be Governor of the local grammar school, lead fundraising for local sports facilities, be President of the local Red Cross. People came to me as a representative of the local big family. I enjoy being able to help, giving time and attending events. My father was similarly involved and held those positions before me. It was part of one's role in a community. We were significant employers in the area. We helped create the infrastructure for our staff.
(Male, 50s, inherited and grew family business)

It was a family tradition. My grandfather gave large amounts of wealth to promoting housing and education to the working class population in [Xtown] so that charitable giving was part and parcel of life... but religion is not important now. I was not brought up as a Quaker.
(Male, 60s, inherited and grew family business)
[This interviewee had grandparents who were strong Quakers.]

Involvement with the community was also closely tied to responsibility for those who worked for the family, whether in a factory or on the land.

I was very influenced by my grandmother who was a very philanthropic person. The duty to society was learnt through the family. It's very important to the family that we continue to support the community in which we all live.
(Male, 50s, inherited and grew family business)
[This interviewee lives in the same house in Wales in which he was born.]

There's a very strong tradition of philanthropy on both sides of my family. There is a strong sense of looking after people who worked for them. A sense of commitment. The family was imbued with the protestant work ethic. They provided social housing in [X town]. Every family was touched by X [family]. I am proud of the tradition of looking after people who work for you. There's a responsibility for your name. There is also the importance of the art collection. If you're lucky enough to have you must go on deserving.
(Female, 30s, inherited)

Several influences are clear in the last passage. As well as the sense of obligation for employees, there is a feeling of pride in the tradition, a responsibility to maintain the reputation of the family name (even though in this case the interviewee uses her married name) and an obligation to maintain and pass on the art collection to the next generation. Like others who had inherited wealth in the form of an estate, this young woman sees herself as holding assets in trust for the next generation. As such, it is a patriotic duty to maintain houses and gardens and art collections as part of a philanthropic obligation to the community in which they live. In several cases, liquid assets were relatively low and significant resources would be released by the sale of the property and art; the responsibility and cost of maintenance would also be removed. However, these benefits were outweighed by a sense of continuity of commitment. This is often demonstrated by giving time, through membership of various local committees, and by financial and other support of individuals in the local community who may have fallen on hard times. The sense of an integration and mutuality between family and community is central.

This commitment to community involvement is by no means limited to those with inherited wealth. It was also expressed by some self-made entrepreneurs with strong local links. Again, all were people born outside the South East of England.

> *My father was a doctor. There was an element of service in his life and wider involvement in the community. There was a belief that charity is a good thing to do and a broad acceptance of wider community responsibility.*
> (Male, 50s, self-made/professional)

> *We have a family engineering company* [in the North West]. *My father gave through the company. He was a Japanese POW and supports army charities. Most of my support is locally based and linked to children.*
> (Female, 50s, inherited and grew family business)

> *I am the result of a lucky sperm count. My father gave wealth to charity. I inherited the idea from my father that wherever the family works you must give back to the community. My family always helped the disabled. We are so lucky. Wealth is a responsibility.*
> (Male, 40s, self-made and inherited)
> [An Asian Muslim]

Outside London, and among those whose faith, if any, was of Christian origin, the expressed sense of community was directed much more to a specific geographical area and reflected more a sense of the obligations of wealth and position – as landowner or employer. With inherited wealth, the obligations are placed in the context of a family tradition, and a sense of pride in continuing to maintain the link with families who have depended on them. In many such cases, the support given may not be perceived as "charitable" and would not attract tax relief. Examples include allowing people to remain in low-rent housing associated with employment after retirement and retaining staff whose employment is not strictly necessary.

Among those who had created businesses, the sense of obligation to the local community which provided their staff and customers was equally strong, particularly away from London.

In some cases the sense of community was strongly allied to a sense of shared traditions and a wider network of obligation or responsibility. This is most powerfully observed within Jewish and Asian communities, and it is difficult, if not impossible, to distinguish between perceptions of those obligations arising from a feeling of religious duty and those which have become expected because of the individual's perceived role and resources. Although the "community" referred to might be associated with the place of worship, the geographic roots, if any, were in the place of origin of the family, particularly among Asian interviewees. This is perhaps not surprising, as their immigration was relatively recent, and was prompted more by economic pressures than by persecution. Even where there had been some experience of persecution, as for Asians from East Africa, there were still members of the extended family in the Indian sub-continent to whom there were ties of blood and duty.

A contribution to society

My parents were generous but not committee people. I was always brought up to do it, it's part of a way of life. It's about sticking to one's own values and helping the less fortunate. It's important to support charities because the state doesn't do a good job.

(Female, 40s, married wealth)

As this shows, some people spoke about a parental influence which brought a sense of responsibility to help the "less fortunate" or disadvantaged within wider society. Sometimes this had arisen within a family of wealth, in other cases not.

> *My parents didn't have much money when I was being brought up so I earned more than I deserved and give some of it back…there was a sense of middle class duty and a background of people who didn't spend on loose living.*
>
> (Male, 50s, self-made/professional)

Similar notions of "deservedness" and avoiding over-indulgent personal spending were expressed by people from a range of religious backgrounds. Others emphasised their independence from religious influences and placed more importance on the personal and political values of their families and the sense of justice these brought.

> *It was a tradition in my family. My grandfather's father set up various trusts and I developed my ideas about the obligations of wealth from the family. Three of my grandparents were very left-wing. I remember conversations in childhood. Philanthropic attitudes were encouraged.*
>
> (Female, 30s, inherited)

> *My parents were active with their time but not money. I always felt obliged to be civic minded. My parents were always involved politically (liberal, anti-Vietnam).*
>
> (Female, 30s, self-made/professional)

Ideas about the social obligations of wealth are explored in more detail in Chapter Nine.

The immigrant experience

Another early experience or influence which was centrally important for some people from Jewish or Asian communities was that of being an immigrant to the UK – either themselves or their parents. As we have seen, there are deeply held cultural and religious values within such communities and it is difficult to disentangle the factors surrounding immigration. Nevertheless, some talked explicitly about the influence of their family coming to a new country and wanting to contribute to the society which had given refuge.

A key factor was a feeling of debt to the country which had offered security and opportunity. Strongly linked to this was parental encouragement to achieve and be successful from an early age.

> *I am the son of a refugee. It was probably of influence when I was growing up. There was parental encouragement and support to do well.*
>
> (Male, 50s, self-made/entrepreneur)

The moral preoccupations behind all religions were there when I was
growing up. My father was a holocaust child. The adult lives of my
parents were devoted to public service. I came from a solid middle class
background. At the age of 14 my pocket money was stopped. I was told if
I wanted something I had to work for it. I was told I wouldn't inherit and
had to get on with it. 'Make yourself financially independent by the time
you're 40 and then do something worthwhile'.

(Male, 42, self-made/entrepreneur)

This experience encapsulates those of many people who very much value
and respect the traditions and the sense of community of their country and
culture of family origin, even if they have no personal experience or
memory of that background. And for some there was a direct association
between the feeling of individual good fortune and the recognition of
owing what is seen as a very personal debt.

It's always been something that we've done in my family. There is a strong
sense in the immigrant community of putting something back. There is a
sense of 'there but for the grace of God'. I do a lot for England, not just
Jews but English people. It is hard to distinguish between an immigrant
putting something back into the community and Jewish tradition.

(Female, 50s, inherited)

Asian immigrants were less likely to talk about "putting something back",
but emphasised the importance of making a contribution to society and
supporting the family and local community.

My father came with virtually nothing. I would say we were not
observant but God-fearing. The overriding ethos around which the family
is constituted is integrity, its strong value system and the Indian culture.
This means love and support for the family, respect for elders and each
other. I come from a country with extremes of wealth and poverty. One
learns to see this but not register because it's part of the landscape but
still one has to contribute. There are so many deserving causes; the
question is how to choose.

(Male, 40s, self-made/entrepreneur)

Influence of the family discounted

A few people claimed that neither religion nor family upbringing had
influenced them.

There was no tradition in my family and none of my interests would be attributed to family upbringing. My father was rich for a short time but then lost his money.

(Male, 50s, self-made/professional)

The only link they could identify that related to their family or upbringing, albeit a weak one, lay in a generosity of spirit in their parents.

I was brought up as a Catholic but I don't think it influenced my giving unless you believe that being Christian makes people different. There was no tradition of philanthropy, there was no money. My parents were always generous by nature. I think there is a link between being generous in spirit and being generous in the rest of their life.

(Male, 50s, self-made/professional)

Whatever their personal reasons for resisting the idea that childhood experience might have affected their adult attitudes, no-one in this small group had alternative theories as to the origins of their values and approach. In fact, they almost contradicted themselves in explaining the position.

I was brought up with no tradition of giving and I have no children, but my attitudes do come from my upbringing. It's not about helping people less fortunate but that if one can do something, one should.

(Male, 50s, self-made/entrepreneur)

Key points

Parental influence, religious affiliation and membership of a close-knit community are powerful drivers to philanthropy.

Families with a strong base in a community are likely to inculcate the concept of responsibility to that community, which may well include employees and their families. Not all such support is necessarily counted as "charitable" giving, and will not be tax-deductible. It may include time and provision for individuals.

A strong sense of community is more manifest as the area of origin moves further from London.

For people who claim no influence from family or religious upbringing, there is a different kind of imperative, linking perception of need, awareness of their own good fortune and realisation that something could and should be done. People in this position refer to spiritual, ethical or moral codes which may be based on the influence of previous generations, although they do not currently practise any religion.

The reported influence of religion, however latent or from previous generations, is surprisingly high. However, by taking part in this research, interviewees were demonstrating a sense of duty to help in the development of philanthropy, and it may be that people find it easier to identify with this than broader spiritual, ethical or moral codes.

This may reflect the fact that some 72% of the population report themselves as Christian, but well under 10% attend church regularly. As we see in Chapter Two, whereas about 80% of interviewees claimed that religion was significant in their upbringing, it is now important for less than 50%. This decline was unrelated to age and gender.

4

Early experiences of giving – developing a philosophy of philanthropy

While the attitudes to giving of some interviewees were influenced by early childhood, others were affected by their experience at school, university or at work. Yet others made their first major donations after realising significant wealth. In the course of creating wealth or managing their resources, some recognised that they might have more than they need, and over the same period – which might be several years – began to be aware of what their money could achieve. This awareness was raised in a variety of ways.

An individual's process of deciding philanthropic potential is a combination of self-analysis and external factors. For some, the combination of having time to think about wider society (for example having sold a business) and the realisation of just how much money they have, linked to existing interests, was sufficient to activate their charitable impulses.

Others required an external stimulus – a dynamic individual, or a life-changing experience – to point the way. For a tiny number that individual influence was Margaret Thatcher, who they believed had created an environment in which they could make money, with the implication that if they succeeded they should help the less fortunate.

Some people had developed a philosophy of giving, or even a structured framework to assess requests, either initially or as their experience of giving developed. Others responded to the requests of people they know and respect, a feature that is more fully explored in Chapter Seven.

Early experiences of giving

Chapter Three showed that family, cultural and religious values in childhood have an important influence on people's underlying motivations to give to charitable causes. It is therefore not surprising to find that a number of people said their earliest experience of giving was as a child or in their teenage years.

> *At the age of nine I organised a swimming day in aid of Guide Dogs for the Blind because it was the only charity I knew about.*
>
> (Male, 40s, self-made/entrepreneur)

> *I started by giving time. When I was 12, I started a free helpline for teenagers telling them about what public services were available.*
>
> (Male, 40s, self-made/professional)

There was often an element of naivety in these early experiences, either raising money for a cause they were personally involved in or as a result of seeing adult behaviour. Others referred to episodes later in their teens or early twenties, where the giving was more associated with joining a religiously-linked youth organisation, a feature that was particularly strong within the Jewish community.

> *I was asked to join a fundraising committee of a Jewish old people's home at the age of 20. That's where I met my wife; it became part of my culture.*
>
> (Male, 50s, self-made/entrepreneur)

School and university

Although religion, upbringing and family traditions were by far the most frequently cited factors in influencing early attitudes to philanthropy, there were some who identified school experience as having the most, or earliest, effect on their giving. This is perhaps not surprising as, in many cases, the parents had chosen the school on the premise that it would instill and reinforce their own values. A number mentioned the importance of school reinforcing family influences.

In several examples, the interviewee had attended a fee-paying or religious school in which "community work" was compulsory or strongly encouraged. They recognised that such activities were not always popular, or were popular for the wrong reasons ("*playing chess with someone living in Peabody Trust accommodation where you were allowed to smoke*"). But those who had this experience were convinced of its importance and the positive influence of teachers.

> *We were encouraged at school to help old people; the housemaster was a very humane man, a great influence. One's experiences as a child, what one sees one's parents doing, conditions you. I am a huge believer in the importance of the formative years; it becomes the basis of one's principles.*
>
> (Male, 50s, self-made professional)

Those who had attended, or whose children had attended, academic institutions in the US mentioned the way these establishments went about fundraising.

> *I went to Harvard Business School in 1975. I have been trained by them to give money annually. There are 10 sections of 80 people in each year. Each section had responsibility for its own fund. There is an element of competition. It is the most effective fundraising institution in the world.*
>
> (Male, 50s, self-made professional)

He went on to say:

> *I was then on the boards of two schools attended by my children in the US. It was expected as part of one's duty as a parent. I got experience raising money for endowment and annual giving. They aim to have one capital campaign within the lifetime of each parent/student. The school has $180m endowment for bursaries – it offers needs-blind entry. The key is development – having a relationship whilst you are at the institution. Since then my children are at university in the US, and I became involved in the [XYZ orchestra in London] through a contact in New York. We can use it for client entertaining but I also give it personal support. They have a music education programme in deprived areas. I played the bassoon and used to sing in the ABC Choir but they have never asked me* [for money or involvement].

This quote encapsulates several interlocked ideas. Perhaps most significantly, it suggests that in the US people are expected to give financial support to their school or university, even if it is already well-endowed and fees are also being paid. The interviewee also recognises that people develop a habit or practice of giving by being "trained", and having the relationship reinforced through the process of "development". This "development" is based on the concept of building lasting relationships – the concept which underpins fundraising. It is used to describe the fundraising profession in the US – and increasingly in the UK. Chapter Fourteen looks at differences in the practice of elite philanthropy between the UK and the US.

Interviewees also voiced experiences in the UK of giving to educational institutions in which there was a personal interest.

> When my daughter [now 17] was in infants' class, a letter was sent to parents asking for money. I thought that if I didn't give it may affect my daughter! I did a four-year covenant for £700 a year.
>
> (Female, 50s, inherited and grew family business)

This woman, who is running her own company, moved on from reactive giving such as this to develop a more strategic approach, a feature discussed below. For another person there were several motivating factors to giving to educational establishments, linking his own university education, his professional activity, tax relief and a persuasive advocate. This theme of multiple influences, with a single imperative hard to identify, recurs frequently.

The following interviewee had specialist links with the world of academia:

> My first experience was the Oxford campaign in 1988: Henry Drucker explained that £100,000 would cost less than £60,000 after tax relief: this was only £12,000 a year for five years which I knew I could afford. I split it 50/50 between the Bodleian and the Pitt Rivers Museum.
>
> (Male, 60s, self-made and inherited)

We return to the impact of tax relief in Chapter Seven.

Workplace initiatives

Few people mentioned their early work experience as a major influence on their giving. Among those who did, most referred specifically to working in the US, or for a US employer. Some of these initially resented what they saw as undue pressure in an area they regarded as essentially private, but having seen the results of their giving were reconciled to and indeed positive about the effect of workplace persuasion and expectation. At least two people mentioned their community work experience. Both are employed by US banks.

> *The programme at [X Bank] community team works. Everyone in the company spends a day a year – about 20,000 people around the world. This was an introduction to charity. I was a partner for eight years and have just retired having been very fortunate with markets. Also, I have made lots of money and should give some away.*
>
> (Male, 40s, self-made/professional)

Another US bank employee (a young British woman) spoke of the expectation that senior staff would set a good example of giving. This is perceived to have a positive impact on the corporate culture.

> *At [Y Bank] senior people earning over $1/2m are expected to give 3% of their income to charity; this means the top 300 people have to give, of which 20 are in the UK. This makes it a more personal and friendly company.*
>
> (Female, 30s, self-made/professional)

The realisation of wealth

The theme of having been lucky and, linked to that, the idea that people who had – or had made – money should in some way be benevolent in order to "deserve" their wealth (and continue to be lucky) features in Chapter Three. Several people began thinking about giving to charitable causes at the point when they acknowledged their luck to themselves. This is a typical example:

> *I started in 1977. I did a job because it was interesting and it turned out to be a goldmine. I was in the right place at the right time. I was particularly fortunate. I got the first bonus in 1984/85 and then it just went up and up.*
>
> (Male, 50s, self-made/professional)

Having gone into the City, this contributor found himself much wealthier than his friends and contemporaries who went into professions such as medicine or the law. When he made his career decision, banking was perceived as a lucrative profession but there was no expectation of the phenomenal bonuses which were to transform City earnings. The turning point for his giving was the realisation that he had amassed capital assets and the fact that he had links to networks, including American colleagues, in which giving was a norm. It was a combination of capacity, cause and opportunity.

Some interviewees explored their thinking about the links between building a business, success in business and the development of a philanthropic instinct.

> *People who develop their business from scratch, the sort of people who are old-fashioned entrepreneurs, are paternal to their staff and carry the HR responsibility in their companies. They apply the same ideas when they realise a capital sum. They do it because of the feel-good factor, not because philanthropy is part of the upbringing.*
>
> (Male, 50s, self-made/entrepreneur)

This idea, which was mentioned in different ways by others who had built businesses, echoes some of the ideas of responsibility to staff discussed earlier. However, for these interviewees, support of others is not linked to family tradition or expectation from the community, but to the feelings of satisfaction and self-worth philanthropy brings.

Many people who had set up a business aimed to sell it by a given date or when a certain sum could be realised. Not all stuck to their original plan, but some had an idea of making sufficient money to be independent by a certain age in order to engage in other, potentially more interesting or worthwhile, activities.

> *When I set up my business my aim was to be financially independent. That was 16 years ago. I overshot my target wealth, making £36m before tax – the target was under £10m. The question was how much to give. The closest I got to advice was the historical tithe. The problem is that the more you have, the bigger the percentage you could give. There are no guidelines – there should be: what do you need and what do you want to keep?*
>
> (Male, 40s, self-made/entrepreneur)

Several factors triggered thoughts about philanthropy after making money through business or enterprise. But to an extent, all are underpinned by people's realisation that they had more money than they felt they needed combined with having time to think about how their money might be used – or how they, personally, could be useful.

I first became involved by making money. I developed my personal philosophy of philanthropy in the last 10 years. Ideas about the obligations of wealth came from generating more than I needed and then figuring out the options – consumption, inheritance and charity. I became involved with [a performing arts organisation] in the mid-late 80s. They were very enthusiastic. I enjoyed getting to know people, understanding the economics. I started to think about arts organisations – they're not independently commercial in trying to raise money. One had to do a bit oneself.

(Male, 50s, self-made/entrepreneur)

This person is still working in the City, although he allocates a significant proportion of his time to non-profit activities. Others started thinking about philanthropy after the sale of their business. But irrespective of when the moment of reflection arrived, several ideas or options were often being considered at the same time. These included the allocation of resources and practical ways of continuing to use their business skills but within activities that gave further expression to their values or own self development.

We sold the business in 1988. I didn't work for the new owners. I was then 45 and had only briefly been involved in the voluntary sector and had lived abroad. I had to think about what to do with the next 40 years. I didn't have to work and thought about putting something back. My husband felt the same. We saw an article in the FT about the Network for Social Change and responded because we thought we might get engaged as well as interested. So we went along. The first presentation was from [ABC]. I was interested in the overseas work so I volunteered to be the liaison between [ABC] and NSC. I started doing work for [ABC]... working in a volunteer capacity. So I was involved and then a trustee for about nine years. This was the start of my active engagement in the voluntary sector in the UK. Also at NSC there is a funding cycle. I was so excited by the projects, I gave about £2,000. This was the first step, and I felt good so I went on from there. I joined NSC, not to be philanthropic but to find out what to do with our lives – both in terms of time and money.

(Female, 50s, self-made/entrepreneur)

As this illustrates, specific events, encounters or engagements, coming at these significant times of reflection, had often sparked the beginnings of philanthropic activity. Sometimes these arose through becoming involved with a particular organisation and building a relationship with it, so reinforcing the feel-good factor; the interest strengthened through the development of an intellectual understanding of the business model underpinning the charity and the application of business experience.

Some interviewees recognised that although they had apparently large sums, it was essential to be focused if they wanted to make a real impact. For some this led to the selection of a cause based on perceived need and the challenge of supporting something that others would not.

> *After I sold my company, I wanted to change the world. I put £6m into the [X] Charitable Trust. There's so much wrong with the world one can't address it all. At the time I felt that international work – overseas aid – was too big and too far away (although having met someone involved in that field last year I now have a different view), so I confined my giving to the UK. Then I looked for people who wouldn't get funding otherwise and focused on young, adult, male homeless people.*
>
> (Male, 40s, self-made/entrepreneur)

A few people explicitly acknowledged a debt to Margaret Thatcher. Within the interview sample, these were all based in the North East or North West. In the North East all mentioned the very powerful advocacy of the head of the Tyne and Wear Community Foundation.

A typical illustration comes from an entrepreneur based in the North East who, starting in 1976, built his business in the 80s and 90s. During this time he had been involved in the local chamber of commerce and the CBI. He described how his thinking developed:

> *Until fairly recently I hadn't really had that much time to see as much of the local community or the wider world as I would have liked. During that time Margaret Thatcher took away many of the shackles and restrictions that hindered people like me from building their businesses, making money, creating jobs... the horrendous tax rates we experienced 25 years ago have gone... the Conservative philosophy, I believe, includes the better off accepting some individual responsibility for the local community. With the opportunity to create wealth comes an obligation not just to earn it but to enjoy it and make good use of it.*
>
> *One of the many changes in the fiscal regime... was the introduction of greater tax incentives for charitable giving. This was meant to encourage us to share some of our wealth with others – those who could benefit much more than we or our children are ever likely to do from just a small part of our savings.*

I was attracted to the idea of the Tyne and Wear Foundation when it was set up [in 1988]*... I had just sold my company... I agreed to set up a personal endowment fund pledging £5,000 a year less tax for five years... There was the incentive of a challenge fund from the US which would give £2m to the first community foundation to raise £1m... I received a list of projects each year... My wife and I were invited to a number of Foundation events and we met many of the people receiving its grants. I also attended a short residential conference organised by the Foundation about how to use charitable funds more effectively.*

I stayed on in the business... I had been thinking about selling [again] *for a while but one of my concerns had always been what I would do and how I would occupy myself. I quite looked forward to creating a blank page in my life and seeing what turned up, but I did feel I needed an interest which would be central to my life...something which would avoid me rushing into other commitments I might later regret.*

From this the idea of setting up my own charitable foundation evolved... partly to give me something to do; partly because I had seen how much good a little extra money can do in our society, certainly in relation to the needs of my by now very comfortably placed family; partly because of the very worthwhile tax reliefs and partly because of the influence of Margaret Thatcher. During Mrs Thatcher's successful mission to revitalise our country, I particularly remember her saying that she hoped and expected that those who derived extra wealth from her policies would in turn want to help those less fortunate than themselves.

(Male, 60s, self-made self-made/entrepreneur)

In the event this person has created a designated and named foundation within the Community Foundation, which handles the administration.

This extract is extensive because it captures a number of themes raised in different ways by many people who had created and built up their own businesses. In addition to those already discussed, these include having developed confidence and understanding through starting giving at a relatively low level; the leverage of the tax benefits; the significance of another person who pointed the way and guided the donor; and the importance of supporting the local area in which the business operated.

Several made the point that they embarked on their giving in a relatively small way and then developed it with experience. This expansion was in part spurred by the realisation that giving small amounts brought considerable enjoyment and having more to give would be even better. This applies to those who created significant wealth from business, but is also the case for others, including many with much smaller resources. For some the creation of a trust enabled them to provide a "pot" for periodic windfalls, freelance earnings, or the odd bonus. In all cases such trusts had benefited from rising stock market and property values.

> *I formed the charitable trust in 1968. We* [interviewee and wife] *put in £400 each. We wanted to form a trust. We were increasingly being asked to covenant and thought it would be fun to try to build capital in order to have more to give. It increased over the years by investment and has been added to by gifts from myself and my wife. The value is now greater than £1m.*
>
> (Male, 60s, self-made/professional)

Developing a philanthropic strategy

It is evident from this discussion that several interviewees had developed a strategy for their giving. In some cases, this had developed from when an event, such as selling a business, allowed time to plan. In others, it occurred in a more gradual way, as the scale of charitable donations grew. The woman, described earlier, who started by giving a covenant to her daughter's school, described how her approach evolved:

> *Then,* [after giving to her daughter's school] *a friend who runs a fundraising consultancy which raises money for education and the arts asked for help with ABC theatre. I visited the theatre and thought I could help both corporately and as an individual. At that point I was asked to join the board but said no because I was too busy... Then three or four years ago I thought I could be more strategic and set up the XYZ Charitable Trust... I add to it when I can. I have put in £75,000 so far. I tend to give from that and put in £25,000 a year.*
>
> (Female, 50s, inherited and grew family business)

In another example, a significant increase in wealth took an already developed approach to a higher level:

> *From my first employment I decided I would give 10% of my income, not just to Jewish causes. I became friendly with a Mormon in my first job. There is a deep American tradition of helping through the church. I decided to do this anonymously. This was 1983. I married in 1989.*

We reached agreement that we would set up a family foundation and put in 10% of our after-tax income. [They were both working at a City bank.] *My husband didn't believe in giving anonymously so we are giving through our foundation. We were working all the time and moving around the world so all we did was write cheques in December. In the middle of this I left banking for a bit.* ["Banking is a feminist issue because in banking I could support myself, but there are heroes in public service"] *So I was writing cheques and giving to my university but it was not strategic and the rest built up as capital. As time went on and the children were growing up we had more money and then came into substantial money… and we were able to move a substantial block of shares into the foundation. It now has more than £8m and is growing all the time. I decided to become more involved and develop a plan.*

(Female, 30s, self-made/professional)

Conversely, others had been very strategic in approach from an early stage. They intended their giving to be as effective and focused as their business, and were very clear about how they wanted it to develop.

The first stages [of my giving] *were small projects at my university and Business School – I made reasonable gifts. Then I put £25m, which came from selling my shares, into a trust. I was 48. I needed to think about: a) how to manage this money and all the rest I am going to earn; b) what about my children; c) being purposeful and focused. It wasn't a St Paul conversion; I made money from founding a company and taking it public four years ago. I wasn't penniless before and had realised that a substantial amount of money would be coming. I had set up the foundation four years earlier. The Charity Commission suggested a general grant-giving organisation, but I wanted to have a focus because I realised that although it seemed a lot of money, it wasn't really a lot. I wanted to focus on secondary education and wanted it to help people and not buildings so I engaged somebody to run the trust. I have an advisory panel of experts and appointed my children as trustees.*

(Male, 50s, self-made/entrepreneur)

This passage expands on many themes noted above but in this case the trust provides a framework for direct intervention in a chosen area of activity. Characteristic of this type of approach is the combination of passionate personal engagement with a business-like approach to structure and the use of expertise.

Others were at an earlier stage of defining how best they can use their wealth to have an impact in specific fields. In one very wealthy family, for example, one of several siblings in their 30s is, by agreement with the others, allocating significant time (about 30%) to research in order to refine a family strategy for philanthropy. However, as in other cases, the structure or framework for charitable giving was established some time ago.

> It is something we do. It is a private family business. We set up our own foundation nine or 10 years ago. After our parents died [in the 90s] we decided to step up the level of giving. Once you're comfortable with giving money away, adding another nought is not difficult. We are gradually giving away real money allocated from the profits of the business. We put a large amount into the foundation and as it is spent we shall put more in.
>
> (Male, 30s, inherited and grew family business)

A small minority referred to the fact that they had inherited significant funds when relatively young and had set up a trust at that stage. But although some were following a strong family philanthropic tradition, they were exploring their own approach.

A personal response

In a quite different group are those who were first moved to give significant sums through personal experiences or circumstances they had encountered. That is not to say that they had given nothing beforehand, but their early giving was an emotional response to an event or personal involvement in a cause, rather than an intellectual or detached analysis of the process.

For several people, the personal experience was a serious illness, either suffered by themselves, a child or a close friend. This had had a profound effect on them and was crucial to their early giving.

> My wife and I have been giving since the mid 80s. I was involved with charities in raising money since the early 80s. In the 70s one of our children was ill and only just survived. Her life was saved by Great Ormond Street and through my connection with the hospital I became the first Chairman of a charity established to help the families of sick children. From the mid 80s we started to have money to give on a modest scale.
>
> (Male, 50s, self-made/professional)

I had a kidney operation, found my notes and ended up funding a particular scientist involved in basic research. I got involved in the cancer surgery centre because I discovered that 90% of cancer cures are attributable to surgery but of worldwide spending on R & D in cancer, only 1% is on surgery research. Then I was on a boat with people who had their own project and I merged mine with theirs…

(Male, 50s, self-made/professional)

As in the above case, several people allied their personal response with an investigation into what needed to be done and how they could help most effectively.

Others reported personal involvement in a political or social cause which had prompted early giving and led to later donation. For some this was giving to the Labour Party, or a broader commitment to social justice as the start of their civic engagement.

I was a founder member of an organisation providing Christmas breakfasts for the unemployed. In early years I was interested in Quaker work and international reconciliation rather than broader social welfare. My wife was on the committee of [Xtown] CVS and helped them to build up links with others who shared common ideas – for example, Catholic Church Action on Poverty.

(Male, 80s, self-made/entrepreneur)

Being engaged by a specific cause or an organisation was also important in a few cases.

In 1985 I became involved with the Aga Khan Foundation programme. This was not particularly religious. It's a programme for Bombay Street Dwellers – 'socialising' them by building flats. I became passionate about this and gave 1% of the turnover of my company. I gave £100,000 a year for four years between 1985 and 1989. This was stopped by the recession.

(Male, 40s, self-made/entrepreneur)

[1] A creative social entrepreneur who created Comic Relief and later Pilotlight, which brings together high net worth individuals and charities needing expert help to develop their potential.

I got involved through Jane Tewson[1]. I went to Centrepoint and was gob-smacked and gave one day a week. It was proactive, creative and there was leverage. This was intelligent engagement.

(Female, 30s, married wealthy entrepreneur)

This is another example of the crucial importance of the influential ambassador. For one person, seeing such need led to a life-style change:

*I went to India in 1987 and saw poverty in India for the first time.
I became angry and thought I would do something. I gave up my job,
sold my shares and decided to change my life; I had plenty to live on.
Rich Christians in an Age of Hunger[2] says freeze where you are, cut
back to where you are comfortable and hold that. That's what I did. I
sold shares, sold the second car, gave up my job with seven-figure
earning potential; my wife is also committed. I didn't think it was better
to earn more and give that away, I wanted to commit my life; I wanted
to use my entrepreneurial skills to create leverage and imbue the
sector with business skills.*

(Male, 50s, self-made/entrepreneur)

What all these have in common is an emotional response to an experience, coupled with an understanding, or at least a perception, of how they could make a difference. Perhaps most crucially, a relationship with an organisation had developed which responded to and reinforced their interest. There is "intelligent engagement" and it becomes personally rewarding.

Key points

Several recurrent findings in the above analysis hold important messages for different constituencies in the UK. These include:

◆ People do not, on the whole, start as strategic givers. Even those who come from families with a strong philanthropic tradition want to develop their own approach and philosophy.

◆ Among people who are not members of a family or community with a strong philanthropic tradition, few start serious giving at a very early stage. They embark on a significant philanthropic commitment when they are moved by a cause, realise that they have more than they need or when they have sold a business and want to use their time effectively.

◆ Almost all of the experience of early workplace giving was based in US institutions.

◆ Being introduced, asked and managed effectively can be an important early experience.

◆ Very few people had been encouraged or counselled by a professional adviser.

[2] Book by Ronald Sider on subject of poverty with practical advice on making change according to Christian teachings.

One implication of these findings and those in Chapter Three is that in order to encourage philanthropy we need to create a culture in which it is expected that people of means will give. As we have seen, such expectations are prevalent in certain cultures and faiths, and still apply to traditional institutions such as "the big house" and major local employers. The challenge is to generate this same culture in the City and business, so that senior employees lead by example and make a commitment to philanthropy in their personal capacity which may complement and enhance the corporate social responsibility programme of the company, if there is one.

There are a number of steps which could be taken to develop a stronger culture of giving among the wealthy in the UK. These are discussed in Chapter 15. They require committed and sustained investment by a number of players – the government, the education sector, employers, community foundations, and professional advisers. However, there is one course of action that is entirely within the control of charities themselves. They need to use the most important trigger to substantial giving – being moved by a cause. This is explored in Chapter Five.

In some cases – having hospital treatment, attending an arts event – the personal experience itself is enough to stimulate future engagement. But charities in all sectors could do much more to make people aware of an issue or opportunity, to produce a reaction of anger, amazement, passion or enthusiasm, to provoke the response that something should and could be done, and to provide an effective means for the individual to become involved in a way which is appropriate for them.

5

Motivations, incentives and rewards

W hether donating time or money, most people have a range of motivations for giving. The influences operate at different levels and along varying dimensions. They are also intertwined in the explanations people gave of what underlies their charitable giving. This has made the key issues difficult to disentangle and complex to present.

We focus on general motivations rather than why people support specific causes, although there is sometimes an inextricable overlap. General attitudes and motivations are strongly linked to upbringing and family, religious and community traditions and expectations, as explored in Chapter Four. Criteria for selecting specific causes can be associated with these factors, but also with personal and business experience, social networks, and where people live and work. Personal experience may include a specific trigger – for example a child's illness, being moved by a great artistic performance, or coming face to face with perceived injustice or waste of talent. The relationship with the cause may also have started in a number of other ways – through an introduction from a friend or business acquaintance or attendance at an event, for example.

Looking at motivations on an individual basis, we see that no-one had just one impulse to give. It is also vital to distinguish between the passions and personal experiences which may lead an individual to become a giver, and the reinforcement donors get in knowing that they are making a difference, being properly thanked and meeting like-minded people. In this chapter we also look at the significance of incentives such as extended networks, social engagement, and privileged access to services (educational, cultural, healthcare) provided by the beneficiaries, and consider the extent of altruism in giving. We explore the factors which would change the level of people's giving, and in the final section we look in some detail at the giving of time.

Why people give

This first section explores why people give money. We look both at people's underlying motivations and at what triggers particular interests. Although multiple in their origin and variable in their manifestation, the influences that emerge fall under five broad headings:

◆ Belief in the cause.
◆ Being a catalyst for change.
◆ Self-actualisation.
◆ Duty and responsibility.
◆ Relationships.

The chart opposite shows the way these influences interlock. Each is explored in turn.

Belief in the cause

The cause is the motivation.

(Male, 60s, inherited and grew family business)

Without a doubt, the key impetus for the majority of people is belief in the cause. For many, a passion for a specific cause is inseparable from motivation; the enthusiasm underpins and is reinforced by the affinity for and relationship with the individual organisations which focus on the subjects of concern to the donor. Donors who care deeply about a generic cause, whether child poverty or opera, may well support more than one charity or institution addressing those issues.

The inter-locking influences

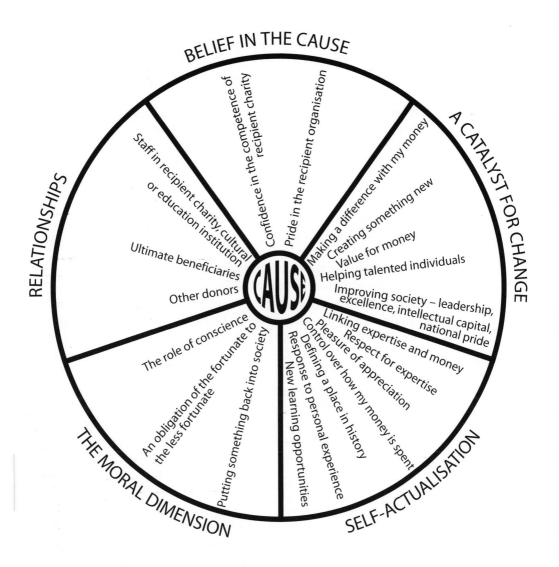

One gives because one believes in the organisations to which one is giving. One believes that they are worth supporting and encouraging and they are initiating new things. I am keen to give with knowledge. There has to be an interest combined with emotional involvement. Charity allows people to respond to emotional and intellectual feelings. We are putting money back in to things that have uplifted us and challenged us and horrified us.

(Male, 60s, inherited wealth)

This interviewee comes from a family with a tradition of philanthropy and inherited wealth, but the views were echoed by most people, irrespective of their background or source of affluence. It was common to see issues surrounding "putting something back" into society and a response to both emotional and intellectual engagement melded together. We also see a recurring combination of belief in the cause supported by confidence in the organisations supported.

The ties and influences which link people to particular charities are explored in detail in Chapter Six. But essentially the choice of a cause is often influenced by a wish to change or enhance society's systems or structures in line with a particular interest or belief. Although some denied a political agenda in their desire to influence change, others recognised in themselves an ethical imperative in their support of particular causes. This applied on both a national and international basis.

> It's immoral that there's a bunch of people who don't get a realistic chance – the disadvantages of being poor. There's also the economic perspective – wasting talent is stupid – but the driving force is moral. Social mobility has become worse. That's the crux of what I'm trying to do, to break down barriers to social mobility.
>
> (Male, 50s, self-made/entrepreneur)

> I'm interested in social justice, redressing inequalities, compassion, reconciliation. I don't respond to pressure but to the need. South Asia is now a big cause. I wasn't aware having come from Africa but I was shown how I could make an impact. I am now strategic and focused on the South Asian diaspora.
>
> (Male, 50s, self-made/entrepreneur)

For some, the chosen cause was support of major institutions, particularly those with an educational, medical or cultural base. This was often linked to a sense of national as well as personal pride. London, or Manchester, or the North East, or the UK, were felt to benefit from and "deserve" outstanding hospitals, art galleries and so on.

Belief in a cause is not the only reason for giving, and certainly not for continuing to give. The level and continuity of commitment is closely correlated to the degree to which the recipient is able to awaken and sustain a passion for the cause, a subject we explore in Chapter Six.

Being a catalyst for change

I like being a catalyst, not just maintaining the status quo. Time plus money equals change. A lot of what I do is to do with supporting self-esteem and dignity.

(Male, 40s, self-made/professional)

A related theme concerned people's desire to see "something that otherwise wouldn't have happened". This was sometimes expressed as "helping to create change", sometimes as "having an impact", but always with the underlying wish to make a "real" difference.

We try to make a real difference to small organisations doing really good work, so we fund small organisations in the Notting Hill area. I am concerned with issues such as human rights, drugs/alcohol/eating disorders, and issues in the community to do with ethnic minorities.

(Female, 50s, married wealthy entrepreneur)

Some wish to provide opportunities for individuals, others to facilitate change around a cause or a social problem, and some want a blend of the two.

I begin to identify with the cause. It's the will to succeed... I am helping people towards independence. The great thing about having lots of money is the ability it gives you to solve problems. Charity is one way of doing that.

(Male, 50s, self-made entrepreneur)

I feel good, I like making a difference. I am interested in educational charities because I am an unreconstructed elitist – I see myself as training the next elite.

(Male, 50s, self-made/professional)

The wish to have an impact on individual lives – whether disadvantaged young people, talented artists, or people who lack opportunity more generally – was expressed by several. Many linked their support of individuals to the benefits to society, partly to redress inequality but also to allow recipients to become more independent or to develop "intellectual capital". Others emphasised the satisfaction of observing the effects of their philanthropy – seeing the beneficiaries flourish, creating a better society and satisfying their consciences at the same time.

> *What motivates me is doing some good for children. Putting some money into individuals and seeing them do well. It's good fun to give money away. It's quite pleasant. There is satisfaction in thinking of doing something and satisfying that part of one's conscience. I get quite worked up. Education guarantees a fairer society. Seeing these kids at these great schools is great. There is no political axe. It's about individuals and how to work within the system.*
>
> (Male, 50s, self-made/entrepreneur)

This relatively widespread interest in making a difference to educational opportunities is perhaps not surprising given the nature of causes that attract significant attention. We note in Chapter Two that education and other opportunities for disadvantaged children in deprived areas were high on the agenda: for many this was about prevention of a "waste of talent". But others were interested in providing opportunities for people across a range of different spheres – and not just for those from more deprived backgrounds.

> *I help young people to help themselves, not just the most deprived. It could be comfortable families where my help will make a difference to do better. It's easier to help organisations for the disadvantaged because an infrastructure exists. It's harder to help those who want to better themselves. I like to help individuals to go on Project Trust or Operation Raleigh. I help with college fees; I've helped musicians (I helped with a violin and a bow), someone go to dance school or athletes.*
>
> (Male, 60s, self-made/entrepreneur)

Another recurring theme in facilitating change was the wish to get "value for money" – effective and direct use of a financial contribution.

> *For fairly modest amounts one can make a real difference. I feel ashamed if we don't have a world class opera house in London and if foreigners are expected to provide the money.*
>
> (Male, 50s, self-made/professional)

That person added that he *"wanted to make a difference in keeping London a great world city"*. He was not alone in citing national pride as a factor in his giving.

For some who wanted to see their money put to effective use, a dislike of supporting large social welfare charities with what were seen as relatively small amounts was a common concern.

I am motivated by need. The first question is 'what is it for?'. I like things where less money goes far. It's harder to support charities such as [examples of major UK charities] where you feel it is a drop in the bucket.
(Male, 60s, inherited and grew family business)

For some, an underlying motivation to effect change was a wish to invest in the future. Some saw this as about the protecting the country's cultural heritage, others about developing a "better" or more equitable society.

Both corporately and personally I work on the principle that if you want to defend prosperity you have to attack poverty. If people want to protect what they have they must be actively engaged in this. So what I give must in some meaningful sense cover the responsibility to others and the responsibility to ourselves to help the attack on poverty. This is not just in the UK, I see myself as an international citizen.
(Male, self -made/professional)

Self-actualisation

It's a personal way of changing things.
(Male, 50s, self-made/professional)

You become involved at a certain age. When you have achieved as much as you can in your job you look for psychic benefit: there's a feeling you could contribute and make things happen. It's an antidote to business life. It would be unusual if that was before your forties.
(Male, 50s, self-made/professional)

A number of drivers can be categorised under the general heading of self-actualisation – the realisation of an individual's personality and development of some or all of its aspects. They involve issues surrounding integrity, personal engagement and commitment, as well as responses to intellectual and emotional sentiments. Although for most people self-actualisation is not the initial motivator, the experience of the "psychic" benefits sustains their giving and is the basis for recurring commitment.

Linking expertise, time and money

We have observed that there was often a surge in philanthropic activity when reaching a particular stage in life. Having more time – and perhaps occupying time – was regularly mentioned as a contributory factor, as was the idea that making money is not enough for a complete life.

> *I have to do something when I get up in the morning! When I had done my bit on the City treadmill I had energy and resources and can't think of a better or more interesting way to spend my time. It's not about creating an edifice for posterity... I'd like to think my children will continue, but what I like is helping the arts and people who do wonderful things for inadequate levels of compensation, or sitting in front of something worthwhile – a person or event – which couldn't have happened without my support or in part at least because of what I was asked to contribute.*
>
> (Male, 50s, self -made/entrepreneur)

Some people emphasised that it may not be possible to give time unless an individual has inherited money, is a non-working partner or has retired. But many who give time in the form of professional expertise are at the top of their profession, and the satisfaction of applying skills learnt in business to the non-profit sector was often mentioned.

> *I am in a very privileged profession. What redeems me is being able to offer ideas for fundraising operations or cause related initiatives. It's hard to say no a) because of the client and b) as a human being. I feel honoured and privileged to be involved with XYZ. It is an unmitigated joy because of all involved. It is socially focused and they are keen to put something back.*
>
> (Male, 30s, self-made/entrepreneur)

In this case and many others people felt satisfaction – almost a sense of "redemption" – from using professional expertise, often in finance or law, to help others. The satisfaction was reinforced when there was obvious value placed on the advice or when it was implemented. All who were members of the Chancellor's Court of Benefactors at Oxford University, for example, referred positively to their experience of being asked for ideas as well as money. But the reverse could be equally influential in an adverse way – one potential donor with expertise in property management was asked for money to repair badly managed properties but his offer of advice about how to reduce the risk of this happening in the future was rejected. He did not become a committed giver to this institution.

Appreciation

Although people need respect for advice and expertise, the main appreciation they receive is of course for money, and the motivating power of that reinforcement cannot be overstated. Most people emphasised the pleasure of being valued for their donations, and being respected by other donors, which in turn contributed to feelings of self-worth.

> *Anyone who has more than they need should give some of it away. I get a tremendous amount back from making a significant donation. If you have money and want to be liked and respected, give money to charity. You get genuine affection and respect. It's much better than a Rolls Royce. People have lost sight of the need to make substantial donations... If you haven't much to offer in terms of intellect, power or influence and you want to get involved in institutions in the UK, the easiest way to get accepted and respected is to give money.*
> (Male, 60s, self-made and inherited wealth)

Control over how money is spent

People used to leadership and decision-making gain an additional satisfaction by allocating money which would otherwise go to the government. Chapter Seven explores in more detail what this might mean in practice. This is in part about keeping control and influence over the way their money is spent. It is also about competence, and the idea that giving money in a tax-efficient way is a better alternative to paying more taxes and having "Gordon Brown spending it".

> *It's better for people to decide individually what to give to rather than for the government to take it and give it to charities. That is very inefficient.*
> (Male, 60s, self-made/professional)

Defining a place in history

> *It's a personal way of changing things. This is very difficult in the modern world... My dream is to have funded the person who got the basic biology of cancer sorted out. Most times it won't happen but it's worth anything.*
> (Male, 50s, self-made/professional)

This passage, from someone who made money in the City and immediately allocated a significant amount to a trust, highlights another significant issue – the dream of the philanthropic legacy.

Although many interviewees could celebrate major commercial and entrepreneurial achievements, and a few had made significant contributions in creative fields, there was the strong implication that the highest recognition of posterity would lie in what benefactors were able to do for others. No-one cited the Medici, but some mentioned great British or American philanthropists when talking about philanthropy generally, and their spirit lingered. This issue was discussed in depth when we asked about people's desire for recognition, a subject covered in Chapter Six.

Response to personal experience

At the other end of the spectrum of motivation is the response to personal or family experience – often illness or an accident. Much support for causes addressing specific medical or social conditions is linked to this. Many people supported hospitals where a child had been cured, or an organisation which helps specific disabilities or illnesses. Support for the educational establishments attended by the donor or their children is in this category.

> *I give money to ABC, which helps people feeling suicidal in the Y area. My brother committed suicide so I can relate to it. People can achieve their objectives with your money. I can afford it. I have enough to achieve my objectives.*
>
> (Male, 60s, inherited and grew family business)

A tiny number admitted to involvement in a social care or health related charity as a form of enlightened self-interest – although many were happy to identify this as a factor in supporting the arts.

In terms of personal motivation there is a difference between supporting a cancer charity because someone one loves has experience of cancer, and supporting it because one thinks it might ensure better or quicker care should one need it. This may have practical implications for the recipient if there is a real expectation of reciprocity: for example a university place. This question is considered in more detail later in this chapter.

New learning opportunities

It is clear that people engage in a learning process about their philanthropy, developing an understanding that comes with the ability to give it time and attention.

> *I left XYZ Bank last year. I wanted to pursue interests in philanthropy and the governance sphere and am exploring what to do... I am just coming*

*up the learning curve but it's not yet a strategy. I feel better than I did a
year ago.*

(Female, 30s, self-made/professional)

Several people mentioned the reinforcing effect of acquiring knowledge
about a subject and gaining more insight into the philanthropic process.
Such insights also give pleasure.

The moral dimension

The role of conscience
We noted earlier the feeling of "redemption" felt by someone whose
privileged position was somehow mitigated by their support of a major
social cause. Giving time, expertise and money makes them feel a better
person. For them and many others one factor in their motivations was the
satisfaction – to a greater or lesser extent – of their conscience. This was
not to do with any perception that their wealth was ill-gotten; indeed,
although many people mentioned the fact that they are fortunate as being
one of the reasons for their philanthropy, only one in the entire study used
the word "guilt". For most people the basis of the values which prompted
feelings of obligation were the influences explored in Chapter Three – of
faith, family or community.

An obligation of the fortunate to the less fortunate
Some linked their sense of being privileged both to an obligation to those
less fortunate and to wanting to help rebalance a sense of social injustice.

*It's natural. I am fortunate and should therefore share with others less
fortunate. There is no philosophical base but it has a relation to justice
and fairness and rebellion against the establishment and hypocrisy. I am
pleased to have the opportunity and pleased to be able to help. I would
feel bad if I didn't give and I don't give as much as I ought to.*

(Male, 60s, self-made/professional)

The identification of others "less fortunate" varies. For many it covered a
wide range, from family to community to wider society. In some cases it
included staff, extended family and friends in financial difficulty.

Such giving may not be "charitable" in the sense of giving to registered
charities or supporting people who would be regarded as disadvantaged.
However, it is nevertheless philanthropic and poses its own challenges:

how to manage wealth (particularly self-made) and retain your relationships, especially with siblings and close friends.

Financial support of those with much less, or going through hard times, is seen as part of the responsibility of wealth, and in some cases is a family tradition. This transcends cultures: it is as true in the Jewish and Asian communities as for those who have inherited traditional family estates in the UK, and the support is seen as reinforcing mutual ties.

> *Generations of the family have given. It's a family tradition. What makes it worth it is the continuity with the people who receive it.*
>
> (Male, 40s, self-made and inherited wealth)

For those who had inherited or created wealth locally and those with a strong religious background, the notion of other people's expectations could further fuel a sense of obligation.

> *Doing something for others, the less fortunate and the wider community. It's time and money but many do more than me. It's expected among the people in the community with whom I mix. I thought it would be nice to get involved with youth in the community in the North West.*
>
> (Male, 50s, self-made/professional)

Putting something back into society
The theme of "putting something back" was mentioned by many, especially those who were immigrant in origin. Not surprisingly, this features very prominently in US research, and is explored in Chapter Fourteen. However, not everyone explained their philanthropy in those terms.

> *I sense I have been fortunate to be in the right place at the right time. We have a high income and now have capital. My wife doesn't want to be conspicuous. There's no way of spending it all. There's a huge number of deserving causes, but I don't have a burning sense that I must give something back to the community. There's a feeling of satisfaction, making a difference to something worthwhile.*
>
> (Male, 50s, self-made/professional)

The point that they had been "in the right place at the right time" was made by several who had made money in the City or high technology in the 90s, or who had benefited from what they saw as Thatcher-influenced opportunities to grow their businesses.

A significant minority, including some who had made money and some who inherited, linked their belief that they had been fortunate with the obligation to share.

> *It's right that you should do something if you have been blessed. People in this country are generous even with high taxation. The higher the tax rate, the easier it is to give. You might create something for the future which will be beneficial for someone. You get to know people better. It's a good opportunity to reinforce relationships.*
>
> (Male, 60s, self-made/professional)

This sense of "deserving one's luck" was manifest across all religious backgrounds. While there were major contributions to the local community in the North-East from self-made entrepreneurs, the evidence suggests that this sense of duty to society or community was particularly strong among those who had inherited their wealth, although the level of giving varied.

> *I am absorbing my inheritance. It's a way of putting money to good use. I have plenty for a nice life and care passionately about the environment. It's passion and making the world a better place. It's a role for those who don't have to work to have a chance to look at things at large, and hopefully with wisdom, to try to influence changes.*
>
> (Female, 30s, inherited wealth)

The moral dimension and the role of conscience are not confined to those who claim strong family, faith or community traditions. However, it is more pronounced or explicit among those from that category, and we observe in Chapter Four that some who had made money were unclear as to what level of giving might be appropriate. This was a different issue from the question of financial security, and what people could "afford', which is explored in Chapter Eight.

Relationships

> *The cause is the motivation. Plus satisfying peripherals: the relationships with beneficiaries and the people administering the charities.*
>
> (Male, 60s, inherited and grew family business)

It is not surprising that one of the major motivating factors reported by respondents across all categories is the fun, enjoyment and personal fulfilment of relationships with a range of people that charitable activity brings. Recognition of this by those seeking support and the importance of the personal approach is explored in Chapter Six.

The pleasure in part derives from the broadening of perspective engendered by meeting those from a completely contrasting walk of life, often creative and dedicated to different goals. The sense of working in partnership with those who deliver the mission is very important for many donors: it is the idea that philanthropy is the successful integration of money (the donor's), commitment (donor and recipient) and professional expertise (recipient), with money as the enabler or facilitator.

> *The sense of making some real difference, whether large or small. Satisfaction, getting to know some extraordinary people... who are now friends. Fun with a capital F. You can't buy it and it's unobtainable elsewhere.*
> (Male, 50s, self-made/professional)

Such "extraordinary people" may be those working for the charity or a cultural or education institution or the ultimate beneficiaries. They might also be other donors. Retaining a place among a lively community of exemplary givers is a major motivator. The nature of relationships with other donors is explored in more detail opposite.

Throughout this section we have seen that there is rarely a single motivation to give but rather a mix of motives and reinforcements. Both initial motivations and motivations for continuing to be involved are identified and many of the emotions and responses expressed are reactions to how the recipient manages the relationship with the donor. Whereas the initial gift may be the product of one set of ideas, continuing to give depends also on the donor feeling that their motives have been understood and respected. One of the participants very ably draws all these factors together.

> *The cause. Making a difference is important. A sort of pleasure, satisfaction, conscience, fulfilment of duty and the pleasure from that... and the appreciation. You don't get that once you're dead. The [named] room at the [major museum] gives me a buzz. It's not a condition but it's fun. Fun and angst balance. I would feel an absolute shit if I didn't do it. I would love to do more but I'm too idle to be richer.*
> (Male, 70s, self-made/entrepreneur)

Extended networks and social engagement

This section explores how giving is linked to social engagement and the desire or influence of joining networks. This is crucial to what constitutes or encourages a culture of giving. Culture, amongst other things, is about the attitudes, values, norms and "rules" which inform a society, and membership of a group within society (faith, family or community) which creates expectations of charitable giving is, as we see in Chapter Three, a key determinant of philanthropy. In the absence of any such membership, joining and participating in a network or set of relationships in which giving is an essential and pleasurable component is a major step to normalising such behaviour.

The donor network

All who were experienced donors, irrespective of their backgrounds or origins of wealth, knew other donors to their causes.

I sit on the same board, I get invited to functions [examples given in the arts and heritage]. It's recognition of my support of music. With the [named charity – a children's welfare organisation] *the pressure comes from one's own desire to help – you must feel a strong link. I hate dinners. The most recent event was last night. It's the same people. It's easy to get in if you want. Young people must be targeted more. Older people experienced the war and its aftermath. Younger people are not interested in charity. One must make US style planned giving possible here.*

(Female, 70s, self-made/entrepreneur)

I know other donors through [my family's] social circle. Emotionally, I would support the arts. I enjoy some events and share this with my husband. We like meeting other people. It can be very amusing. Last night we attended the Beaumont group at the National Gallery. Yes, there is a network and it can seem elitist and exclusive. It depends where you look. You find giving people popping up. It is big in opera and music. New donors would be well received.

(Female, 30s, inherited wealth)

These two respondents raise important issues that were recurrent in other responses. First, there is a strong perception of a group or network of donors whose interests span several organisations or causes. This is also true of boards where there is felt to be overlapping membership, particularly in the arts[1]. But both people emphasised, as indeed did many others, that the network is not exclusive and there is a need to draw in new people, particularly of a younger age.

[1] It is not possible from the evidence from this study to provide a detailed analysis of the extent of overlap between board membership and donations.

A second feature is the obvious pleasure that some people experience through attending events or getting to know people within the donor network. Although some people "hate dinners", there are many other types of social events that may engage an individual's interest. The opportunity to share giving and personal engagement with a partner can also be very important, particularly for busy people. The event reinforces the personal as well as the philanthropic relationship.

While many individual charities may create and nurture their own networks, those which transcend single institutions are again more common in the arts. The arts also provide, in their venue or mission, ready-made opportunities to share the passion for the cause with fellow and prospective donors, meet other supporters and reinforce relationships. This is less easy in other areas – "*the pressure comes from one's own desire to help*". Perhaps because of this several people felt that the pressure – or at least encouragement – they experienced was stronger in the arts than with social welfare causes.

The importance of existing networks in providing a natural community for philanthropy was discussed in Chapter Three. The Jewish community was frequently mentioned as a strength within the donor network, both from within and outside the Jewish population.

> *I get pressure from [fellow professionals], other board members. I suspect there is a network and I would love to be able to afford to give more. I would love to win the lottery and be able to give. The ability to share philanthropy is very important. The Jewish experience is so important.*
> (Male, 50s, self-made/professional, Church of England)

The Jewish experience extends beyond synagogue to social welfare organisations and arts institutions, both in the UK and Israel. The dinners and other events which reinforce commitment to the cause also provide a mechanism for strengthening the community itself. Some respondents saw the existence of such networks – and the opportunity they offer to widen contacts – as potentially helpful beyond the immediate focus of giving.

> *I know givers in the Jewish world, yes. 20 to 30 people give 80% of the large donations. I meet them at events organised by the charity. I am building up a network and getting to meet influential people. I am not sure how or why it might be useful. It's a question of reciprocity.*
> (Male, 30s, self-made/entrepreneur, non-observant Jew)

Several people who had inherited wealth, or were in strong communities, or were already major donors, made the point that they "knew the people anyway". Those in this position see themselves as detached from the need to respond to social pressure, although they might support something for other reasons.

> *I am above the battle. It depends what I want out of someone – for example, reciprocity. I don't like first nights and that kind of thing. I miss quite a lot of them. I like the privileges such as rehearsals, early morning visits, touring buildings while being built, directors explaining things. There is a network but it is not getting bigger.*
>
> (Female, 50s, inherited)

Some who claimed not to respond to such pressure still enjoy meeting others. But being on the receiving end of strong reciprocal expectations may require people to support causes even though they do not believe in them passionately. This is a challenge, notwithstanding the opportunities to exchange ideas with like-minded people, and to demonstrate their commitment to their community.

The issue of reciprocity in the context of asking for money is considered in Chapter Six.

The role of events
People are divided in their views about attending events, whether to be solicited or thanked. Some enjoy them both for the event itself and for the social engagement they offer, some are less enthusiastic but find them hard to resist, while others are very selective about what they will attend.

> *Sometimes it's fun but personally there are events I prefer not to go to and make a donation for the amount.*
>
> (Male, 50s, self-made/professional)

> *I don't mind them* [events] *but I would equally be happy never to go again. I despise balls which raise pathetically little money and seem engineered primarily for the activity and profile of the under-occupied. The last event I attended was [a major anniversary celebration] because I am on the advisory board of XYZ.*
>
> (Male, 50s, self -made/professional)

People who were established and confident socially were more likely to resist fundraising events – but this was equally a matter of personal temperament. Perhaps the most common aversion was to formal dinners, where people often stayed for drinks only, and preferred to make a donation rather than attend. This is particularly true of busy people who are reluctant to give up an entire evening for what may be an indifferent meal.

As in the above passage, the task of attending events as a responsibility of board membership was sometimes mentioned. While some enjoyed this "because I am with friends", others reported "pressure" that they should support organisations on whose board they sit. Unlike in the US, it is not assumed in the UK that financial contributions are an inherent and implicit commitment of board membership. This is discussed in Chapter Fourteen.

Social opportunities and aspirations

Although not all donors enjoy charitable events, the successful giving network can become an enjoyable social network. Those who are members are seen as friends – and the encouragement and example of friends is not necessarily seen as "pressure".

> *I do not respond to social pressure, but I enjoy getting to know other givers. This becomes an important part of life. It becomes a community. I like people who like musicians... it's a congenial group. I enjoy the social aspects in moderation. We invite musicians to our home.*
>
> (Male, 50s, self-made/entrepreneur)

The integration of social and philanthropic life is particularly strong in certain groups – the Jewish community, as we have seen, certain City networks and supporters of major arts institutions in London, for example. For people who have a wide range of social opportunities, relatively routine events are not a draw; indeed, those invited may be well aware that it is their presence which is required to attract others. They understand that their attendance is genuinely to benefit the cause and not a personal "reward".

As well as the opportunity to meet new people, some of those who had created their own wealth found an extra incentive in the opportunities to visit great venues and meet influential or socially impressive people. It can be hard to resist.

> *I try not to be affected by who asks, but for example I was invited by the Duke of Westminster and felt I was put under pressure.*
>
> (Male, 60s, self-made/entrepreneur)

It's an active stimulant: for example events at Chatsworth for [named] hospital. Charles and Camilla were there. I get a real buzz from working with non-Jewish charities. I meet new people. The social reward is considerable. The [arts institution he chairs] had a reception at Downing Street. It's fun. It's not an incentive but it is a reward. Intellectual stimulus is only good for me.

(Male, 60s, inherited and grew family business)

Others mentioned accepting invitations to events attended by a member of the royal family they wanted to meet (either The Prince of Wales or The Princess Royal). But others had different reactions, and disliked the assumption that the presence of a member of the royal family would affect their giving decision.

Some people observed that the exploitation of social aspirations was a legitimate incentive, and should be incorporated into a strategy for developing a culture of giving. More commonly, people made the point that a "special" invitation would not of itself affect their major or repeated giving. As we have seen, this requires engagement over and above attendance at events, unless the event is either part of a community activity and/or provides the opportunity to see the quality and nature of the work.

People may attend an event or presentation of a project because of the origin of the invitation, or who else may be there. But they will only commit significant sums if they are sincerely moved, and only continue to give if there is a solid relationship.

Giving circles

In recent years a number of more or less formal networks have developed for people at various levels of net worth to explore their attitudes to and responsibilities of wealth. One of these is the Network for Social Change, which offers members opportunities to discuss such matters among themselves in private, and to support a range of social causes. A small number of those interviewed are members.

I regard networks as very important in most human activity. I benefit from good networks among grant makers nationally and locally and among grant seekers in particular fields. The Network for Social Change is a special case. For some members, not myself, it is vital to exchange views with other donors. Apart from that, people bring a wealth of knowledge about a great number of worthwhile projects.

(Male, 80s, self-made/entrepreneur)

There is perhaps a paradox in the evident importance of a sense of community in building up networks, and the observation by more than one person that the need for philanthropic networking was often less outside London. This may be related to the reported existence of strong alternative local networks, with more stable and smaller communities. However, in the North East, where there is a strong community foundation, several people mentioned the opportunity provided through the foundation for networking and learning.

> *I know other givers through business or friendship and then ask them for money. There is a constant flow of mainly minor local and relatively small causes. It's a local, not a major network. I love meeting people, new people but it's not the reason I do it. I don't think there is a network of big givers, not that I have found. I don't want to be part of it. To me, giving is very personal. When we decide to do something it is because we want to do it. It is very private.*
>
> (Male, 50s, inherited and grew family business)

Widening the set of contacts

While some donors were concerned that new members were not joining their giving circles, everyone suggested that such networks are open to all who are willing to contribute. The challenge is not to open closed doors, but to attract the donors in the first place. This was seen as the responsibility of those soliciting support, whether voluntary or paid.

The task is to match prospect and cause, and other supporters of that cause, and to look beyond the immediate supporter group.

> *It's about social level and shared interests and values. Friendships form among givers; anyone can join as long as they pay. They are always looking for new money; they are desperate for new blood. It is great if you can identify and welcome someone to the club. People are often very enthusiastic about their first charity. When I first made money, people didn't ask me for money for about 10 years.*
>
> (Male, 50s, self-made creative)

There is a strong suggestion here that, at least in some cases, the net is being cast too narrowly. While working outwards from the associates of existing supporters is a necessary component of any strategy to broaden the circle of givers, clearly this approach may not capture the newly wealthy, the person in a "solo" career (such as the interviewee last quoted, a writer), or perhaps people outside the mainstream of city life.

Once engaged in a new network there is a double reinforcement, reported particularly by the recently wealthy: the rewards of the support of the cause and the expansion of the circle of acquaintance.

> *I have enjoyed meeting lots of interesting people and some real dogs at all levels. It has broadened my life. Some friends have only been to the golf club. I have various sets of friends and that is a benefit.*
>
> (Male, 50s, self-made/entrepreneur)

It is difficult to anticipate how any individual will respond to social aspects of the donor network, since personal inclination and appetite for social engagements are such important factors. We have noted that people vary in the types of events they enjoy, although for people who are socially ambitious or who want to extend their circles of acquaintance, an interesting and unusual venue, access to people of "influence", and the opportunity to become part of a new network, all hold attractions.

Perhaps more crucially, the point was made that it is the responsibility of fundraisers to ensure that networks function and new people are welcomed and absorbed. People who have created their own wealth, and particularly those outside the "mainstream", may not be identified through the usual channels, and may respond very positively to the first organisation which takes an interest.

There is therefore a complex response to the question of how people react to social pressure and peer group expectations, and whether they enjoy networking, meeting other people and so on. As with all giving, it is important to distinguish between motivations for the initial commitment, and the reinforcing effect of the inclusion in a circle of like-minded people.

Special access

> *They should definitely offer hooks for people who give time and money. Organisations are not very good at saying thank you. If you give money and can't get a ticket, it's a poor do. It's a way of saying thank you and can be a motivation to give more.*
>
> (Male, 50s, self-made/entrepreneur)

I don't expect it but I do appreciate it. I well accept that there is privileged access for people who give money.

(Female, 50s, self-made/entrepreneur)

People were asked whether or not donors should be offered special access to the services provided by the beneficiary. For many, it was not seen as a significant issue. This was either because they were supporting an organisation (heritage or cultural) precisely to obtain the benefits offered by the charity, often for membership; or they did not regard themselves as sufficiently major a donor to qualify for personalised or tailored privileges. But others, particularly those supporting the arts or higher education, thought that the organisation should certainly provide some form of access.

There were important differences between special access in arts and education.

The arts
Many people took the view that benefits, while not being a determining factor, were important.

I am more inclined to give money if they don't promise special access, but in practice having a special phone line for ticket booking is very nice.
(Male, 50s, self-made/professional)

For some major givers, such arrangements would be part of the overall package of recognition and involvement to be negotiated between donor and recipient.

It's not a condition but I want things clarified beforehand – if my name will be on display, if there's special access etc.
(Male, 40s, self-made and inherited wealth)

Because most arts organisations offer a range of special privileges, donors come to expect it. The forms of special access might include:
♦ Attendance at rehearsals.
♦ Visits to exhibitions outside public opening hours.
♦ Visiting projects under construction.
♦ Seeing behind the scenes, such as building work in progress, rehearsals, conservation activity or other specialist operations.

◆ The personal attention of the director.
◆ Avoiding the crowds, primarily attending exhibitions and other visual arts displays through, for example, private views (for high level supporters) or personal tours, escorted by curator or director (for major donors).
◆ Saving time and obtaining fast-track servicing. Examples included:

✦ A hotline for tickets.
✦ A special bar or bar area.
✦ A special area for collection of programmes and tickets.
✦ A designated cloakroom (to save queuing at the end).
✦ Free parking.

Those who were givers and also had experience as fundraisers were particularly emphatic about the importance of looking after major donors.

You must nurture people, not drop them when you have got the money.
They must be included in the future even if they do not continue to give.
It is not about one-off deal-making. You must make them feel special.
(Female, 70s, self-made/entrepreneur).

The relationships which people seek with the organisations they support, and the importance of looking after donors, is explored in Chapter Six.

Donation as membership

Some individuals were explicit about their expectations that giving at a certain level is about buying privileged access. At a low level it is simply a good deal – membership of the National Trust or the Royal Academy was seen as being in this category. It was noted that the tax treatment of such contributions was inconsistent, some being payable through Gift Aid or trusts and others not, and some organisations having to pay VAT in some cases.

People expect to pay more for an allocation of scarce resources – usually tickets. At this level of support it was not expected that the tickets would be free, just available. Some recognised that this was a mutually beneficial arrangement and should not be counted as charity in the same way as gifts to causes where there was no self-interest.

I am a founder member of Glyndebourne[2]. I don't consider that charity.
I pay the premium to jump the queue. It's the same as being friends of
English National Opera or the Royal Opera House. If you get the benefit,
it's not charity.
(Male, 50s, self-made)

----
[2] An opera house in East Sussex.

Others stated that they did not expect special access and condemned those who do, although, as we see, some recognised that this is not "charity". It was also noted that organisations need to ensure a committed donor base. For those receiving no public funds it is about securing a recurring income base on which to plan. Examples cited included the Royal Academy and Glyndebourne.

Four key points emerge from people's discussion of special access in the arts:

◆ Lower level givers may see themselves as buying a service – a ticket hotline, a fast-track cloakroom – as much as being "charitable".

◆ Partly in response to promotion by arts organisations themselves, expectation of such services are widespread, and those involved with fundraising strongly advocate their continuation.

◆ Donors see themselves as potential ambassadors, and argue that to perform that role well they need frequent (privileged) access.

◆ Some higher level donors are very irritated by what they see as pettiness about charging for small things. They are not interested in the finer points of the rules related to tax issues. Some expect to negotiate terms for access as part of the overall management of the relationship.

Education
Compared with the arts, far fewer interviewees had made significant donations to schools or universities. Within the group who had, there was a major divide between those who felt that donations should not buy access and those who believed they should. The issues discussed related entirely to university places, and specifically Oxford and Cambridge.

Examples of two very different views are shown below. In the first, a donor to the arts who had also given significant support to his old college contrasted his attitudes to the different sectors:

Social access such as post-performance dinners for high level donors is harmless. It's a good reason to give money to arts organisations. It's like a subscription, not charitable, but I look at it in terms of value for money – for example Friends of the Royal Opera House... [but] there should not be preferential access that matters.

(Male, 50s, self-made/professional)

This is someone for whom academic excellence is important and who had had a brilliant career at a leading Oxbridge college, to which he had given significant support. The college did not accept his only son and he has never mentioned it to the college nor suggested preferential treatment.

At the other end of the spectrum, there were those – a few – who felt that if the child in question had achieved the necessary entrance qualifications, it was not at all inappropriate to allocate one or more spaces for the children of major donors. It was evident that the US experience was influential in such a view – those who felt strongly about this had lived in the US or were aware of US friends with relevant experience. In one case the individual had children at both US and UK universities.

This same attitude was shared by those who had no children, although some claimed they would not adopt this approach themselves.

> *Take university entrance: I have no problem with, for example, Oxford allocating one or two places for wealthy, bright kids. Would I purchase a place? No.*
>
> (Male, 30s, self-made/professional)

No-one mentioned hospitals and hospices in the context of special access but we have noted the "insurance" factor in donations. Those with experience in fundraising for hospitals reported that major donors expected that they or members of their family would receive not so much special treatment as expert advice, for example, in cases where cancer is diagnosed.

Altruism and giving

Altruism may be defined as either giving which involves financial sacrifice (as perceived by the donor), or giving to causes in which the donor has no direct interest.

Donors who recognise in themselves the mix of motivating factors we have considered all saw giving as relating to one of the five main drivers. To that extent it could be said that no giving is entirely altruistic, since all donations generate "psychic" benefits and feelings of self-worth. This is a very significant point, since as we have seen many have observed that a key factor in encouraging others is to show them how to get in, and to demonstrate the fun, pleasure and satisfaction which people experience when they give.

What varies enormously is the relative importance of each element, and there is clearly a range of perspectives.

While a few interviewees recognised the moral content of foregoing something desirable, and regretted that they did not give more, no-one reported giving at a level which involved real sacrifice.

> *Supporting the arts is a bit of a luxury, as is giving a bursary to my children's old school. That's not what it's all about. There is a spectrum. It's not completely altruistic if you get looked after. I should be tackling hard, social problems. Giving a scholarship to a violinist is very important but it doesn't feel the same way as supporting the disadvantaged. I tend to ration that kind of giving. If I get pleasure out of it, it is not quite right. It's about the importance of the success and wellbeing of the city in the round. It leads to the success and wellbeing of the company.*
>
> (Male, 60s, self-made/entrepreneur)

This contributor is a leading businessman in a northern city and several in his position made the link between the wellbeing of a person's city or community and the success of their business.

People were asked whether they made a distinction between supporting organisations from which they had benefited or expect to benefit (such as educational or cultural institutions) and those with which they have no personal links (such as environmental or political disasters overseas, medical research, inner city playgrounds, and the homeless). The spectrum of response ranged from a tiny minority who only support the arts, to an equally small number who only support social welfare, with varying mixes of the two in-between.

> *The enjoyment of music has always been important in my life. The musicians are right in front of you. Other causes are too remote. You have to make decisions.*
>
> (Male, 50s, self-made/entrepreneur)

This donor highlights the response to a personal passion, the immediacy of the experience – you are involved with the performance and, by implication, can see where your money is going – and the idea that, with limited resources, choices have to be made. Others report no expectation of benefit other than the pleasure of involvement and recognition.

I expect no personal benefit. I give to social causes in the developing world. It [my support] funds improved quality of life, human rights, micro-finance and social change.

(Male, 60s, self-made/professional)

Apart from the fun and buzz of writing a cheque and getting recognition for one's time, the giving is totally altruistic. The buzz is private.

(Female, 50s, self-made/entrepreneur)

As we saw earlier, some charitable support is linked to personal experience rather potential benefits – for example, supporting research into diseases or conditions suffered by a close relation, usually a child of the donor. We have also noted that some giving to medical or social causes can be seen as a form of "insurance policy".

However, much more commonly people said that they supported charities where they enjoyed a benefit as well as causes where there was no immediate or personal return and they made no distinction in their decision-making between the two. They felt that their giving benefited others, as well as benefiting themselves. As we have seen, supporting the arts, heritage and the environment was often about sharing the enjoyment with others as well as providing opportunities.

We do benefit because we enjoy the arts. I want to give more people the choice of experiencing the thrill of a live performance at a theatre or experiencing first-hand the wonders of Shakespeare. We want every child in Wales to experience one live theatre performance.

(Male, 50s, inherited and grew family business)

This kind of double benefit is not confined to the arts.

There was an example last year of a mesh between self-interest and charity. I wanted to buy a wood, eventually a wood came up and I helped the Woodland Trust to buy it. The public can walk around it. What is ownership?

(Male, 60s, self-made and inherited wealth)

One major giver to a range of causes and sectors speculated that giving with self-interest may increase.

The Royal Opera House is a selfish cause which is not improving the lot of the poor. With people living longer and having more leisure, 'selfish'

*causes may benefit more. It may lead to more support of private
hospitals, golf clubs and the like. But the prosperous may become more
charitable. They may support the enhancement of life such as
beautifying the countryside. The National Trust is doing well because of
leisure in the country, but social causes are suffering.*

(Female, 50s, inherited wealth)

Others felt it was invidious to draw an altruistic/non-altruistic distinction as
it implied that some charities are more deserving than others.

*The distinction makes no difference. The question is, does one want to
support the purpose? If it is a compelling purpose I will still support it.
I dread the day when some charities will be seen as more virtuous than
others. You must apply the public benefit test to what is charitable.*

(Male, 50s, self-made/professional)

Changes which would be likely to increase the overall amount given to charitable causes

As we review in the Chapter Seven, less than 60% of respondents
expressed themselves as very satisfied with the effectiveness of their
donations. A significant proportion believed that their donations could be
more effective, although very few considered the risks of financial
mismanagement at an unacceptable level.

In this context it is interesting to consider which changes might increase
the overall level of giving. This question was designed to echo the
question asked in the research by Paul Schervish in the US in 2001,
reported in *The Mind of the Millionaire*[3]. A multiple choice of options was
offered, and respondents could select one or more of the alternatives.

It is clear from the chart opposite that most people say having more
money would make the biggest difference. This was likely or very likely to
make a difference for over 75% of those interviewed, with a slightly higher
proportion of women. Finding a new cause about which people care
passionately is the next most important change, and a factor for over half
those who responded.

Better tax incentives are important for about a third of these interviewees.
Some who made this point were among those who complained about the
complexity of Gift Aid, and the fact that not all the tax relief comes to the

[3] *The Mind of the
Millionaire: Findings
from a National
Survey on Wealth
with Responsibility*
Paul Schervish and
John Havens,
Boston College,
January 2002.

What changes would increase the overall amount you give?

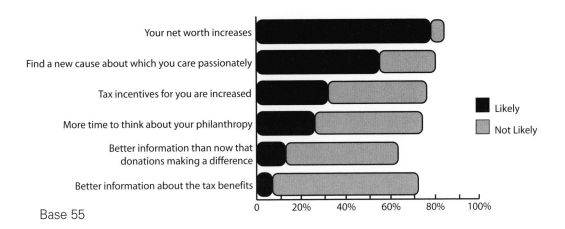

Base 55

donor (as discussed in Chapter Seven). A few were aware of the opportunities available in the US for planning gifts of capital in their lifetime. However, this category also includes those who are not aware of, or "cannot be bothered with" all the tax incentives currently available.

By contrast, better information about tax reliefs was the least likely to be a factor in increasing giving. Mainly, this group of donors feel they have all the information they need, and many in this group have charitable trusts.

Around one in ten said they would be likely to give more if they had more information that their donations were making a difference. Women were more prevalent in this category. A similar proportion did not feel confident that their donations were effective.

Having more time to think about their philanthropy would be likely to make a difference to the level of giving for about a quarter of respondents, although this was less important for women.

Comparisons with views expressed in the US on the same issues are explored in Chapter Fourteen.

This evidence suggests that increasing wealth and confidence in the security of that wealth, combined with improving tax benefits, provide the basis for increasing the potential level of giving. In the US, the period of wealth creation, and of the availability of tax incentives for the wealthy, has been longer. But in both countries the wealthy are expressing a combination of financial security with the desire to be emotionally involved with a cause. It is the combination of perceived material capacity and an awakened passion or interest which unlocks additional generosity.

Giving time

Time + money = change.

(Male, 45, self made/professional)

Volunteer activities which involve giving time reflect the range of motivations and interests demonstrated in giving money, and the same triggers and influences. For some this is linked to the idea that money alone is not enough: to drive change there must be ideas – by implication from the donor. So it is not that the giving of time is always the end in itself; it is more the satisfaction of adding value to the donation by providing expertise and participation, for example as a board or committee member, as well as the realisation that creative use of time will lead to a change in daily routines and priorities.

Feelings about giving time are much the same whether the initial impetus has come from the charity itself or whether the donor was already giving financial support and offered time and expertise on the basis of his or her perception of the needs. It is not surprising that the motivations or triggers for giving time echo those identified for giving money. But there are additional rewards and incentives for having direct involvement. These include:

◆ Applying business skills or professional expertise.
◆ Adding value to their financial support.
◆ Personal involvement in making things happen.
◆ Wanting some change in activity or lifestyle.
◆ Learning something new.
◆ Appreciating an opportunity to be creative.

As with giving money, for most people there is a mix of motives and reinforcements. Here is a typical example which encapsulates several themes:

Why do I give time? I was asked and I enjoy it. It's a small way to contribute. It's easy for me to give financial advice. I can add value.

I meet people from different backgrounds and learn about a different world. It is also an intellectual interest. My work with them is the best way to contribute.

(Male, 40s, self-made/professional)

Some people suggested that time, in the form of specialist and focused expertise, was more valuable to the recipient.

Time can be more costly to the giver, and more valuable to the recipient, than money. Personal volunteering can go along with philanthropy, and the former sometimes leads the latter. I have given voluntary service, hence time, to many bodies, mainly as committee member or honorary officer or speaker/author. Why? The pay-off for volunteering can be satisfaction in helping a good cause, the interest of the issues and the calibre of one's colleagues.

(Male, 80s, self-made/entrepreneur)

In many cases, the donors concerned have been very successful in their own spheres and were confident that the application of their expertise and tenacity would help to drive the organisation more effectively.

I volunteered to be the first chair of the XYZ Foundation. Why? I wanted to serve the community. I thought it was more likely to be a success if I was the chair and no one else. I had the time and had just sold my business and was only 66.

(Male, 60s, self-made/entrepreneur)

As this shows, board membership can play a crucial part in the time given to supported organisations. Issues surrounding board membership are discussed in Chapter Six.

For some people, giving time was linked to the process of learning more about matters surrounding their giving which they had mapped out for themselves – for example a banker who was "curious" about how the art world works. And others, women in particular, mentioned the opportunity for creativity in the context of planning and managing fundraising events.

I plan to do up my garden with a view to opening it for charity. This will both be a new skill and a personal satisfaction as well as giving to charity. You have to get something out of it yourself.

(Female, 50s, married entrepreneur)

However, some added a cautionary note that giving time could only be expected for a finite period – particularly for fundraising. "Networks dry up", raising money is time-consuming, and people feel they have done their bit.

> *I think one can only give time for up to five years. I have given contacts, expertise and enthusiasm.*
>
> (Female, 50s, inherited and grew family business)

We see here that the drivers for giving time echo those for giving money. In most cases the well managed rewards for giving time – appreciation, recognition, respect, success – will reinforce the feelings of involvement, and ownership, and are likely to encourage more financial support as well.

How much time do people give?

Interviewees were asked to estimate the amount of time they spent on charitable and other non-profit activities.

Giving time

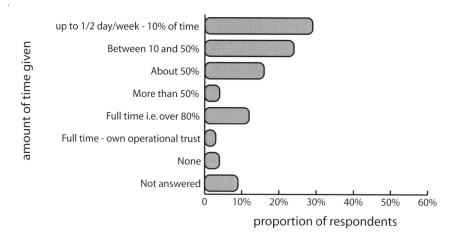

The largest group consisted of those who often have a full-time occupation but give up to about half a day a week or 10% of their time. One in this category mentioned that visiting projects they support was in addition to this, although it might be argued that this is time invested in being an effective grant-giver. Almost as large a group consisted of those who give more than 10% of their time and up to 2.5 days or 50%. Some of these have their own trust with an active involvement in the organisations that they support.

Next in size comes the group who give about 50% of their time. At least one person in this category noted that he also gave the time of his staff. Around one in 10 of those interviewed said they allocated most of their time to philanthropic activities. These divided into those who volunteer on a range of activities including their own trust and the very few who direct the work of their own operational trust.

Less than 5% said that they gave no time whatsoever to volunteer activities. While there were exceptions, it is not surprising that those giving less time tended to be women with young families and men in full-time employment, often with young families too.

> *Time is the most precious commodity. I don't see my son awake from week to week. It can be frustrating. I am much more willing to give money than time. My son deserves my time. I go to dinners if I can bring my wife and I know the table host and the tone which will be set for the evening.*
>
> (Male, 30s, self-made/professional)

On the whole, giving time was correlated with age, or with women having inherited wealth.

Key points

A real commitment to the cause is the underlying motivation for all significant giving, whether of money or time. Because people care fervently they want to make a difference, and giving money, and sometimes expertise, is a way they can change things for the better. The initial impetus may have come from individual experience, from an ethical imperative or from a private passion.

The sense of personal satisfaction and self-worth that comes from the appreciation and respect shown by recipients and other donors sustains their philanthropy and becomes the motivator for further giving. Membership of networks with in-built expectations of philanthropic behaviour underpins and reinforces a practice of giving. Invitations to participate in such networks can be enticing. As well as spiritual and social rewards, some people have practical motivations for their support, such as privileged access or anticipated reciprocity of donation. Apart from having more money, the most important influence in increasing individual generosity is the identification of a cause. But after the initial engagement, it is the relationship with the recipient which is the key to recurring and increasing giving, and it is this that which we explore in Chapter Six.

6

Relationships with recipients

The way the recipient organisation manages the relationship with the donor is a crucial element in the successful development of a sustained commitment to a particular organisation, and by extension to the practice of philanthropy generally. A key aspect of that relationship is that the donors want to feel they are valued members of the team. They want to be appreciated for more than their money. They know that money is one of the essential strands for a project – others being strategy, expertise, design, management and effective implementation. More than one person referred to Margaret Thatcher's observation that The Good Samaritan could not have helped unless he had money. But donors also want recognition for the interest, concern and passion which motivates them, and which they assume they share with trustees and staff of the recipient organisation (and, in some sectors, with the ultimate beneficiaries), and for the expertise which is often the source of their wealth.

In this chapter we explore the various ways people associate with the organisations they support. We look in depth at the nature of the participation sought by donors and consider what people expect from their beneficiaries, including attitudes to recognition. We analyse the perspectives of major donors in some detail. Concerns about financial mismanagement are also reviewed. We explore people's views about governance and their involvement as volunteer leaders of the organisations they support, as well as their experience in soliciting commitment from others for such organisations.

Essential features of the donor-beneficiary relationship

Good communications

The importance of effective communication was constantly stressed in discussions about the management of the relationship between donor and recipient.

I want a personal letter of thanks, that's all. I don't want to be deluged with stuff.

(Male, 50s, self-made/professional)

You can't thank people enough, charities shouldn't be afraid to write too often. Too many charities become production lines. You lose people if you don't really make it personal. They must keep in touch regularly, make people feel part of the team, keep people informed. I want to know we are getting value for money and review the audited accounts. It is important to see what you are giving to.

(Male, 50s, self-made/entrepreneur)

I would give 10/10 to an organisation which came back after a year and asked for 30 minutes of my time to explain what happened to the money and project and what was achieved. I have very little experience of this happening.

(Male, 70s, self-made/entrepreneur)

I want to be appreciated and not taken for granted. I expect no say in how the money is spent. I back an organisation, project or person; it's for them to decide. I want a continuing relationship. Some organisations are much better than others.

(Male, 50s, self-made/professional)

As we will show, the preferred content of the communication and the forms it should take vary between individuals, but the need for ongoing connection was firmly emphasised. Interviewees repeatedly mentioned the importance of establishing good contact at the outset, of maintaining it throughout the relationship and giving time and thought to the process.

There was also recurrent reference to the need for personalised communication rather than "production lines".

Some suggested that recipient organisations should try to avoid asking for money in "every" communication they send. Many complained that too often written feedback was coupled with a request for more. They felt that this could be handled with more subtlety – and certainly without any feeling of pressure.

> *If I give four figures or more I feel I should understand where the money is going. It's the Private Eye test. The more information the better. But sometimes I think 'please take my money and leave me alone'. This is particularly the case with people who think that because I gave £100 last year I will give again. It's presumptuous.*
>
> (Male, 50s, self-made/professional)

Information

There was a widespread call from donors for the provision of regular – and useful – information about the progress of the recipient organisation or cause. The nature of the information required varied but among the more common suggestions were:

◆ Succinct reports of achievements against targets, and any setbacks, with an explanation of what is being done to address problems.
◆ A financial update.
◆ The impact on the people affected by the work, with an individual story or two if appropriate.
◆ An account of what the organisation has learned.

People spoke with appreciation of the unexpected short and personal note or phone call or even email about a success or milestone in the project, and their regret at careless or mass-produced data bearing little or no relation to the project they had supported.

Several respondents suggested that it would be very helpful to have standard components in feedback – a process which would be encouraged if major institutional funders could agree on what these should be.

> *There's a need for different forms of feedback at different levels of donation. We need monitoring with a light touch and a good risk*

management strategy. Feedback to donors should be much simpler and less bureaucratic and appropriate for the amounts received. It's difficult to get the balance right. We do research in advance so when we have decided to give money, we don't interfere.

(Female, 50s, married wealth)

Many made the point that information is important but should be appropriate for the gift level. Major gifts are discussed later in this chapter.

Appreciation and recognition

Few people interviewed did not want some form of appreciation or recognition for their charitable giving from the recipient organisation. But there was a wide spectrum of views about the form this should take, from a private expression of appreciation at one end to public and publicised recognition at the other.

As we have seen, some felt that there should be a clear – and personalised – "thank you" from beneficiaries for their contributions. Although this seems a fairly modest request, several people spoke of inadequate expressions of gratitude for major gifts – standard letters for six-figure sums. Mostly these referred to large charities, since small organisations are less likely to receive such sizeable amounts.

The response from the people I help is 99.99% of what is needed. I like it when people thank me and say they could never have done it without me.

(Male, 50s, self-made/entrepreneur)

The UK is hopeless at saying thank you, but it is too far the other way in the US. There, money buys respectability and a place in society. One mustn't let it dominate. Organisations that don't thank you tend to be corporate such as [a range of major social welfare charities]. I gave £¹/4m to [a major charity] and didn't hear anything after the initial acknowledgement. I go back to grateful charities.

(Female, 50s, inherited)

In addition to appreciation, some wanted some form of recognition of the significance of their contributions.

I would expect to be taken seriously and would expect recognition by the director giving me time. The Oxford Court of Benefactors is a brilliant idea: a) there's amour propre – how one sees oneself and how one is seen; b) I know it is a construct but I still warm to it; they have taken trouble and it makes me feel special; c) I have given more and in the end will give just as much as new members; d) this is forever, whereas other charities look after you only for a while.

(Male, 60s, self-made and inherited)

As this shows, the recognition required is not simply about money but also about respect for an individual's intellectual or business achievements. Other members of the Oxford University Court of Benefactors reported similar approval of the mechanisms in place, with emphasis on the apparent solicitation of advice and engagement, and the permanence of the arrangement.

The importance of such effective donor management – and the negative consequences of its absence – was repeatedly emphasised.

It's not about recognition, but if people treat donors so carelessly do they really need the money? A three-line hand-written letter would have been better. I even wrote to [the director] offering constructive help. I got a reply from someone else – not encouraging.

(Male, 50s, self-made/professional)

It could be argued that there is a difference between recognition by posterity, in terms of leaving an impact on society, and current recognition – with the family name on a building or plaque, for example. For some, the concern was approval of their family, while for others the audience for their philanthropy was their peer group: members of their community, other major donors, or others in the same profession or business (important to some who had made money). Relatively few were concerned about the posthumous approval of later generations outside the family.

Views were very divided about how public any recognition needed to be. In some cases, donors take active steps to avoid publicity or recognition for some or all of their donations. We see in Chapter Seven that many have sought anonymity in certain cases, and there are a few whose giving is channelled through a trust whose name could not be associated with the family name. Others saw quiet giving as a private family matter or as part of their faith. In one or two cases their non-domiciled status was a possible further reason for discretion.

> *I understand the need for recognition but giving is part of my belief;*
> *I prefer to be low profile and am wary of press and media. I don't like to*
> *be in the press. I like to control my environment.*
>
> (Male, 40s, self-made/entrepreneur)

For others, a good report of the work of the organisation in the media provided the kind of recognition they required.

> *There is great satisfaction in seeing the media report good work by bodies*
> *one has supported, especially if it refers to the outcome of a particular grant.*
>
> (Male, 80s, self-made/entrepreneur)

However, in many cases the situation is more complex than a simple denial of interest in recognition. Several people are already nationally known, either as business or City leaders and/or as donors, and many are known locally. A few have an international reputation. Many of these pointed out that they *"don't need it"*. As one well-known donor said *"the curse of the name – they keep coming back"*. Others pointed out that the leading givers would be identified in some way anyway.

Those with experience of supporting both social welfare and cultural or educational organisations pointed out that venues visited by the general public provide opportunities for the recognition of a range of gifts, as do guidebooks, exhibition catalogues and programmes for performing arts events. Among those who see the plaques and list of donors will be peers and fellow donors. Such recognition is reinforced and recurring. Similarly, fundraisers will try to persuade donors to allow their name to be publicised, as an endorsement and to encourage others.

A comparable or much bigger gift to a social welfare institution is quite different. Even with a capital project such as equipment or a specialist unit at a hospital, the constituency of those who use the scanner, for example, is unrelated to the donor community, and the motivation of the donor (for example family experience of cancer) will be quite different. With social welfare organisations such as children's charities, public recognition may be thought inappropriate by both donor and beneficiary.

> *The [ABC national children's charity] has a policy of not recognising*
> *people who do good. It's a huge organisation and there is always*
> *someone else who has done just as much. It is a huge problem –*
> *it causes more problems than it solves.*
>
> (Male, 60s, self-made/entrepreneur)

A number said that while public recognition would not influence a giving decision, it was a bonus – rather like a courtesy present wrapping service for an expensive gift. The bonus lies in the reinforcement of the desire for recognition not just for giving, but for having made a difference. For some, it is evidence for posterity of the footprints in history which acts as a motivator, a factor which is explored more fully in Chapter Five.

> It's not a deciding factor, having one's name on a building, but it would be nice to leave something more permanent.
>
> (Male, 50s, self-made/professional)

> I like the odd plaque. It's very nice – especially for the children. I want to be independent so I don't go for honours. The children will see their father's name on things and feel proud. They will give when they are older.
>
> (Male, 60s, self-made/entrepreneur)

People also found themselves not wanting to be left out of the lists of donors. This was not so much for recognition by the general public as a desire that their peers should not think that they (alone) had not contributed. They didn't necessarily like this characteristic in themselves. It has become a circle with both virtuous and vicious elements. The virtue is to encourage and be an example to others. Some younger people and newer donors were in the process of learning about the importance of recognition to achieve this.

> We want to encourage people to give and to give more responsibly so we will raise our profile to provide a role model and an example. It's nice to give quietly but it is important to be seen doing the right thing. I want to do well, make more, have security and show everyone how things can work better, but I do realise that I have my place at the table because I have money. At 38, I am much too young to be looking at recognition in the form of honours.
>
> (Male, 30s, self-made/entrepreneur)

This young donor is involved in running a family business. There is also a special situation when the wealth comes from a company which also bears the name of the benefactor, and where the company might also benefit from being associated with charitable giving.

> *I would be very happy if, in the long term, the ABC Trust would do something about social deprivation in the [part of the country]. I am not bothered about my name, I don't seek publicity unless it would benefit the recipient, that is if ABC support gives the project credibility, but it is a benefit to the ABC company to be seen to be socially responsible.*
>
> (Male, 60s, self-made/entrepreneur)

It should be noted that while many did not seek and had not anticipated the increased status which recognition for giving provides, they had enjoyed it once they had it.

> *Having a not-for-profit career is much more interesting than I would have thought possible. My standing has increased because people have heard. That is the reward. I don't expect it but I enjoy it. It is quite a reward that the achievement is recognised – the increased standing. I should be ashamed.*
>
> (Female, 50s, self-made/entrepreneur)

While that person was in two minds about her feelings of self-satisfaction, others, particularly more experienced donors, were more detached – and resigned to the fact that such recognition made other organisations aware of the potential for support.

> *The ABC Room at X art gallery encourages others and clearly denotes the room. It is setting an example. Of course, people see the name on the board and it produces other applications but there is a feeling of warmth.*
>
> (Male, 60s, self-made/professional)

It was noted that invariably nowadays it is the organisations seeking funds which incorporate "naming opportunities" and other benefits and options for recognition into their proposals requesting support. They are an integral element of the shopping list. Some people appeared almost to resent the implicit assumption that these factors, rather than a passion for the cause, would be decisive. Others suggested that while they were not themselves interested, public acknowledgement might be attractive to some people.

As we see, the interest in or desire for recognition is entirely a matter of personal style, character and preference. Even for those who wish others to be aware of their major gifts, the audience for their philanthropy is usually confined to their family, peers and community, rather than the general public. However, people do want to feel appreciated and acknowledged, and if the recipient makes a habit of recognising major donors in some way, and offers such recognition as part of the solicitation process, then most do not want to be left out. Recognition is a means to an end – a validation of their own actions which sustains their self-esteem and gains approval by those whose opinion they value. It is noteworthy that so many who have been great achievers in business want their children to be proud of their contribution to the public good, and their reputational legacy to be based on their philanthropy.

Consultation and influence

Some donors wanted to "have a say" in how their donations were allocated and spent. Most commonly, this was a wish for some consultation over the allocated expenditure, rather than directing how money was spent. Moreover, more than one person observed that at least appearing to take notice of major donors was the best way to retain them.

I would lose interest if no one took any notice of what I say.
(Male, 50s, self-made/entrepreneur)

Some expressed this more strongly, moving from the idea of consultation to influence. But several noted the inherent tensions and difficulties built within this.

So far, I see myself as subscribing to their goals. I just expect newsletters and so on telling me how it is going. I don't expect to be Top Gun; I expect to be told about the outcome, and I don't want to influence the staff. Where the work is of life-changing importance, the donor should not be able to influence, but I would be surprised if they are not accommodated. I see there is an intellectual and emotional contradiction here.
(Male, 40s, self-made/entrepreneur)

If you want to you should have a right to ask or have a say in how it is spent. There is a tension between the 'no strings' wanted by the charity and the interests of the donor. I would expect some flexibility in determining how the money is spent within the mission. I would expect feedback and reports as though I had made an investment.
(Male, 40s, self-made/professional)

With giving you lose control. You've had nothing in return. When you are purchasing you have something in return which is economic activity and that in itself is a social good. There is a huge fuzzy area between the purchasing of goods and services and altruism.
(Male, 30s, self-made/professional)

Although the word "control" was used here, in none of the actual cases discussed was expenditure donor-driven, beyond responding to the core mission or project or "shopping list" provided by the beneficiary. What was important was the feeling of involvement or being asked for advice.

People give because they care about the cause, and want to be involved. Donors of all types and interests care how the money is spent. They feel that opportunities should be created to draw the donor into the work or project. Donors want to pass on expertise as well as money, but do not expect to influence the allocation of the money. They look for respect for that expertise, and appreciation for the giving of time which is involved in major philanthropy.

Governance

Many compared their position in relation to a charity with that of being an investor in a business. Those making this point included experienced donors from a range of sources of wealth as well as new donors with new money.

> With ARK [Absolute Return for Kids, the charity established by the hedge fund industry] there is complete involvement in how the money is spent – choosing the recipient, evaluating needs, measuring impact and outcome, being cost-effective. Guys in the City are concerned about administration costs. They want to feel that they can meet the director but in fact they may not have time. Board seats shouldn't be bought but there must be an understanding that a donation is an investment and that one wants to be involved in governance. There is also the importance of the symbolism of giving being equivalent to being a major shareholder. Major donors should want to be involved and charities should want them to be involved. If you are a major shareholder in a start-up you have a lot to say. Most of these things are about sensible governance – fiscal probity, periodic reporting, openness in how you treat employees and a known budget and investment policy.
>
> (Female, 30s, self-made/professional)

Although ARK is a particular case, this contributor echoes the thoughts of donors from a range of backgrounds. First, we see that the donation is viewed as an investment and the donor as a partner in the enterprise – something which the recipient should see as a positive factor. There are concerns about administrative costs, a desire to meet those who deliver the mission, as well as for other involvement, and a clear recognition that there may be a lack of time. It also reinforces the evidence that the areas in which donors want some kind of involvement are to do with governance and reporting, not the methodology for the delivery of the core mission.

For all donors who are also board members, the essence of their involvement was related to governance. A sizeable group of respondents (about a fifth) reported a strong association between their involvement as a member of the board or committee and their giving. (Not everyone who is a board member feels an obligation to give, as we see below.) By being a member of the board they were by definition involved in the decision-making.

> *I am proactively involved as a board member. I am provided with information through regular meetings. The benefactor should be treated as one of the constituents. There's a difference between arse-licking and being part of a family. People want to be included, they want a flow of information; there should be a respect for knowledge.*
> (Male, 40s, self-made/professional)

> *These three organisations are the recipients of my biggest gifts. In all three I have been encouraged and wanted to be involved. The fact of my involvement makes me more generous than if I were not involved. I like to be able to add value to my donations. For example with X* [an organisation with whose start-up he was involved] *it was governance, better management, better strategy. With Y* [which he chairs and for which he leads a major capital appeal] *it's about giving and getting – being a catalyst for change. With Z* [an education institution] *it's about setting up scholarships and lectureships to encourage people to study [subject].*
> *I give several small gifts to organisations where I don't need to be involved.*
> (Male, 50s, self-made/entrepreneur)

Although many of those who sat on boards or committees of organisations give a major share of their donations to the same institution, some people are unhappy with the expectation that board members should give money as well as time.

> *I am uncomfortable with the expectation that board members should give money because I think if people give time they shouldn't have to give money. Also, you risk ending up with a narrow board. Organisations should try to be more inclusive. You shouldn't just have bankers, but fundraising is a major element so you need some who can make a contribution.*
> (Female, 50s, married wealth)

For many people the giving of time and money is interlinked. They may have given time first – formally becoming a member of a board or committee, and attending meetings – but did so in the expectation, or at least acceptance of the position, that they would sooner or later make a financial gift as well.

Experienced board members were clear that donors had a right to expect competence, and it was the responsibility of the board to see that it was delivered, particularly if new investment was being sought.

> In some organisations there is a need to improve the quality of management as a quid pro quo. The Chairman has an obligation to manage the affairs well. There needs to be a rigorous examination – are they cost-effective? They need to analyse exactly how much money is needed and look at their core funding.
>
> (Male, 60s, self-made/professional)

Backing effective people is important to all supporters. Those who are both donors and board members could see several facets. As private donors they can trust their own assessment; as a board member, and especially as a chair, they have a duty not only to other donors, but also to those whom the charity exists to serve. They see themselves as moving from a personal to a public sphere.

> I try to back people rather than organisations. When I come across someone who is able to do things, I give them the money and let them get on with it. It's a question of judgement. It's different with other people's money. ABC [a major charity he chairs] must be cost-effective, offer value for money and be able to measure the impact. As a board, there is a responsibility to be accountable to donors; the problem is responsibility to beneficiaries.
>
> (Male, 60s, self-made/professional)

In discussing governance, we should mention donors' concerns about the possibilities of financial mismanagement. Although none of the donations that interviewees regretted (reported in Chapter Seven) were associated directly with financial mismanagement, some donors said that actual or potential concerns had influenced a decision, and some gave specific examples or reasons. These included:
   ◆ Generic anxiety about overseas aid, especially in Africa, with India also being mentioned. Issues included corruption, diversion of funds to other projects, lack of long-term impact ("*it won't make a real*

difference"), and lack of suitable and effective local infrastructure. These concerns were mentioned by several people.

◆ Concern about the quality of leadership and governance at the head office.
◆ A perception that the organisation is raising money when it need not.
◆ A perception that too much is spent on fundraising or aspects of administration.
◆ Concern about charities which were too small.

Several people mentioned these or similar factors as issues they might need to think about. It was said that giving to charity is inherently risky, just like investing in business. Many donors therefore make careful checks before they commit to an organisation.

> *I don't give to any charity if there is a risk of mismanagement. I always look at the accounts and the percentage spent on administration and fundraising beforehand. It depends on the nature of the work. Some have heavier overheads: for example, homelessness. Once I've given I don't ask for the accounts because I make a long-term commitment and keep in touch with the recipients.*
>
> (Male, 50s, self-made/professional)

> *I always check. The Charity Commission should tidy up the register and should close tiny charities. Charity governance is very complicated.*
> (Male, 50s, self-made/entrepreneur)

It was also noted that making a detailed assessment and developing confidence in an organisation tended to be associated with repeat gifts and long-term commitment. It was suggested that once you have made an investment in or given support to a charity, you should trust the leadership. This trust can be reinforced by keeping in touch with what is going on.

As we see, many donors are concerned about issues of competence and governance, particularly where the donation is large, and see their position as analogous to that of a major shareholder in a business. Some board members expect to focus their donations on the organisations with which they are involved, but there is a significant minority who do not believe this is the role of charitable trustees.

Major gifts

> *I work it out with each one. I think I am a fair person and can see both sides. I wouldn't give money if I thought they couldn't manage the project. It's very important to feel appreciated. I expect to be listened to.*
>
> (Male, 30s, self-made/entrepreneur)
>
> *I don't believe in strings being attached, but as the sums increase I would want more of a say.*
>
> (Male, 40s, self-made/entrepreneur)

The requirements of major donors for good communication, acknowledgement, recognition, and good governance are similar to those sought by people who give smaller amounts to an organisation or cause. But there was also evidence to suggest that the desire for influence and direction is heightened when major gifts are awarded, although always within the mission of the charity.

These feelings were expressed either by donors with relevant expertise (for example in building works), or by those who had supported many similar projects and had learned from the experience. In these cases the desired influence was not so much related to the core programme as to a desire to ensure that the project they were funding would be successful. Many experienced major donors took time to set up a framework for the whole relationship.

> *I look at every project. There is a contract with every charity based on experience. It covers standards, recognition, the timing of payments, what the gift will cover and feedback. One gets embroiled in affairs. The more embroiled, the more one gives. Does £10m give you the right to interfere? I used to think it did, but now I don't think so even if one knows better.*
>
> (Female, 50s, inherited)

Those with family businesses considered influence on project design or management as protecting the family name; if the family business is associated with best practice, then the organisations they endow or support should be too. They are willing to be flexible about arrangements but also want them clarified in advance.

*In India, for the college in [place], we wanted influence on the institution.
It was our name and we wanted a representative on the management
board. It was a question of quality control. Once we have made up our
mind there are no conditions; we want things clarified beforehand, for
example about name, representation and so on. It's not a condition but
we want to know.*

(Male, 40s, self-made and inherited)

In more than one case a large gift led to the recipient not so much wanting
a say but asking fairly fundamental questions. The following example was
someone, a relatively new donor, who supported and raised money for a
performing arts organisation outside London.

*I don't expect to have a say – except perhaps where I have made a huge
donation like to the [ABC theatre]. When I had raised the money I asked
how it had got into that state in the first place and looked at the weak board.*

(Female, 50s, inherited and grew family business)

In the case of a really major gift to create a new venture – for example, a
building in a health or educational institution – the donor may require
involvement from the start. This is particularly true where the support
arises out of the expertise and wealth basis of the donor. Examples
include new university faculties.

*For the [named] Centre for [Y discipline] [investment of £12m by donor]
we have had an impact on the design to ensure an open free flow of
communications. We brought in architects at our own expense to ensure
that the building works. [Husband] will be a board member of the centre.
He insisted there should be a separate board and it was set up with the
Vice-Chancellor of the university. You must have entrepreneurs as well
as academics on boards.*

(Female, 50s, married wealth)

Experienced donors were sensitive to the accusation that they expected to
influence activities outside their expertise. But where they had such
expertise they believed they had a right to be heard. Having been targeted
and motivated to make a difference, they see – as in their businesses –
that the difference may be made not only with money, but with the
application of the business skills which is the source of the wealth. This is
very important. Some charities are seen to solicit money but appear to
reject expertise. This is viewed as a lack of the respect which is crucial to
a successful partnership.

Several people made the point that giving money with this kind of involvement requires real commitment from the donor as well as the recipient, and that the fact and nature of this engagement was not always appreciated, particularly if the donors are not board or committee members. Because of the time required, some experienced and strategic donors limit the number of organisations they support.

The responsibility and experience of the involvement brings pleasure from the relationship with those who run the organisation – a factor we have seen as important in motivating recurring giving.

However, some people noted that it was important not to patronise the recipients or to influence the design of the core activities. Implicit in such views is the recognition that the leaders and senior staff of the organisations they support bring their own expertise and commitment. One person with experience as a trustee of a major institutional funder talked about the value of this type of experience, and made the same point about the risks of seeming to be patronising in relation to his own giving.

> *Relationships with grantees often developed into close personal friendships as between people sharing the same social ideals and objectives, and broadly the same views on strategies for furthering them, though with different contributions to make (respectively, money, and talents/skills/dedication/service). With [our own foundation], where the role of a single family has become known, the problems are greater. I tend to respond to expressions of thanks from grant holders by referring to the different and complementary contributions to common purposes, just noted. Without their work, our money would be sterile.*
>
> (Male, 80s, self-made/entrepreneur)

Major donors, and those with the potential to become major donors or leave a significant bequest, believe they merit an individual programme of engagement. It is important for recipients and donors to take time getting to know each other. For major gifts there should be agreement in advance on how the relationship is to work.

Decision-making in family trusts is shared, and other family members may have to be persuaded. There may be tensions when specific pots are allocated to children who do not share parental passions.

Asking for money

Around half the interviewees discussed their experience in asking for money for the organisations they support with major gifts[1]. Most had some experience in asking for money, or at least in introducing or cultivating prospects. Only a few reported no experience at all, either because they were spending virtually all of their time actively engaged in the operational activities of their own trust or their business life and/or they did not feel it appropriate, or were reluctant, to ask. For some the reluctance was associated with the potential expectation of a reciprocal donation which they might not want to offer. In some cases they ended up making a higher contribution themselves.

There was no doubt that most of those who had experience of asking others for donations found little enjoyment in it. Essentially, the reasons were a combination of not knowing where to start, not believing themselves to be socially adept or a good networker, embarrassment, not feeling properly briefed about the prospect and unsatisfactory past experience. The basis of the disappointment in past encounters lay either with the response of the prospects or with the inadequate level of support provided by the organisation seeking funds.

In many cases, lack of preparation and knowledge of the prospect, particularly of their financial circumstances, led to embarrassment and fear of "getting it wrong". Many recognised that if they did ask, people might give for the "wrong" reasons – not for the cause but because of the asker. That gave little satisfaction to the asker, and not much to the donor. This was particularly the case with events and small gifts. Some refuse to engage in this kind of approach and say they would "rather write a cheque myself".

A few, including experienced askers, reported various examples of lack of adequate professional support from the fundraising staff, lack of research and appropriate targeting, lack of involvement from senior management and lack of flexibility about visiting projects.

The frustration is with the administrators, not the donors.
(Male, 40s, self-made/entrepreneur)

However, where people do care passionately for a particular organisation or cause, they may overcome their reluctance. This is much more likely to happen where people have a formal relationship, such as board or committee membership.

[1] Many of those who did not discuss this question had already commented that they did not get involved in asking for money; in other cases there was insufficient time to explore it in depth.

The analysis of what makes donor asking effective was similar across the range of experiences and attitudes to asking for money. Several factors were seen as contributing to a successful outcome to requests.

Being a donor as well

Peer pressure is essential. I have given, why don't you? The fact that we have given to our maximum is impressive and we can endorse the work of [major charity]. Donor get donor is the best mechanism for charities to use.
(Female, 50s, inherited)

You need to get the message across about why there is a need. I don't feel embarrassed if it's a good cause. You must put the message across very quickly and capture the imagination. It helps if you can use your own example as a giver, especially if it's a woman asking a man.
(Female, 60s, self-made/entrepreneur)

Styles of asking

Various suggestions were made as to how to "get the message across" and "capture the imagination". For many with experience it was essential to find a way to involve people. One is to show them the actual work on the ground; the challenge is that many do not have time – at least in the working day. We saw the reverse of this in exploring how people became involved – "*I saw Centrepoint and I was gob-smacked*".

Even with an appropriate hook it was recognised that there still might be issues of feelings of financial insecurity to be overcome and a lack of opportunity to show that giving can be fun.

The rich who don't give are in two categories: a) people who feel vulnerable, which I understand; and b) those who haven't enjoyed the thrill of helping people with their money.
(Male, 60s, self-made/professional)

At the ABC charity we needed to think up a message to keep the gifts abreast of needs. 'Would you deny an hour to a friend in need? Why not give an hour's earnings to ABC?' How do we reinforce the human conscience? An explanation of why it is fun and therefore in one's own self-interest should tell you that the best use for £1,000 may not a holiday in Spain but giving to the hospice.
(Male, 50s, self-made/professional)

As well as showing the rewards, some suggested that a useful tactic, particularly with smaller gifts, was to identify the amount sought in terms of the prospect's income – an appeal to conscience.

Targeting and timing

One should never ask one's friends; one should start with a project and be transparent. Good fundraising is about matching people, timing and knowing the project. It's a question of finding the right people, they are there.
(Male, 40s, self-made/professional)

Half of the business about giving is who asks and the rest is how interested people are in the cause. Most of the computer millionaires want to give something back. Lots are still thinking about it but they are not quite ready. They are giving time and expertise.
(Male, 60s, self-made and inherited)

Building on that, several with knowledge of high earners such as those in the high-tech sector or hedge fund industry suggested that it was a matter of stage in life. Many were not ready for major philanthropy and the best approach was to get people involved through giving time and expertise.

Awakening an interest

Everyone recognised that major gifts come from those who are fired by the project. The challenge is to awaken the interest. They also made the point that this kind of fundraising is hard work and very demanding. In the Jewish community in particular this was seen as a burden which should be shared. This is more akin to the American approach.

In Jewish Care everybody has responsibility for fundraising.
(Male, 50s, self-made/entrepreneur)

Some causes have prospered because of the application of marketing and PR skills learned in commerce and entertainment, often given as a gift in kind. These were implemented in projects and causes which had harnessed celebrity involvement.

I use the same skills to get people to care about [cause] as for selling a movie or celebrity.
(Male, 30s, self-made/entrepreneur)

Offering public recognition

The interviewee quoted above referred to an event at which the combination of a very glitzy and exclusive party, including a royal guest, a compelling cause and heavy-duty asking had influenced the outcome – a total of some £3m raised. In this case of a social welfare charity there would not be recurring opportunities for public recognition, as there are in the arts, heritage and education. Yet although, as we have seen, there are virtually no cases in which recognition is reported as a primary motivator, more than one asker suggested that, together with the nature of the cause, recognition is an important trigger. It is as though people are saying "*I am not influenced by this, but others may be*" – as indeed seems to be the case from the earlier discussion.

Strategic support from the recipient organisation

A key success factor mentioned by several interviewees was the quality and nature of support received from the charity. This was about staff competence, preparatory research and prospect information, and information about the charity itself.

> *Charities are good at extracting small amounts of money. The challenge is to get large amounts of money. The US is better at getting intellectual people involved with a hands-on job in the non-profit sector or in fundraising. They are giving back their intellectual capacities and city skills.*
>
> (Female, 30s, self-made/professional)

Several made the point that information is needed not only for themselves but to enable them to be an effective ambassador. They know that those who are asked for money by a friend or business colleague see that person's support as endorsement of the effectiveness of the organisation. The more senior and respected the advocate, the more important it is that they are well briefed.

> *When asking for donations one must be satisfied that money is being used in a sensible and positive manner. You must know what will happen to it. People will expect me to have done due diligence. I want to be involved with the [XYZ charity] and see the impact in the schools it supports. One must have access to information.*
>
> (Male, 50s, inherited and grew family business)

We see that in the opinion of givers who are also askers, those who ask for money should be givers themselves. All recognise that there is a major difference between persuading friends to give relatively small amounts and the long-term nurturing that goes into obtaining a big gift. Such nurturing needs preparation and research, the full engagement of highly competent professional staff, not only fundraisers, and flexibility about project visits and briefings.

Attitudes to responses
People were asked about their reaction to responses they received to requests for donations. Inevitably, these varied, but there was much discussion about the people who "could well afford to give" but do not do so – and generally a rather negative view of such responses.

I know lots who don't give who could afford to give and think they're shits.
(Male, 50s, self-made/entrepreneur)

They are missing out on one of the most interesting things that wealthy people can do so I feel sorry for them.
(Male, 50s, self-made/entrepreneur)

They say 'I pay my tax – why should I give more?' My role is to educate them so that they see a bigger picture. We need a major education exercise. They have been conditioned. It's not their fault.
(Male, 50s, self-made/entrepreneur)

There were perceptions that certain categories of people do not give, or have mixed motives. This comment was from someone based in the North West, but the core sentiments were echoed by several:

From my experience, people in the arts and sports don't give.
The justification is that they don't know where their next pay cheque
is coming from. There is an element of truth in that. If they turn up at
an event it facilitates raising money. At the top end of the scale,
if people have significant incomes and don't give, who the hell do they
think they are? I object to that attitude. I give time as well as money.
(Male, 50s, self-made/entrepreneur)

Although a few expressed their views directly to those who decline to give, most did not advocate this strategy.

> *The danger is that you become an arbiter e.g. 'x is good for £10k'. I had a friend who told others what he thought of ungenerous people but you must take it or leave it. The only way to handle people is to get them interested and make them aware but if they don't give, leave it.*
>
> (Male, 50s, self-made/professional)

A sizeable group was not judgmental, although disappointed at a negative response. Many of these pointed out that one cannot know the range of commitments or personal circumstances of a prospect. They might be puzzled about the reaction but it does not affect their attitude to the individual. Indeed it may be the fault of the asker and the way the proposal was presented. These and others made an effort not to take it personally, nor let it affect their relationship with the prospect. They make a distinction between refusal and bad manners – for example, when people do not reply at all.

Where most people are asking friends and colleagues, it was suggested that irritation with non-givers would seriously diminish an individual's social network.

> *You would fall out with a lot of friends.*
>
> (Male, 50s, inherited and grew family business).

They learn from the encounter, try not to be "shaken by some people's attitudes" and target them for something more appropriate. A few claim never to be surprised – they somehow expect the rich not to give.

> *I have never been surprised by some reactions so my attitude won't change. There is a strong correlation between being rich and being mean.*
>
> (Male, 40s, self-made/entrepreneur)

A few took the approach of being a role model and "leading by example and encouraging people", a policy that received some strength of support. A minority expressed concern for those who were not giving – either because they were missing an opportunity, or because they "don't understand the bigger picture" and their role within it, or the limited role of the state. The need for an "education exercise" also relates to the level at which they should give.

> *I wish that more people did give; it's a pity but that's for them. Their lives are poorer and I feel sorry for them. It's a question of perception. Some very rich people would think they are being very generous if they give £1,000.*
>
> (Male, 50s, self-made/professional)

As with many issues, there is a spectrum of reactions to non-givers, from contempt to resignation. People who ask for money are giving time and expertise to a cause about which they care passionately, and are usually experienced givers. When their solicitation is successful it provides a great sense of achievement. As much as anything they want to share the sense of satisfaction, self-respect and enjoyment which they experience from their relationships with recipients and fellow donors.

The experience of those with in-depth experience of asking for money is explored in Chapter Eleven.

Key points

The management of the relationship with the donor is one of the most important elements in creating and sustaining a commitment to philanthropy. An incompetent or insensitive approach to communications can have a seriously adverse impact on future giving. Someone interested in a particular cause, but who had a disappointing relationship with a specific recipient, could often find an alternative beneficiary. There was a range of good and bad examples across a number of sectors. Those with charitable trusts who had bad experiences needed to find alternative beneficiaries at some point, but for many the option was to give less, or not at all.

At major donor levels the links should be with director or chief executive and senior management, not only the fundraising staff. High level givers expect a personal programme of information feedback and engagement which demonstrates respect and desire for a genuine partnership in delivering the mission. They do not expect to influence the programme of the charity, but want to be able to share their expertise in, for example, governance, financial management, IT or property maintenance. Many, particularly younger donors, see their position as analogous to that of investors in a business.

The extent to which donors desire public recognition, as opposed to private expressions of appreciation, very much depends on personal preference. However, where recognition is offered by the recipient charity, few wish to be left out. But the recognition is like "gift-wrapping", a confirmation for those whose good opinion they value – themselves, their family, their peers and, very occasionally the general public – that they are making a difference.

First-class relationship management and appropriate recognition by the recipient organisations together underpin and reinforce the philanthropic inclination. They transform what might start as a one-off impulsive response into an integral and important part of people's discretionary expenditure. More than that, they validate the choices people have made and ensure that charitable commitments continue because the donor gets such pleasure from the experience. They address the five key motivating triggers identified in Chapter Five and are the most important factors in sustaining a culture of giving.

7

The practice of giving

In this chapter we look at a number of topics surrounding the practice of giving. The first part considers how people respond to requests, the basis of their reactions, how they decide what to support and what influences their choices. We also explore their degree of satisfaction with their donations, and what people might do differently. The extent to which people give anonymously, and in what circumstances, is also reviewed.

The second part of the chapter is a detailed discussion of people's experience of the various mechanisms available for tax-efficient charitable giving.

The significance of the source and method of approach of the request varies – for some it is all-important, and few claim not to be influenced in any way by the person soliciting support or the design and focus of the proposal. Those who claimed not to be influenced had all established charitable trusts, and developed a clear framework for their philanthropy. For some the filter of the office provides a protection from the importuning of personal contacts.

For major gifts and experienced donors the nature of the cause is paramount. Even if the cause is one which the donor supports in principle, the determining factor is the donor's conviction that the gift will make a difference. However, in some circumstances virtually everyone can be influenced by the origin and style of an unsolicited request, and we start with consideration of these.

Response to unsolicited requests

There needs to be a personal approach or the cause must be very compelling.

(Male, 60s, self-made and inherited)

We consider it if friends are involved, if it touches the heart, if we feel we could make a difference. I reject it if my name is wrong and if it's a standard letter. I don't give to large conglomerate charities... for example, a friend did a hospice in mid-Wales, I wrote a big cheque, more than we could afford, because it was making a difference.

(Male, 40s, self-made/entrepreneur)

Most interviewees receive a large number of unsolicited requests every year (although, surprisingly perhaps, some, including some of the wealthier, do not). Well established personal trusts or well known philanthropists can expect up to 1,000 letters a year – indeed, one interviewee said they received 10 requests a day.

Some people review every request they receive. More commonly, they select ones to consider and unsolicited applications and "junk mail" all "go to the bin". For those with established foundations and an administrative infrastructure, the requests may be filtered by a lawyer or administrator, on the basis of known criteria.

Most people who give regularly have a clearly defined set of priorities. However, many of those interviewed are not regular or strategic givers, and may be in the process of developing their approach to philanthropy. But in assessing requests, two criteria are central – who asks and the nature of the cause.

The importance of a personal and appropriate approach

Many of those interviewed enjoy a close and long-term relationship with one or more charities. In these cases, they are more likely to be aware of needs and projects on offer, and while they may at some stage receive a formal application for support, it will be either invited or, at least, expected.

In this section we focus more on unsolicited and unplanned requests from organisations not previously supported, or from those with which there may have been limited contact.

The personal approach

People reported huge irritation at unsolicited mailings which are incorrectly spelt or addressed, have been clearly produced by a mail-merge programme, cannot cope with titles and honours or, even worse, open with "dear friend", or "dear [first name]" from a stranger or junior staff member. Having a donor or supporter number quoted by a charity they had supported in the past was seen by some to belie the individuality of the relationship.

People expect a personalised approach, with some understanding as to why the project or cause may be of interest. A hand-written covering letter is desirable but at the very least a hand-written note was expected to complement and reinforce a standard mailing.

Who should make the approach

The friend as endorser is crucial because the friend has invested personal capital – time and emotion – so I will help.

(Female, 30s, self-made/professional)

A second major factor is where people I know are asking for money. It's about respect, and their involvement endorses the cause and the relationship.

(Male, 60s, inherited and grew family business)

Virtually everyone interviewed will at least review and respond to a request that comes from a person or organisation they know and respect. The endorsement of someone known was important because some reliance could be placed on the diligence of the asker. This was particularly the case where the request was from a respected professional or business colleague, or someone who had a track record as a leader in the world of charities.

If the asker has also given money, so much the better; several people alluded to this.

I get 10 requests a day. The question of who asks counts more than anything else. Is the person who asks a giver? The asker must be a lay/volunteer leader, not a professional. Is it someone who has given to charities I want to support? Most people who ask do so for worthy motives but sometimes ego gets in the middle.

(Male, 70s, self-made/entrepreneur)

The experience of asking for money is discussed at length in Chapter Eleven. What we see here is a reflection of that analysis from the perspective of those being asked. Their comments are entirely consistent with the views of askers. Among the main factors that emerge is that the endorsement of someone known and respected is crucial. This is because it is assumed that the known asker will have checked and confirmed that the cause is worthy of support and this saves time. The effect of this is reinforced if the asker is also a giver, not only to the cause for which support is being solicited, but to the causes supported by the prospect. For major gifts the asker should be a "lay" person – that is, not a paid member of staff, and by implication a peer of the prospect.

A few people claimed not to be influenced even if it is a friend or known contact who asks. For them the most important factors are the cause, the extent to which it fits pre-existing criteria and the quality of the specific project, as discussed more fully below. But even then, if a known intermediary is involved, it is more likely that the request will at least be considered.

Some donors feel money is wasted on unsolicited approaches, especially if they appear unnecessarily glossy or expensive. This was a recurring comment.

The nature of the cause

The main focus of my support is already decided… the area of work, for example health and so on, is considered, as is the geographic basis of the work and the performance of the recipient in using grants wisely and economically.

(Male, 50s, self-made/entrepreneur)

We are proactive givers. First it must be about social change – that's fundamental. Then it must be run by good people. Also I must be interested in what they do.

(Female, 50s, self-made/entrepreneur)

Most people who are thoughtful about their philanthropy have already decided their broad areas of interest. Indeed, it would be surprising if that were not the case because, as we have seen, the impetus in early giving is to do with being moved to a particular cause or interest. So while people will look at causes outside their area of interest if the proposal comes from a respected contact, most people who have already decided on their priorities will ask whether it fits within their criteria and chosen focus.

Many of those interviewed had also determined the main sectors or charities they wanted to support. This is not confined to those who have established trusts, and indeed the aims of most trusts are widely drawn enough to allow for giving to any UK charity or cause. Older people were also more likely to have decided their priorities and preferences, as were those who had set up a regular mechanism for giving such as a Charities Aid Foundation (CAF) account. (See later in this chapter for details of mechanisms for giving.)

Having said all this, a few admit that there are sometimes irrational factors at play as well, including whim and mood. Such factors lead to a more reactive and immediate response to an unsolicited mailing.

> *It's related to profit and whim. I don't have a strategy. In each case I was asked by someone I know. I rarely give without a personal link but I got something in the post about disfigured children. It touched my imagination and my heart so I gave.*
> (Male, 50s, self-made/entrepreneur)

This was a very rare occurrence for a significant donation (another similar trigger was a newspaper report), but it highlights a most important point; philanthropy combines intellectual understanding, the imagination, the capacity to give and the heart.

Most people will consider a request for support for a cause operating in a sector to which they are committed. But closely linked to this, they will want to know how their money will be used and how it will make a difference. We see in Chapter Five that making a difference, expressed in varying ways, was a key factor in both motivating a donor and sustaining continued interest.

> *[I ask myself] Is it making a real difference if I give or not? Many organisations have lots of money and are able to raise it from elsewhere; the money I put in must make a real difference. It's not just money: I may be able to help with fundraising and make suggestions of other funders and endorse the project.*
> (Male, 70s, self-made/entrepreneur)

We try to give it to organisations doing really good work where, say £10,000 a year over three years will make a real difference, so we fund small organisations in the [London borough where resident] area.

(Female, 50s, married wealth)

Whether or not people have decided on a few chosen causes, or are still in the process of considering how to focus their giving, most people will give where they feel they can make a bigger difference and have a recognisable effect. This desire to focus on impact and obtain what was seen as value for money can sometimes militate against big charities. Associated with large charities were perceptions of unnecessary bureaucracy. A reluctance to fund core costs, for small as well as large organisations, was mentioned frequently. This was seen as the responsibility of institutional grant-makers or government (where applicable), even by experienced donors who understand the complexities of managing a charity. However, some accepted that there might be an allocation of core costs within a total project budget. This attitude was common to people from a range of backgrounds and familiarity with the charity sector, from those starting on the road to strategic philanthropy to experienced donors.

If the cause is of interest, the donors may well have made significant commitments to one or more charities operating in the field. Many of these may be recurring, or at least allocations over two or three years. An apparently sizeable trust with objectives entirely consistent with those of the charity soliciting support may have very limited uncommitted funds. Indeed, from the perspective of the applicant there may be a paradox: the more involved and engaged the donor, the less likely, in some cases, they are to be able to make substantial commitments to a new recipient, however deserving.

Other factors

Potential donors will want to consider a number of other factors once the nature of the cause is seen as relevant to their interests: whether it represents value for money; the competence of the organisation and who is leading the initiative; and the kinds of involvement it will require from them. These issues are explored in depth in earlier chapters.

The evidence suggests strongly that in considering an unsolicited request for significant sums, potential donors will wish to gauge their interest in the project and be clear about the impact their contribution will have or the difference it will make. They will also want to be assured that it is value for money. Information to help them decide is therefore crucial, particularly as they may be considering many such requests. Those soliciting funds should ensure that they have built in mechanisms to measure the difference the donor's contribution can make and be willing to share that information with them.

Small gifts

Marathon sponsorship, sponsorship of Commonwealth veterans. I make such gifts when they don't fit in with the main policy of the trust. There are no criteria but the personal approach. Sometimes such giving is to encourage.

(Male, 60s, self-made/ professional)

When people I know ask for help I give £1,000 or less. In 90% of the cases the cause is almost immaterial.

(Male, 40s, self-made/entrepreneur)

It is clear that being asked by the right person is never a sufficient condition for a significant donation. Nevertheless, being asked by "someone I know" is often the key determinant for small gifts, although there are other factors in play as well. In an exceptional case, one donor has a policy of directing most of his charitable giving through many small gifts.

It was recognised that small payment philanthropy is essential to values in society, but unlike most major donations, smaller gifts – apart from membership contributions – are often made to causes outside the donor's main field of interest. Interviewees were asked about the circumstances in which they made small donations, and to describe the most recent gifts in that category, which were defined as below £1,000. For many a donation at this level was "a token gift" and there was a mix of pressures and influences on a decision to give. These are briefly considered below.

Sponsorship

I haven't given anything below that threshold [£1,000], *unless you count charity tickets or marathon sponsorship*

(Male, 50s, self-made/professional)

Much small gift support was for events and sponsorship, although many did not really count supporting fundraising events as serious giving. A significant minority cited sponsorship of activities such as marathons as examples of small donations. The cause was often immaterial and in many cases the respondent could not remember what it was. Such sponsorship was accepted as part of life, but some irritation was expressed with sponsorship forms, particularly as used by children. Many doubted whether the approach could "inculcate values of giving and sacrifice in these children". More often it seen as a form of licensed blackmail of the family and friends of the child, with a certain amount of competitiveness thrown in.

Social giving

Social giving – that is giving when relatives, friends, colleagues or perhaps another donor asks – is discussed in Chapter Five. Generally sums are small, causes are diverse and it was sometimes felt to be part of what is expected within the donor "network". This is exemplified in the passage below, although the level of donation considered as "small" by this individual was exceptional.

> *If a friend asks I give. I don't enjoy the social side but I recognise that it's part of the role of mixing with the great and the good. Part of the role is to give. A lot of it is pocket money giving – £5,000 here, £5,000 there. This probably amounts to £250,000 a year. My primary giving areas are education and health.*
>
> (Male, 40s, self-made/entrepreneur)

When small gifts are appropriate

> *I do when a friend asks or because sometimes that's what's asked for. For a small organisation that size of gift may be very important.*
>
> (Male, 70s, self-made and inherited)

Many small donations were made to support specific activities of individuals or organisations. Mainly, this was where a small donation was perceived to be all that was necessary or appropriate for the recipient.

> *The local village church: the person running the fund used to be my secretary. I gave £100 in sponsorship to the husband of somebody in my book club who was running an event. £50 to a disaster appeal. And not forgetting the Christian Aid envelope.*
>
> (Female, 50s, married wealth)

My last three were a music student, to support a horse rider and to sponsor marathon runners.

(Male, 50s, self-made/entrepreneur)

Many pointed out that for a small or new organisation, a gift at or below £1,000 could be very encouraging, and would encourage others. More than one person gave donations at this level to projects in their place of birth or upbringing. Some people were fairly strategic about such giving. Just as people had set aside money for requests from friends, some set aside money to be able to give small amounts for local causes.

I give… 10 to 20 small grants to self-help regional or local groups with low overheads, volunteer-run. These will be one-offs from between £100 to £500. It's less than 5% of my total giving and I don't monitor the effectiveness.

(Female, 60s, self-made/entrepreneur)

Resources committed elsewhere
In more specific circumstances, donors said they might make such a small gift if they had already allocated their charitable giving for the year, but felt the cause was worth supporting.

I make such gifts to a good cause I know nothing about, or to a tiny charity, or when I am short of money but I want to give something. I sometimes give money to individuals through another trust: for example, an overseas student at an Oxbridge college.

(Male, 70s, self-made/entrepreneur)

Large charities
Whereas many focused small gifts on individuals or small charities, they and others might also give small amounts to major charities. This may be because they feel that it will be easier for such organisations to raise money elsewhere or that with larger charities there is less potential "to make a difference". Others limited their donations to larger charities in the social welfare sector because they were seen as increasingly acting on behalf of, and funded by, the public sector. Limiting their contributions was seen as "not letting the government off the hook".

Encouraging children
Many pointed out the importance of encouraging philanthropy and starting with small contributions in order to develop the habit of giving. This was particularly the view of people with children, who use small gifts as opportunities to set an example and provoke discussion.

> *I always give £2 to the man on the street.*
>
> (Male, 30s, self-made/professional)

Process for small gifts

As may already be evident, those who have become more strategic or experienced in their giving often allocate a specific budget for smaller gifts, usually give the same amount irrespective of the cause and sometimes organise a separate process and account from which to make the gifts.

> *I put £10,000 a year into a pot for local gifts to organisations in and around [X town]. I approve of opportunities like gap years. I support things like Drake and Raleigh, giving kids a chance.*
>
> (Male, 50s, self-made/entrepreneur)

Similarly, some of those who wish to support causes or people outside the focus of their trusts may give through a separate mechanism.

> *If a friend is involved and it doesn't fit the criteria I might give personally and not through the foundation.*
>
> (Male, 40s, self-made and inherited)

Like this contributor, others set aside specific budgets for supporting friends and other unplanned giving, and might, for example, use a CAF account for such purposes. Some have arranged their affairs so that even with a trust they can make small grants on an individual basis. In other cases, major donors have recognised the different nature of small giving and have adopted a strategic approach, setting up not only a separate account but an allocation and monitoring structure. Mechanisms for giving are explored later in this chapter.

> *I have a pot for small gifts. I put £100,000 into an account at 21. It's now worth over £1m and has given away more than £1m. It always gives income. At the start the limit was £500 and occasionally £1,000. One gets appeals one can't resist: for example the [local] music festival.*
>
> (Female, 50s, inherited)

Key points

Everyone makes what they regard as small donations. When they do so it is usually in response to requests from people they know. Nearly all the marathon sponsorships and similar events were in response to requests from friends or the children of friends. Many recognised the element of reciprocity here.

A few set aside a pot for gifts to causes or projects where a gift below £1,000 will be appropriate – local causes, support of gap years and travel scholarships, hardship cases and disaster appeals.

But as we see in Chapter Five when we look directly at triggers to giving, in many cases of requests made by friends for small amounts the cause is almost immaterial. It can certainly not be assumed that because a friend has asked, what starts as a small one-off gift will become a bigger gift. Indeed, some complained that they felt pursued by charities with whom they felt no connection whatsoever because they had sponsored an event of some kind.

The nature of feedback and involvement expected from small donations is quite different, and minimal, compared with that for giving to causes where there is a real commitment. With very few exceptions, this type of giving does not lead to a major engagement, unless the passion or interests of the donor have been aroused.

Sharing the giving decision

A majority of those who responded to a question about joint giving involved their partner and in some cases other members of the family in their philanthropic activity. One person said: "*I would consult my wife but wouldn't be deterred if she disagreed*", and one couple interviewed mentioned the director of the community foundation whom they would consult.

Some people talked about making sure that all members of the immediate family were agreed on the allocation of the donations. Part of the reason for this was to ensure shared ownership of the giving and to pass on what are seen to be the appropriate attitudes to the children. We look in greater detail at what people think about passing values and attitudes on to their children in Chapter Eight.

A minority of respondents said that they did not involve others in their giving decisions. In addressing this question, a few referred to specific projects which had been funded jointly with others or where people had led or responded to a challenge grant. One example was a public pledge of £100,000 if the charity could find four other similar gifts.

It may well be that those who said they did not involve others assumed that the question related to people who were not members of the family.

In any case, the research indicates that irrespective of their method of giving, a significant majority of donors do involve their partner and, in some cases, their children in their decision-making. This is not surprising, but it certainly is something fundraisers should consider in their strategies for engaging donors.

Giving allocation

Involvement

People were asked to estimate the proportion of their giving which goes to organisations with which they, their partner or children are or have been directly involved as volunteers, members, participants or trustees.

Giving to organisations where donors are directly involved

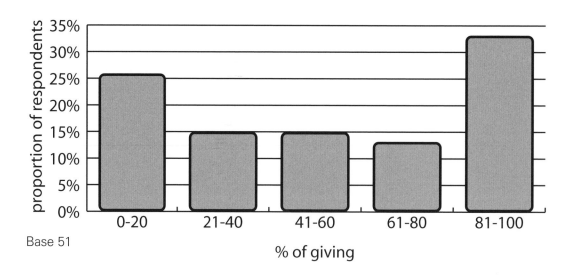

Base 51

Whereas about a quarter of respondents allocated 20% or less of their support to organisations where there was a direct family connection, about one-third directed more than 80% of their giving in this way. Much of the latter was accounted for by major gifts to capital projects or major appeals where the interviewee was a board member, or was a member of a fundraising committee of some kind.

Extent of passionate commitment

We have seen that the nature of the cause is the most important factor in continuing giving. Interviewees were asked how their donations in the previous year had been distributed between giving about which they felt passionate and the giving they felt less passionate about.

Giving donors feel passionate about

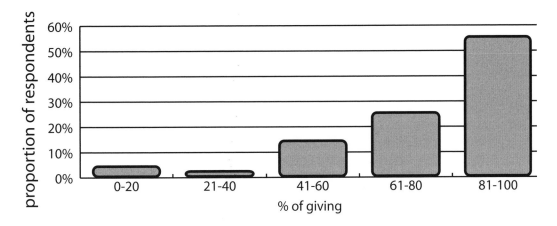

Base 51

We see that three-quarters of the respondents felt passionately about 60% or more of their giving, with well over half ardently supportive of causes receiving at least 80% of their donations.

Most satisfying donations

Interviewees were asked about the donations which had given them most satisfaction. Many did not identify a specific gift or recipient. For them it was the act of giving which was satisfying.

> *All are pleasing. I give large amounts to a few places. I know why I am doing it and why it is worthwhile. I feel a strong commitment and am pleased before I give.*
>
> (Male, 40s, self-made/entrepreneur)

An equal number reported particular cases. Although undoubtedly for the majority of people the most satisfying gifts were linked to larger donations, for a significant number it was smaller gifts which were most rewarding. A number of factors combined to give satisfaction over particular donations.

Support of individuals
Of particular reward was the support of individuals.

> *The biggest buzz was a small grant to sponsor a couple of doctors from the third world at the School of Tropical Medicine in Liverpool. Each year we have dinner with them. You really feel good. We will increase our support.*
> (Male, 60s, self-made/entrepreneur)

Supporting talented individuals who would not otherwise get a chance, and who will then make a contribution to society, was very gratifying for all who gave in this way. The pleasure and reward from helping new work or new talent develop was a theme from several. The donors feel that they make a continuing contribution to society through the individuals who have benefited. Such support covers a wide field – science and medicine, sports, the arts and specialist education were all cited.

The relationships with the individuals are not always personal. Sometimes the donor and beneficiary never meet.

> *I have two examples: a) I came to the UK on a business trip, I didn't have a lot of money. Someone introduced me to a young medical student. His parents were from East Africa and they needed help with the fees. I didn't have much money but I offered a monthly payment. I didn't know the name of the person. Ten years later I was introduced to the young doctor. It was a very nice feeling; b) Fifteen years ago I was involved in an organisation promoting early childhood education. A very concentrated course had to be devised. There were two US trainers and 12 places. A young girl from Bristol desperately wanted to attend the course. I gave her a scholarship. Every now and then I see her name as a star in that field. It gives me a sense that I made a difference.*
> (Male, 70s, self-made/entrepreneur)

In specific circumstances, support for individuals had been derived from gifts made in memory or in honour of a specific person – and these held particular attachment. The people concerned were mostly related – father, grandfather and brothers being cited. In one case a scholarship was set up in the name of a hero of the donor.

Making something happen

Very few of our sample were actively engaged politically or supported political parties to any extent, but several mentioned the satisfaction of knowing that their donations or involvement had had an impact on government policy and strategy.

> *The government has picked up my scheme. The leverage impact is very satisfying. It was about persuading the government to give money to universities to provide access.*
>
> (Male, 50s, self-made/entrepreneur)

The combination of involvement and leverage, particularly of government money, is particularly fulfilling. Related to this is the satisfaction of supporting successful campaigning organisations. One example influenced not only public policy but also that of a major corporate. Another person who had helped fund a major university faculty not only enjoyed the government support and the academic success of the Centre but also an honorary degree. As we have seen, recognition is an important element in satisfaction for some.

Others also mentioned the satisfaction of using their expertise to make the charitable sector more effective. This was more common among those with IT skills.

> *The application of IT skills to the creation of an international network so that researchers and funders can make more effective links. I'm trying to make the sector more business-like.*
>
> (Female, 60s, self-made entrepreneur)

For others it was the reward of seeing a new venture develop and flourish.

> *The ABC project – to create something from nothing. It's had 3m visitors by now. That is an achievement. I enjoy looking back on donations to the things I was involved with.*
>
> (Female, 50s, inherited)

Effective fundraising

Similar feelings of achievement resulted from major fundraising activities or leading a successful fundraising endeavour. People looked back with pleasure on the relationships they had developed with others, the sense of community involvement generated and the creativity required to be innovative. One interviewee, for example, had been crucial to a major transformation of the image of a particular art form, as well as initiating an innovative fundraising activity which is now replicated throughout the country and repeated each year.

Local support
Several people made similar points about the difference that a small gift to the local community can make.

> *Individual small gifts can be the most satisfying. We gave £100 to the local church when our housekeeper died in Scotland. We had an ecstatic letter which showed what a difference it would make. It's not a drop in the ocean like the Royal Opera House. Or we gave £200 for the local vicar. It's upholding something worthwhile in the fabric of society.*
>
> (Female, 30s, inherited)

It is not surprising there is a strong overlap between the rewards of giving, the factors that stimulate giving and the motivations for philanthropy explored in Chapter Five.

Satisfaction

Respondents were asked how satisfied they were with the current effectiveness of their donations, on a scale of one to ten. Just under 60% expressed themselves as very satisfied (eight to ten on the scale). About a third were in the medium category (five to seven) while under 10% reported a low degree of satisfaction (under five on the scale).

The factors which would make people give more, explored later in this chapter, should be considered in this context.

Regretted donations

Occasionally to established charities. I hate the ritualistic formal thank you where I don't feel I have made any real difference.

(Male, 50s, self-made/professional)

When interviewees were asked whether they regretted any donations, some 40% of respondents had no regrets. Of those that did, more than half had graphic stories about their experiences with named charities. Essentially these were concerned with:

◆ Relationships – they felt that they were not appreciated or were taken for granted.
◆ Lack of confidence that they had made any difference.
◆ Procedures which were extremely cumbersome and inefficient.

These factors are discussed fully in other parts of the report and will not be repeated here. But it is important to emphasise that a sense of real disappointment accompanied such experiences – although, fortunately, this did not appear to taint the feelings of reward from other more successful donations.

A number of donors were fairly resigned about the less successful outcomes from their giving. Some observed that occasional disappointments were to be expected, while others noted there was always some risk involved. Of those who said they had not had any occasion to regret a donation, a few added "*not yet*", with a clear implication that it might happen in the future and they would not be surprised if it did. More than one person compared it to being a high-risk entrepreneur putting in venture capital.

> *There is a danger that a charity takes you for granted and they assume that you will always continue to give. You need to know that you are allowed to choose each time.*
> (Male, 50s, self-made/professional)

> *When you start giving you don't realise how much trickles away. You blunt the risk of disappointment if you give money and let them decide. If one motivation is to make a difference there may be a problem; if, for example, you fund medical research which turns out to be rubbish even if there was an expert doctor on the board.*
> (Male, 50s, self-made/professional)

Similar examples were associated with larger gifts or bigger charities. Frequent disappointments were also reported with NHS projects.

Others made the point that such experiences provided the opportunity to learn; for many this amounted to the need to be clearer about the focus of the donation and the content and timing of feedback. Some even attributed their disappointment, which they had written off and forgotten about, to their own lack of forethought. Experienced donors suggested that the problems were due to lack of organisational capacity on the part of the charity concerned and have learned to consider this element when assessing applications.

Similarly, in funding capital projects, a few people blamed themselves for not thinking through the implications of the need for ongoing funding.

What people would do differently

I don't have any regrets about donations we have made in the past but I know we can do better in the future.

(Female, self-made/professional)

I would like to spend more time to visit projects and on administration.

(Female, 50s, inherited and grew family business)

I should be more proactive. The problem is time and I don't know how I would go about it.

(Male, 50s, self-made/professional)

I would get the children more involved. I would like to see some projects I support attracting other money. I would like my personal foundation to get better and more professional.

(Male, 50s, self-made/entrepreneur)

People were asked if they would approach the practice of their giving differently. A very significant minority said they would change nothing.

The rest were divided into those who felt it was too soon to consider the question and those who would like to allocate more time and, in some cases, more money. Very few wished they had been more selective. One regretted that he had not *"gone for anonymity"*.

The wish to give more time to philanthropic activity was a strongly recurring theme, particularly among those who have made their own money in business or the City. This is not so much about being less generous with money, but a perception that applying the business skills that have created their fortunes would improve the effectiveness of the charities they support and so be worth far more that any money they would be able to give.

> *I hope I'm not going to be an M&A banker for ever. I hope to have enough money to have a significant change in lifestyle so I will be more able to give more time to the charitable sector through giving time and money. I have seen that happen – for example with a contemporary who gets £20m a year – but now there are no bonuses.*
>
> (Male, 40s, self-made/professional)

For some, time could also usefully be spent on their own processes. Those who were actively engaged in running their own foundations with a high level of operational focus, and therefore already spending significant time, were thoughtful about how they could improve the effectiveness of their activities. Leveraging other donations to causes they support was also attractive to some.

It was suggested that developing a different approach is associated not only with learning from experience but with age and stage in life. With very few exceptions, all linked to inherited wealth, most people do not start serious giving until their forties at the earliest.

There were some who were unsure about how best to improve the management of their giving, although many recognised that there was room for such enhancement. It was exceptional that people had taken professional advice in this field, but for those that had, it had been a positive experience, in terms of both administration and focus.

In summary, we see a range of aspirations and ideas for improving the focus and process for the allocation of charitable resources. Most of them require more time on the part of the donor, and are associated in the minds of interviewees with a later stage in life – probably retirement or the sale of a business. Very few had engaged expert advice but this may be because they were unaware of the availability of such expertise. It was clear that for all, hands-on involvement was regarded as an integral part of enjoyable and effective philanthropy.

Giving anonymously

Well over half of the respondents have given anonymously at some point, although no-one had made all their gifts anonymously. In the main, the desire was to give discreetly rather than to hide their identity and this was usually related to specific donations. They wanted such discretion in various circumstances:

To avoid being approached by others in the same sector or area

Some people may give significantly to one charity in a sector but do not wish it to be publicised, either because they do not want to be inundated with requests from other charities in the sector, or because they were already supporting another such charity.

In some instances, this was related to giving within a locality and wishing to avoid any publicity or media coverage in the area where they live.

To avoid embarrassment or any sense of patronage

There were various circumstances in which people said they wanted to avoid any embarrassment or feeling of being patronising. Giving to local causes, giving to individuals or gifts closely associated with family members or friends were examples.

> *[I gave anonymously] when I gave to my old school because my daughter is there and I didn't want to embarrass her because it was the biggest donation.*
>
> (Female, 50s, inherited)

To avoid any accusation of ulterior motive

Some were concerned that identified giving might lead others to feel they had unworthy motives. People with children at university were very sensitive to the idea that they may be thought to be trying to buy access, or that it might be thought that the children were not bright enough to gain a place on their own.

> *I gave to X* [Oxford College where his children are students]. *The Principal knows but it's not publicised because people might draw the wrong inferences. People look for nasty motives.*
>
> (Male, 60s, self-made/professional)

In another circumstance, an Asian donor who has a trust in a name completely un-associated with his family was similarly sensitive to people attributing ulterior motives.

*We try to be low profile in the UK. We are publicity-shy because we
don't want people to think we are giving because we want to get known.*
(Male, 40s, self-made and inherited)

To avoid any controversy

There were the occasional references to support of Christian churches
by those of other faiths, mainly Jewish. Even though the support
was essentially a heritage contribution linked to a local connection
or personal friendship, some preferred confidentiality. Several of
the Jewish interviewees were discreet about their giving to Israel.
This was particularly the case for causes perceived to be controversial,
such as projects engaged in work with Palestinians and the search
for reconciliation.

To avoid "fuss"

Similarly, some saw their giving as a private matter and wanted to avoid
publicity or heralding of their donations. This was more often the case for
people with well recognised names.

*Yes. I wanted to give and not have [family name] associated with the gift.
I didn't want a hoo-ha. I had contributed and could sit back quietly.*
(Female, 30s, inherited)

For reasons such as these, some of the interviewees donate through a
charitable trust set up with a name which could not be identified with their
family. It is not always completely anonymous; people within the recipient
organisation and "in the know" might learn the identity of the donor, but
the general public would be unaware. Another person who has not
hitherto given anonymously is actively considering a major anonymous gift
in the name of someone he very much respects.

Others said that they would have preferred anonymity more often.
However, it was sometimes difficult to arrange because donors are often
asked by the recipient to allow their name to be publicised to endorse the
project, even if they didn't want "their name in lights". This was
particularly the case for well known donors to the education and culture
sectors, and has come to the fore with the plethora of recent lottery-
funded capital projects. Such schemes, several for national arts and
heritage institutions, require lottery funds to be matched by private
donations. Many projects were soliciting support in the form of major gifts
in the period immediately prior to this research, and had been supported
by a number of interviewees.

Some were ambivalent about the whole issue of hiding their identity. This is a typical example:

> *Yes, there was an occasion when I didn't ask for my gift to be made public, but there is no principle about this. I don't believe in anonymity, it distorts the market. To put one's name on things is the right thing to do, to encourage others and to inform the market that other people give, but at one level it is very embarrassing. There is a room at our son's school that has our name on it. I don't really get a buzz out of it now, but I might like it when I am 80. I feel squirmy and proud at the same time.*
>
> (Male, 40s, self-made/entrepreneur)

Some went further to suggest that named giving was beneficial as giving publicly encourages others. Indeed, one person saw this as *"part of the point of giving"*.

As we see, over half have wished at some time to remain anonymous, and motives range from what might be perceived as selfish – not wanting to be pursued by others – to sensitivity to appearing to be flaunting one's wealth or being patronising – whether to individuals or local communities.

It is interesting that the fear of being thought to have ulterior motives was raised. This is based on what is thought to be the public perception of – and perhaps cynicism about – people's intentions in their philanthropic activities. This is explored in more detail in Chapter Ten.

Mechanisms for giving

Description of the mechanisms

There is a range of ways through which people can make donations to charitable causes and claim tax relief related to the value of the donation. In most cases the tax relief is equivalent to the tax they would have paid on the income had it not been allocated to charity, and the relief is given to income which would otherwise be taxed. For higher rate taxpayers, the tax rate, and tax relief, was 40% at the time of the research. Tax relief on dividend income is less, and for those with no UK income there is correspondingly no tax relief. The tax relief is an incentive to the extent that there is relevant taxable income against which to offset the release from the obligation to pay.

In brief, people can support a charity either by one-off gifts of money, shares or other assets, or by payroll giving, i.e. regular deductions from salary or company pension. Nobody in this research study was giving through payroll deduction. Giving cash in either of these ways the donor receives income tax relief on the value of the donation. If a charity receives £1,000 from a donor, the donor (if he or she is a higher rate taxpayer) may obtain income tax relief of 40% or £400. The net cost to the donor is £600. In addition, with gifts of shares the donor may also claim capital gains tax relief on the difference in the value of the shares between acquisition and disposition.

However, the process for claiming tax relief depends on the mechanism used. With regular gifts from salary or company pension, the employer automatically allocates the donation from gross income, before tax is deducted. With one-off donations the **Gift Aid** process is used. This distributes the tax relief between the recipient charity, who can claim the basic rate of tax, and the donor, who can claim the difference between the basic rate and the higher tax rate. If the donor wishes the charity to receive £1,000 he or she gives £780 and signs a Gift Aid form. This enables the charity to claim back basic rate tax (currently 22%) on the £1,000, which is £220. The charity "grosses up" the donation. The donor may claim back the difference, 18% or £180, so the net cost to the donor is also £600. However, as many interviewees pointed out, the system is complicated. Their views are explored in detail in the section devoted to Gift Aid later in this chapter.

The Charities Aid Foundation (CAF) provides a range of products which offer donors the benefits of tax relief and administrative support.
The **CAF charity account** works like a bank account designed especially for charitable giving. The donor decides how much they want to give and pays it into the account. Because CAF is a charity, it can claim back the tax on Gift Aid donations and add it to the amount in the account. The account can also be funded through payroll giving or by gifts of shares, exactly as with any other charity. Several of those interviewed have a CAF account.

A **charitable trust or foundation** is a legal organisation that can be set up by anyone who has decided that they want to set aside some of their assets or income for charitable causes. Often, the first endowment is a lump sum from a bonus, an inheritance or the sale of shares. But because a charitable trust is a charity, it can receive money tax-free just like any other charity – for example, using Gift Aid or payroll giving. A charitable trust may be suitable for those who want to give regularly to a number of causes, or to give a reasonable amount as a one-off gift from time to time.

Setting up a personal charitable trust provides a framework for planning charitable giving in a systematic and thoughtful way. The process encourages a long-term commitment to philanthropy, and encourages the donor to set out the aims and priorities for the trust, and the basis on which applications for support will be assessed. Many people involve their family members as trustees and find it a very enjoyable and constructive way of developing a shared family commitment to giving. The main responsibility is to work within the charitable purposes and the powers set out in the trust deed that governs the trust. Apart from the tax relief on donations to the trust, it does not pay tax on its investment income. It does not pay corporation tax or inheritance tax, or business rates if it eventually runs its own office. Also, unless the trust is very large, it does not have to register for VAT.

People can choose what to call their trust, so it can carry the family name or be totally anonymous. Outside supervision comes from the Charity Commission. The trust must be registered with the Commission and it must submit to the Commission a formal report and accounts each year (including a list of the main organisations it has helped), as well as a yearly return and a report of any significant changes. As long as the trust stays within its own rules, the Commission cannot tell the trustees how to apply the trust's money.

The trust can continue after its founder(s) die, and may be the beneficiary of a legacy from their estate (which will be tax-free). The trustees will continue to distribute funds according to the guidelines set out in the constitution.

Community foundations provide a mechanism for individuals (and businesses) to contribute funds that can be focused on the local community. The community foundation provides the trustees, takes care of the administration and manages investments. As with trusts, people may create a named fund or give anonymously. If the family has strong links with a community and has served it well, a named fund in the local community trust can be a permanent memorial.

Many of those interviewed use more than one mechanism for their giving. Those who have a charitable trust will in any case either have contributed and/or continue to contribute to the trust through Gift Aid, or with gifts of shares. Some people with trusts also have a CAF account for small gifts.

I have my own foundation funded through Gift Aid. I am also giving shares to my own foundation. I have had a CAF account for a long time. I have had my own charitable trust for four years. It is very clean, a central mechanism for managing and controlling the whole lot. It means one is a net giver rather than a gross giver; the tax benefits come to the donor. The same mechanism processes everything and one can see what happens. I hope to see my children take it over after my death and involve other trustees.

(Male, 50s, self-made/entrepreneur)

Attitudes to the mechanisms for giving

This section examines people's views about the different mechanisms that exist and the thinking that surrounds their use.

Charitable trusts

Charitable trusts are personal grant-giving charities. Because they are charities they can receive gifts using any mechanism, and the donor gets the tax relief. Even when the mechanism distributes the tax relief between donor and beneficiary, as with Gift Aid, the effect is to ensure that for a given donation the same amount is available for charitable distribution, whatever the mechanism used to fund the trust.

Half of those interviewed had set up a charitable trust and on the whole recognised the benefits of this mechanism. They applaud the tax benefits that trusts allow and the fact that they can involve the whole family. They see it as a strategic commitment to philanthropy, as opposed to the one-off gifts which Gift Aid now allows to be made tax-efficiently.

Most people who have set up trusts have reached what might be called a mature level of charitable giving. They run their own foundations, with the support of an accountant. Other trustees are family members, and often their lawyer and a family friend. A few have trusts of the size which require one or more administrative staff. Those who have set up operational trusts employ staff to run the activities of the trust.

The circumstances in which interviewees set up their trusts varied widely. Donors' decisions to do so were influenced by the following factors:

In anticipation of coming into money

A trust may be planned in anticipation of a flotation, major bonus or other major increase in net worth, and set up before people become "used" to the extra wealth. Once the decision to establish a charitable trust is made, the decision is irrevocable.

> *I set up a charitable trust when I had a huge deferred bonus. It was £8m and is now £14m. I regard it as money I never had. It distributes income and capital. I won't let it go below £5m. I set it up in 1986; I wanted my own vehicle for giving. I thought it would be more rewarding than having a CAF account. I then put in the big windfall in 1997. I can give money now and direct it in future years. I use Gift Aid to add to the trust.*
>
> (Male, 50s, self-made/professional)

This example highlights the rewards of having a trust, clearly linked to control ("*my own vehicle for giving*"). It involved long term planning – over 10 years between the time the trust was set up and when anticipated funds were received. The idea that it is "*money I never had*" was also mentioned by those who set up trusts with money received after they sold their companies.

The idea of using the trust as a repository for "extra" money, while people think about how to use it charitably, was also mentioned in various ways.

Unexpected gains and "extra" money
In much the same way, money acquired through a business activity, such as profit from a takeover, was used for trust development. Several people in this circumstance had built up the value of their trust over many years, through careful investment. A trust may be fed with "extra" money, such as fees and dividends.

> *I have my own charitable trust which I set up in 1965. The source was my own earnings and investment. I had a particular block of shares for which there was a takeover bid so I got £1m profit and set up the trust with that. It was built up by good management. We bought and sold property which increased the endowment. It's now worth about £8m.*
>
> (Male, 70s, self-made and inherited)

Making a major gift

> *We have a Charitable Trust. It was £400,000 initially. It was used as a channel with all to be spent; this was not setting up an endowment. Before that we used to just send cheques which wasn't tax-effective. At the moment small donations don't go through the trust because all three trustees have to sign all cheques. This will be changed. We set up the trust because we were advised to do so for tax benefits because we were making a big £12m gift to the university. We were advised by our financial advisor to set up a foundation and have just done so. This was*

*in cash and not shares because the shares are in unlisted companies.
The trustees are myself, my husband, our lawyer and we are seeking a
fourth, a retired accountant.*

(Female, 50s, married to entrepreneur)

Desire for a committed and strategic approach

Several observed that by its nature and process, setting up a trust
encourages a strategic approach and commitment to philanthropy. It is a
long-term obligation, ensures money is spent charitably and helps to make
spending effective. Careful management can also significantly increase the
value of the trust.

*I have had my foundation for a long time. It is worth about £8m. It is an
easy way of giving money. I would like to see more tax breaks like in the
US. That's what helped me set up the foundation. It also keeps people on
the straight and narrow because the money must be used charitably.*

(Male, 70s, self-made/entrepreneur)

*I have a charitable trust. I wanted to give a focus to my giving instead of
just responding willy-nilly. I am wealthier than I ever imagined I would be.
A key part of what I could contribute was giving and making things better for
others. It's a way of involving the family. It's a good structure. I don't have a
cheque book for my trust; I send details to the lawyer who deals with it.*

(Male, 40s, self-made/entrepreneur)

Wanting to involve family

Many people saw their trust as a way of involving the family. For some this was
linked to the idea that this was a way of letting their sons or daughters have a
say about the spending of money which they might otherwise have inherited.

*We have a charitable trust, a CAF account, use Gift Aid and give shares.
A trust is a good idea for involving children and diverting money which
would otherwise be their inheritance. I give through the family
foundation which I set up, the Network for Social Change and personally.
I will top it up with share transfers.*

(Male, 80s, self-made/entrepreneur)

Seeking or responding to advice

Most of those who set up a trust when they had made a lot of money did
so on the basis of advice from their lawyer, financial adviser or accountant.
A few people already engaged in charitable activities were advised by
fellow board members.

I have a charitable trust and use Gift Aid. Sometimes I give directly through Gift Aid and gifts of shares. I was advised to set up a trust by X [a friend who is a banker and fellow board member – also an interviewee] *so that I could involve my children. They can then put money into the family trust and share decisions about the allocation. Trustees also include my wife, her sister and husband.*

(Male, 50s, self-made/professional)

One interviewee invested in comprehensive research on the various options.

I have a charitable trust. It represents 51% of the business value at the time it was set up. I first commissioned research on how trusts work, for which I paid £8,000 or £9,000. I wanted to run it properly like a business looking at inputs and outputs. I have spent the last three to four years getting it running. The trustees are myself, my wife, plus my daughter and daughter-in-law. The income was £^{1}/4m last year. I plan to build it up to £^{1}/2m over next two years. The ultimate endowment is shares in the company but it is currently funded by cash from the company. I will increase that until it achieves a return equivalent to the long-term return it will get from the shares. The recent legislation hasn't affected the mechanism. I can already see I will have to employ someone to help to run it.

(Male, 60s, self-made/entrepreneur)

In summary, people see a trust as a mechanism for retaining control over their money, and deciding how it should be allocated to charitable purposes. It is a way of outsourcing their philanthropy in a tax-efficient way.

Disadvantages of trusts

I have a charitable trust fed by Gift Aid. It was a small sum to start off with, then I made monthly contributions and put in amounts to top up. It was a sensible mechanism to covenant money each month and get tax relief. Then Gift Aid came along and I used it to top it up. It was a convenient way of keeping track but now it is easy to get tax relief on one-off gifts. I wouldn't set up a trust again because there wouldn't be the motivation to go through the process with the Charity Commission. I would just have a stack of Gift Aid forms. Having a foundation attracts applications – somebody has to deal with them.

(Male, 50s, self-made)

While recognising the benefits of establishing a charitable trust, a fifth of those who have a trust have serious reservations about one or more aspects. The main problems identified were as follows:

Advice and monitoring by the Charity Commission

Apart from the bureaucracy of registration and regular reporting, several mentioned other problems with the Charity Commission, and its approach to investment policy. This was a particular complaint by those who had endowed their trusts with shares in the companies they had created.

The irritation was compounded if it was planned to spend the capital.

> *The Charity Commission is an anonymous bureaucracy...there is minimal value in terms of better performance. It is completely muddled on its investment policy and its diversification policy. If the government wants new entrepreneurs to put, say 10% of the company into a trust and then two years later tells them to diversify, why should they set it up like this in the first place? The Commission shouldn't treat it in the same way as a pension fund. It behaves as if the money has passed to the state.*
> (Male, 60s, inherited and grew business)

Related publicity

People also disapproved of the lack of privacy associated with establishing a trust. The contributor above, who set up a trust in the 70s and now *"greatly regrets"* it, commented with some feeling about this:

> *Since the government encourages charitable giving with Gift Aid, one is much better off not setting up a trust. You could give a fortune to the cats' home and nobody would know. Charitable activities should be private and one should be one's own master. There is pressure to be politically correct. I like the idea of the right to privacy in charity... Why should the public know to whom the gifts go? Information should go to the Charity Commission and the Inland Revenue.*
> (Male, 60s, inherited and grew business)

Outsider scrutiny

Several mentioned their resentment of criticisms, particularly by the Directory of Social Change (DSC). Disapproval was expressed by those with long-standing trusts as well as those who had set them up recently, particularly those who had endowed their trusts with their company shares. Critics included those who had not themselves featured in DSC reports or been otherwise censured. It was felt that if the focus of the giving was one or more registered charities, or individuals covered by the terms of the trust, and the Charity Commission and Inland Revenue were satisfied with the administration of the charitable trust, it was not the business of others ("self-appointed") to tell trustees what they should be doing, and publish negative reports.

Several people pointed out that charitable giving is a private and voluntary activity, and is to be encouraged, not criticised. As we have seen, the impetus is often deep personal experience and passion. Although no-one explicitly said they gave to "the cats' home", several felt that if they did, it should, if they wished, be nobody's business but theirs and their trustees, the Charity Commission, the Inland Revenue and the cats.

These attitudes were reflected by professional advisors, particularly the lawyers.

> *Luke Fitzherbert[1] is intrusive and unkind. Charities must be open to scrutiny and it is useful to show charities which fail to provide information when approached, but he goes beyond that and acts as a disincentive. Poking fun at the area of charity* [chosen by the donor] *is not his business.*
>
> (Solicitor)

Many advisers and some donors pointed out that the criticisms had become counter-productive. Although, as we have seen, people see the creation of a charitable trust as the best infrastructure for a strategic commitment to philanthropy, the principle of the Gift Aid mechanism (tax relief on one-off gifts), if not the administration, is now seen as an attractive alternative. The tax benefits are similar, costs are less, there is no long-term commitment and gifts can be completely private.

As one adviser said:

> *Luke doesn't see that being PC has had a negative effect. I wonder how his Directory is carrying out its charitable objects. How is it within its own objects of educating the public by criticising trusts? He doesn't realise how much has been lost to charities and trusts as a result of his activities.*
>
> (Solicitor)

[1] Luke Fitzherbert, of the Directory of Social Change. See Appendix Four for his response to these comments.

Gift Aid

> *I have always used Gift Aid. It's tax-effective and increases giving.*
>
> (Female, 50s, self-made/entrepreneur)
>
> *Gift Aid is much too complicated. In the US charitable donations are very, very simple. It's easy to understand: the donor gets the full tax deduction.*
>
> (Male, 50s, self-made/entrepreneur)

At least a quarter of those interviewed mentioned using Gift Aid, although the number who do is probably more since those who periodically give cash to their charitable trust may well be using this mechanism. Of those using it, the majority spoke positively about the process and the mechanism, mainly because of privacy and relative simplicity.

Most of those speaking well of the process were comparing it favourably with the cost and complexity of establishing and running a charitable trust. As we have seen, many of those who have established a trust also use Gift Aid, and some would not set up a trust again because they find the Gift Aid process comparatively simple. Some people with a trust use Gift Aid for smaller gifts, additional donations when buying tickets and for support outside the main purposes of their trust.

However, a significant minority of interviewees were strongly critical of the process. Many, while recognising the benefit of some kind of tax-deduction for a one-off gift, with no requirement to make a long-term commitment to philanthropy, complained about the unnecessary complexity for donor and recipient, ignorance on the part of beneficiaries and the fact that the donor does not get all the tax relief, whatever their tax rate.

> *Gift Aid is simplest. I sometimes Gift Aid via CAF. But there is this ridiculous system of clawback of tax by the recipient. Better that either donor or recipient receives the full amount. I thought about setting up a trust but I asked for a package from the Charity Commission. It's a bit of a palaver, so I never did anything about it. There is no need to because a registered charity is always the recipient.*
>
> (Male, 50s, self-made/professional lawyer)

Some expressing adverse views had experience of US giving, to which they compared Gift Aid unfavourably because of its constraints and intricacy. Not only is the tax relief split between recipient and donor, but there appear to be arcane and inconsistent rules about the extent to which benefits may be enjoyed by the donors. In some cases (membership of The National Trust, some Friends schemes or individual visits to places of interest) Gift Aid may be claimed, even when the potential benefits are substantial in relation to the cost of membership. In other cases there are complicated calculations.

> *I find the complexity of the UK system very irritating. I pay tax in both countries and give in the US. It's much simpler in the US. One can make a gift, get tax relief and still have the lifetime use of the money. Also in this country you can't write off the whole value of a ball ticket, just the donation element which makes it more difficult to raise money.*
>
> (Male, 50s, self-made/professional)

It was strongly felt that opportunities are lost because of the complications of the system. These views were particularly prevalent in the City, where the combination of periodic bonuses (mentioned by a few) and lack of time indicated the need for a very simple system which employers could establish and promote.

> *Employers should set up a trust or CAF account for staff. Tapping the bonus doesn't happen; employers don't offer the option of a tax-free donation from the bonus to go to charity. Charities should make it as easy as possible to give tax efficiently; it's completely stupid that either the charity or the individual can't claim the whole 40% – I don't have the time. For us it's £2,000 to £3,000 in the taxman's pocket which shouldn't be there. It should be made easy for the charity to give a voucher which is put back into the tax return. Tax should be seen as hypothecation. The Treasury should tell the top taxpayers 'if you give x we'll give y'.*
>
> (Female, 30s, self-made/professional)

Support for this approach was not only linked to simplicity but to the idea of leverage and hypothecation – that is the tax is "my money", and by allocating it to a chosen cause the donor is directing the Treasury to allocate a further sum to that charity which otherwise would have gone into the general coffers.

Many of those interviewed without trusts give by cheque and only sign a Gift Aid form if the charity asks. A number of charities, including many well known organisations, did not do this, even for sizeable donations.

In a separate part of the interview, people were asked about their views on the impact of tax incentives, and particularly the changes introduced in 2000. We have noted the irritation with the perceived unnecessary complexity of Gift Aid, both in terms of the forms and when dealing with recipients who are unfamiliar with the system. The calculation of the gross cost and net benefits is more complicated for higher rate taxpayers, although most people were able to work out the net cost to them of the charity receiving a given amount. However, they feel much better if they are giving, and are credited with, the gross sum, and many pointed out that this was much simpler, and cheaper, for the beneficiary. Even those who did not feel strongly about it recognised the likely impact of all the benefit going to the benefactor.

Those who are happy with Gift Aid tend to be giving to their own charitable trust or CAF account which enjoys the benefit of the split tax reliefs, or, in a few other cases, are experienced donors supporting larger organisations more accustomed to the administration.

Community foundations

A group of interviewees had had very positive experiences with a community foundation. All are based in the North East, and no-one interviewed from other parts of the country mentioned any kind of association with a community foundation. The interviewees in the North East were introduced via the local community foundation, but nevertheless the study included major donors from other parts of the country where there is a reasonably strong local community foundation presence. Clearly, the experience of those in the North East is a tribute to the strength and effectiveness of the individual community foundation.

> I have a charitable trust, I use Gift Aid and giving shares. I give through the community foundation. I put 40% of the money I made into a charitable trust after the flotation of my business. We have our own trust and fund within the community foundation. There is now £7m in the trust. The income is about £1/2m – that's what we give away annually. It suits my personal circumstances, especially the effect on tax, and it has been very fulfilling; in particular we have been able to target our giving at real projects serving many underprivileged sectors of society.
>
> (Male, 50s, self-made/entrepreneur)

For most people interviewed, giving through the mechanism of a community foundation is exactly like giving through a trust, but with more support and less bureaucracy. People wanting to support their local community perceive it as an excellent structure. Some people have their charitable trust for other causes and a fund within the community foundation for local projects.

> *I use Gift Aid and give shares to a charitable trust and through the community foundation. We are fortunate to have more income and capital than we need…we can think of no better way than investing surplus income or capital in trying to help those less fortunate and trying to improve the quality of life in Cumbria – and at the same time, significantly reducing our personal tax liabilities. The foundation provides a trouble-free way of achieving this – and the comfort that our donations are being carefully and professionally managed. I am no longer a trustee and have no say.*
> (Male, 60s, self-made/entrepreneur)

Many of the advantages cited mirror those expressed about charitable trusts – the sense of control and ability to focus on preferred and targeted local objectives, the possibility of involving family members, tax benefits and an effective administration process. However, the tax benefits vary depending on the source of income (being less for dividend income), which is seen to be anomalous.

CAF accounts

> *Everyone should have a CAF account. I use Gift Aid to put money into a CAF account.*
> (Male, 60s, self-made/professional)

There was explicit reference to the use of a CAF account (always alongside Gift Aid and other mechanisms, and used for small gifts) and nearly all those who use it spoke very positively about it.

> *I have a foundation; it's a good mechanism although it's sometimes unnecessarily difficult to register. I also have a small CAF account with £10,000. I use this for small gifts. It's very neat and minimises paper work.*
> (Male, 60s, self-made/professional)

Most of those who use a CAF account feed it using Gift Aid. A few had experienced administrative problems.

Gifts of shares

Share giving is a huge incentive. The tax benefits are substantial and a good thing.

(Male, 60s, self-made/professional)

Giving shares is an excellent idea which needs to be explained better.

(Male, 60s, self-made/professional)

The assets of the foundation are shares. It is very complicated and cumbersome. The mechanism was used to establish the gift from the donor to the foundation.

(Female, 60s, self-made/entrepreneur)

Income tax relief on giving shares was introduced in 2000. This was on top of the existing capital gains tax relief. In discussing this question people had considered making gifts of shares from their own company either to set up or increase the endowment of their charitable trust or as a donation to a completely unrelated charity. Others had donated shares from a mixed portfolio to a charity, either their own trust or an operating charity.

Some people had given shares as a one-off charitable gift and most of these were positive about the idea in principle. However, there were a few criticisms of the complexity of the process, and the experience of the decline in value of the shares between the announcement of the donation and the realisation of the sale proceeds by the charity. (This was in 2002, when the stock market was falling.)

The concept of giving shares, particularly of companies who have just gone public, is a good thing. The problem is that most people just don't know how to use it and how to create endowment funds for the charity. Asking for shares is a different proposition. The shares could be kept locked in by the charity and the charity could borrow against them. The problem is the Charity Commission attitude to charitable trusts having all or most of their shares in one company.

(Male, 50s, self-made/entrepreneur)

As elsewhere in this report, we note the position of the entrepreneur with a private company who makes decisions about their charitable giving from a strategic perspective. They give individually or corporately depending on their current financial position, the corporate agenda and the optimum tax advantage. Share giving may be considered, but it will be in the context of a review of all the personal and company options.

> *It's very complicated. I may well give shares in the future. I would certainly expect to get tax benefits. I am forming a foundation which would be a proper charity. This is because there is a large mix of activities. I am giving time; others in the company are giving time. Individuals are raising money for the cause, there are also corporate activities to raise money and the company gives money, and sometimes I give. The foundation will be [interviewee] and the company. I could ultimately endow it with shares and it would also be a good way for me and the business to channel work in kind; for example, the graphics department could charge work to the foundation which would be a gift to a charity from the foundation. There would be money from me and the company each year into and from the foundation.*
> (Male, 50s, self-made/entrepreneur)

Some of those who had acted as fundraisers or askers said they had received unclear guidance from the Inland Revenue. In one case, different tax offices had given inconsistent advice to the prospects of someone soliciting support in different areas of the country.

During the period of the interviews, some askers had seen the giver of shares to a charity receive tax relief and recognition for a donation whose nominal value far exceeded the sum actually realised by the charity.

> *I have a very bad experience with gifts of shares. I am involved in a project to convert a chapel into a community centre and we pushed hard for donations in shares. These are now worth a fraction of the value they were when they were given. This is a disaster; having initiated the work we have to seek further funds. Of course, with hindsight we realise the shares should have been cashed in at the time.*
> (Female, 50s, married entrepreneur)

Since income tax relief on giving shares was introduced, there has been general frustration that a scheme which is perceived by most interviewees as excellent in principle is undermined in practice by lack of clarity and inconsistent advice from the Inland Revenue and Charity Commission. As indicated above, this situation is compounded by lack of experience on the part of recipients.

Private company giving

A small number of interviewees give partly or entirely through their company, not giving shares at all. One relatively young entrepreneur channels all donations through the company.

> All our giving is through the family business. It is tax deductible. We have no charitable trust. I keep control of what I want to do and what not. It has the virtue of simplicity. The government has made it easier. In 2001, I gave £200,000 out of the business, and about £60,000 in 2002.
>
> (Male, 50s, self-made/entrepreneur)

Payroll giving

During the period of the research, giving through regular deductions from salary or company pension was the most tax-efficient mechanism for charitable giving of cash. This was due to the additional government incentive to encourage a commitment to this form of giving (10% of the value of the donation to go to the recipient). However, in spite of this inducement, and the fact that payroll giving could be used for a one-off gift, no-one claimed to be using this mechanism currently, although one had in the past. This was the case even where interviewees were working for financial institutions and companies which had such a scheme in place.

Tax incentives

> I feel good about the idea of money levering tax benefits. I wish more people did it. It's better in the US where you get tax relief when the commitment is made, not when the gift is received. It is simple.
>
> (Male, 50s, self-made/professional)

> I like the thought that £200,000 from the XYZ company goes to my charity with no tax payable. I would do it anyway; I think of it as money which we would otherwise have for ourselves.
>
> (Male, 70s, self-made/entrepreneur)

In the US with big money you see the immediacy of the tax break. There is the association with hypothecation and all the benefit goes to the taxpayer. Compare this with Gift Aid.

(Male, 60s, self-made/professional)

I do not give to receive a tax benefit. I would like tax benefits to be good for charities.

(Male, 60s, self-made/professional)

People were asked about their general reaction to the incentive effect of tax-efficient mechanisms for giving, and the impact of the recent (2000) tax changes. The vast majority of respondents thought that such incentives encouraged giving in principle and took advantage of the benefits. It should be emphasised that no-one thought that tax incentives alone would lead to substantial giving; there must still be a charitable impulse, since whatever the tax benefit, the donor is still foregoing disposable income or the use of assets which could otherwise be allocated to non-charitable activities.

For some the personal reward of the tax incentive was reinforced by the feeling that the process is an in-built form of hypothecation or leverage: money which would otherwise go to the Treasury may be directed to a charity of the donor's choice. This was perceived to be an incentive and an opportunity.

It's a useful tool. It gets to hypothecation. If you give x the government will give y to your chosen cause. It's your chance to give something back.
(Male, 30s, self-made/professional)

The main focus of comments about tax incentives concerned Gift Aid and giving shares. Many of the points raised in the previous section were reiterated. Although recognising the improvements in tax incentives, particularly with giving shares, many compared the situation in the UK unfavourably with that in other countries, especially the US.

It was noted that the main tax relief relates to earned income; there are fewer options for those whose UK taxable income is not at a level at which the tax relief would have an impact.

Non-domiciled

A small number of those interviewed were not domiciled in the UK for tax purposes, although they have major corporate interests on which tax is paid. Perhaps slightly tongue-in-cheek, one pointed out that he was not in a position to benefit from tax-related incentives to philanthropy. One interviewee deeply resented the apparent benefits enjoyed by non-domiciled benefactors.

> We would rather pay 0% tax and give away £30m than pay £20m in tax and give away £10m because we think we would spend the money better. We would put a promise in writing to give more money if we paid less tax... There is no recognition for keeping money in the UK. Compare this with the [ABC family] who were knighted while massively offshore. They give a fraction of what they are saving and get rewarded for it. There is no recognition for backing the UK. It is an imbalance. We give lots to charity and pay lots of tax. If we had structured our companies differently we could have given the same amount of money and got lots of plaudits. Charity is equivalent to investing in this country. There needs to be more thought about this.
>
> (Male, 30s, self-made/entrepreneur)

Improvements

Interviewees were not specifically asked for proposals to enhance tax-efficient giving but as we have seen there were many unsolicited ideas. For many who had already established a foundation with a major lump sum (for example from the sale of a business), the issue of further tax incentives was relatively unimportant. Giving through other methods (such as a CAF account, which might be used for small gifts) might be facilitated, but the incentive effects were minimal since by making an irrevocable gift of a large capital sum to their foundation they had already made a significant commitment to philanthropy.

However, while recognising the benefits of legacies to charities, several people suggested what they saw as changes which would enhance the incentives for gifts of capital in the lifetime of the donor.

> People are asset rich and cash poor. Improvements I would like to see are gifts in kind – like the Australian model, and tax relief on lifetime gifts (like charity remainder trusts in the US).
>
> (Male, 60s, self-made/professional)

As we have seen, many echo the advocacy for US-style lifetime giving structures.

There were two main strands to the recommendations:

◆ Simplify the administration of the mechanism for one-off gifts (Gift Aid) for higher rate taxpayers, and ensure that the donor gets the tax relief. There was resentment at the costs which charities had to incur and irritation at the opportunities lost to encourage people to give through the tax return process. The psychological rewards of giving, and being recognised for, the gross amount, were also reported.

◆ Create opportunities for donors to obtain tax relief at the time of an irrevocable pledge of a capital gift made in the lifetime of the donor, allowing the donor or someone designated by the donor to continue to enjoy the income on that capital for a specified period.

A small number of people also referred to the absence of an incentive to give works of art and shares in private companies.

The underlying requirement for tax mechanisms is that they should be consistent in approach and simple to operate.

In addition, several people referred to the incentive effect of the annual tax return as it is managed in the US. This provides the systematic reminder of the gifts made and the tax reclaimed, and the opportunity to make more charitable donations to maximise the tax benefit in the given tax year.

8

Wealth, security and family

Here we explore the attitudes of respondents to their wealth. We look at the basis of their feelings about money and security, and explore how values are passed to their children. We consider attitudes to children and the passing on of wealth, opinions about inheritance taxes, and the consequences of capital transfers for family and society.

Financial security

If you are worth £10m and you have two properties that together are worth say £4m, that leaves £6m for investment. At say 5% this produces £300,000 a year. Are you wanting to retain the £6m and provide houses for your children? If so, you 'only' have £300,000 a year. If you can eat into the capital of both the £6m and your property you could have twice that to spend. The psychology of people in my square is that they are not financially secure enough. The challenge is to make people see that there is an ability to give and that it's fun.

(Asker, ex-banker)

People were asked how secure they feel, on a scale of 0 to 10, where 0 is least secure. This question deliberately echoes one posed by Paul Schervish in his research on US millionaires for Boston College, reported in *The Mind of the Millionaire*[1]. In Chapter Fourteen we consider how the answers compare.

While everyone interviewed would be perceived as wealthy by comparison with the average UK citizen, it is clear that people have very different attitudes to money, confidence in their financial position and sense of what is necessary for them to feel secure. The discussions on feelings of financial security provoked some of the most self-analytical responses in the interviews, as did those on passing money to children. However, whereas most respondents, particularly older ones, had clearly given some thought to issues of inheritance and capital transfer, and discussed them with their partners and advisers, only a tiny minority had discussed their fears and concerns about financial security with anyone.

Many of these feelings are matters of intensely personal judgment and experience. They are not subject to logical analysis, and a number of interviewees acknowledged that their attitudes, fears and insecurities may seem irrational in the context of their actual level of wealth. Their reactions to the question were based on a combination of deeply embedded personal feelings, perceptions of the external marketplace and the political situation, and their ideas about their own long-term prospects.

The chart below groups respondents into low, medium and high security clusters.

How financially secure do you feel?

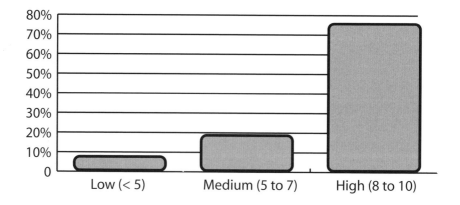

Base 67

We see that about three-quarters of respondents feel reasonably secure. Some made the point that it was not the level of wealth but the level of confidence that matters.

Links to level of wealth

Many people suggested that feelings of financial security are not related to the level of wealth and this was borne out by the analysis.

Level of wealth	
Net worth £m	Proportion of respondents reporting high security level % (50 in total)*
Over 500	0
200 – 500	75
100 – 200	50
50 – 100	65
20 – 50	85
10 – 20	75
5 – 10	65
1 – 5	45
* to nearest 5%	

Sixty-two interviewees reported their net worth, and the number in each category is small or very small: for example, 10 out of the 15 in the category £5m to 10m report themselves as feeling a high level of security, and five out of eight in the £50m to £100m group. Without placing any emphasis on the statistical validity of this small sample, particularly at the top and bottom of the net worth echelons, we can see that perceptions and feelings of security are on the whole unrelated to levels of wealth, except perhaps at the lowest level.

Security and source of wealth

The association between the source of wealth and feelings of security is set out in the following table, covering 76 interviewees.

Source of wealth

Source of wealth		
Source of wealth	Number of respondents	Proportion of respondents reporting high security level %
Self-made professional	29	65
Self-made entrepreneur	25	67
Inherited and grew family business	7	33
Inherited wealth	6	100
Self-made and inherited	4	50
Married wealth	4	100
Self-made – other	1	100

The first two categories account for over two-thirds of the interviewees, with the third category only about 10%. The sample size in each of the last three categories is very small. However, this table would appear to suggest that among these interviewees, those involved in managing and growing family businesses feel less secure than those in other categories. Only about a third in this group felt secure, whereas two-thirds of those who were self-made, whether as an entrepreneur or as a professional, felt reasonably secure. Everyone who inherited or married wealth felt very secure.

Running a business

One of the least secure people in the study ("*about two to three*") was one of the wealthiest, with a net worth of about £650m. His assets were very largely tied up in his business. It will be noted that although those who set up businesses said they did so because of a desire to build capital, to be in control of their own lives and be independent, several people who were running their own family businesses felt relatively less secure, not least because of pressure from other family members. For most entrepreneurs the fear of the failure of their business is clearly about more than the risk of financial loss.

> *I ought to feel 10 but I don't. If anything happened to the business, it would ruin the rest of my life...*
>
> (Male, 50s, self-made/entrepreneur)

One of the differences between the position of a self-made entrepreneur and the person running a family business is the network of family members who are dependent on the success of the company. Some of those running family businesses observed that strategic decisions may be influenced by the differing needs for dividends, and there may be pressure to employ family members whose skills may not be appropriate. So the fear of failure is not only about financial shortfall and loss of prestige and reputation, powerful though those factors are; there is the additional consideration of the impact on the extended family.

For many of those running their own business, the responsibilities and self-esteem balance out; the clear message is that the personal benefits and rewards of running a business are not related to immediate feelings of security, even if the initial and continuing impetus is to build capital. Many people continue to build their businesses long after their self-defined material needs are satisfied; many who have sold businesses invest in or start up others, and for some the return on their investments becomes, as we shall see, a substitute measure of their own continuing effectiveness.

Security and age
We looked at the relationship between age and financial security.

Age		
Age	Number of respondents*	Proportion of respondents reporting high security level %
Under 35	1	100
35 – 44	13	73
45 – 54	22	71
55 – 64	20	71
Over 65	13	58
* 7 declined to give the information		

There was a range of sources of wealth in each age category. However, in the group aged over 65 (13 of the total) there was a higher proportion (11) of self-made entrepreneurs or professional people than in the sample as a whole (about 70%). So although the sample is small, it appears that the feelings of security drop markedly with older respondents. This is the more marked as those in the medium group (five to seven on the security scale) are similar – between 20% and 25% – for every age group. The major drop in feelings of security of those in the oldest age group is reflected in the larger proportion of those in that group with levels of five or below.

In the conversations it was younger people who expressed concern about the range of unknown expenses and family responsibilities for which they might have to provide – children, parents, health risks. But this category was least likely to be considering major gifts, and was more or less confidently engrossed in building their businesses or their careers. Older people were dependent on investments over which they had much less control, and more aware of their own fragility.

Security and gender
There is some indication that the women who responded feel more secure than the men. None were in the low category (against about 10% of the men), with a higher percentage of women in each of the other two groups.

Inconsistency of perception
A small group of people claimed not to feel secure, and yet the figure they gave for the level of net worth they would need to feel completely secure was lower than the level of wealth they reported at a later stage in the interview. One gives a very small proportion of his income (under 0.5%), and claims that having more money would be very likely to make him give more. Another, distributing the income of a trust established by his father, and one of the least secure people interviewed, would not give more in any circumstances. There was a strong Jewish and family business representation in this small group.

Some were clear that their insecurities had complex bases. This was particularly the case for those with Jewish origins, more than one of whom referred to the endemic lack of security felt by Jews[2]. Others showed major inconsistencies in their perceptions about their own levels of wealth and giving. For this group, including those who say that having more money would trigger more philanthropy, it may be possible to raise awareness about their real financial needs and philanthropic opportunities, linked to perceptions about what it is appropriate to give.

[2] For example, see article in *The Telegraph* of 15 January 2004: "Our history has taught us to be insecure, that no place is forever" – Professor Alan Herzberg.

Passing values to children

Values are caught not taught.

(Male, 50s, self-made/entrepreneur)

People were asked whether they had tried to educate their children during their formative years about the family's relative affluence, at what age they thought it appropriate to begin educating children about these things and whether they had done anything to educate them about giving and volunteering. For most people their approach to wealth and their family values were inextricably linked. The largest category included those who felt that educating their children in their family values and making them aware of the responsibilities of wealth is a process which starts from early childhood. For most people it was a question of providing a model, of living the example. One person used the term "osmosis". Many but not all in this category based their life on strong religious beliefs or values.

While many people feel philanthropy should be seen as an essential part of their life, and an integral part of wealth management and allocation, a few think it important that children learn their values but deny the need for a formal process. They think that children will absorb the "right" attitudes; for some this is linked to a reluctance to talk about money. Some wish to protect their children from the knowledge of their wealth and live relatively modestly. But nearly everyone is concerned to teach self-reliance, to encourage their children to earn their own income, and to be aware of and sensitive to those who are far less well-off.

Starting young

> No child likes to see a hurt animal. I wouldn't dissuade them from helping such causes. It's the act of giving. One should start at a very early age: look at Blue Peter appeals. We tend to underestimate the ability of children to give. My children sat through a presentation from the church and came away with questions.
>
> (Male, 30s, self-made/professional)

Several were of the view that there should be an integrated approach to imparting family values of which exemplary philanthropy is a part.

Many, but by no means all, in this category come from backgrounds and childhoods in which there had been a strong religious influence, or awareness of values drawn from a religious tradition of previous generations. One or two from strong traditions thought such matters should be left until later. The values of their faith of origin underpinned their way of life, even if attendance at a place of worship was irregular. For these interviewees, who included some from a cross-section of religious backgrounds and sources of wealth, philanthropy and charitable giving is one aspect of their relationships with each other, their community and wider society. The community tradition was strong among some members of Jewish society.

Sharing the pleasures, responsibilities and rewards of giving is an important component. People referred to support of television appeals when children are very young, and to making them aware of the successes of their charitable trust.

> *We have tried to have an influence on our children. They have seen what works, for example, in marriage. They have seen the pleasure we have from seeing something happen which wouldn't otherwise have been there.*
>
> (Male, 60s, inherited)

Many of those with family foundations mentioned the importance of involving children in the charitable trust from an early stage, well before they can be formal trustees (at the age of 18). Many encourage their children to propose projects, even if they are for causes about which the parents are not enthusiastic.

> *This is important. They are now trustees of the family foundation and I have encouraged them to become involved in proposing projects. One can't start too early in educating them about their relative affluence and about giving time and money.*
>
> (Male, 50s, self-made/entrepreneur)

As well as ensuring that children are aware of charitable activities, many people, particularly in cities, had used the experience of people asking for money on the street to try to inculcate values and encourage discussion of the issues surrounding inequality of wealth. Some people said they give to street requests, and purchase *The Big Issue,* the magazine by and for homeless people, for that reason alone.

Family and school

For many, the type of approach based on practical experience is linked to the school. As we saw in Chapter Four, this had been an influence for many interviewees themselves, and many choose schools for their children in the hope that they will impart the values and sense of priorities and responsibilities desired by the parents. Several emphasised the role of the school in sharing the responsibility of inculcating values, and most parents said that they support their children's schools in their charitable endeavours. The involvement of schools reinforces family values and example. But school alone is not enough. There must be an integrated approach.

However, while supporting the principle of early giving and involvement in school projects, we note in Chapter Seven that some question the mechanisms, and in particular the widespread use of sponsorship forms.

Awareness of wealth

They are aware of our relative affluence because they see newspaper reports about our firm's profits and what partners get, or other schoolchildren tell them what they have read. They see that others have less money. We spend more on computers but don't go to smart hotels.
(Male, 30s, self-made/professional)

Like this donor, others said that, even if they wanted to shield their children from knowledge of their wealth, it was sometimes in the public domain. A few tried to "protect" their children from the knowledge of the family affluence – almost as though it would be a corrupting influence. Others whose lifestyle was one of obvious wealth seemed fairly relaxed about it.

Yes, they see our lifestyle, the Caribbean holidays, the polo, the ponies. They are aware of meetings on the church. Values are imbibed from what children see around them.
(Male, 50s, inherited and grew family business)

But some who had not been wealthy as children had mixed feelings about this.

One can't start too young. We are already trying to educate them about these issues; we tell them that a lot of children are less fortunate and Daddy spends his time trying to help them. We'd like to have the kids treated as we were treated but it's very difficult because of our lifestyle. I feel guilty about the kids enjoying it.
(Male, 50s, self-made/entrepreneur)

However, others who had built up family businesses were confident that their children would not be spoilt by wealth, because of the strong family values.

Self-reliance

Few people mentioned encouraging their young children to manage their wealth, but several had given serious thought about how to handle the situation. Many who had made their own money felt strongly that their children should earn money for themselves. It was seen as part of their character development.

> *I have talked openly about money. They see me on television. I haven't especially talked about values. I wanted them to be independent and earn their own living. Self-reliance is the first thing to teach. They all campaign for the Labour Party and all belong to trade unions so they have absorbed left wing views.*
>
> (Male, 50s, self-made)

The themes of example and self-reliance, linked to the provision of "limited allowances", recur frequently, across a range of backgrounds.

> *They have to save up for things they want.*
>
> (Female, 40s, married entrepreneur)

Involvement of professional advisers

> *We've started thinking about how to educate our children in these matters. We've been to seminars on issues surrounding wealth and children's inheritance in the Caribbean. I take my daughter (aged 16) to some meetings. They have a lower level of pocket money than most of their peers. They were brought up to manage their money and my son will have to work to earn money in the holidays.*
>
> (Female, 50s, married entrepreneur)

Only one person mentioned attending formal courses on family wealth, although a few who had inherited wealth or realised their assets had involved a professional adviser in a more formal or structured approach.

This question of understanding the responsibilities and opportunities of wealth was emphasised by others who had involved their bankers.

The importance of philanthropic example and learning about wealth was mentioned almost in the same breath.

> *They both worked at Rothschild's who managed the trust funds. They*
> *were very helpful. It puts wealth into proportion and educates them.*
>
> (Female, 50s, inherited)

Skipping a generation

Some who have made their own money and were not rich when their children were young emphasised the importance of passing values to their now wealthy grandchildren.

> *We weren't affluent when the children were small. There is no particular*
> *age but we are trying to develop our grandchildren so that they*
> *become increasingly aware of their position but in such a way that fits*
> *with their understanding of the world. Their parents (our children)*
> *strongly agree with this view and educate them in the same way.*
> *We have explained our philosophy to them and invited them to join in the*
> *charitable trust when they are ready. They will certainly take it over*
> *in the future.*
>
> (Male, 50s, self-made/professional)

Does it work?

A small number of people said either that they did not try formally to transmit values or made the point that even in families with strong values and a tradition of giving, children vary enormously in their reactions.

> *My eldest daughter always wastes money. The 19-year-old is already*
> *giving a monthly donation which I am pleased to see.*
>
> (Male, 50s, self-made/entrepreneur)

> *I didn't try to educate them about their relative affluence. One of my*
> *three daughters spent all her money. The other two set up trusts.*
>
> (Male, 60s, self-made/professional)

Many people made the link between passing values and passing money to children, a topic which is addressed in the next section.

Passing money to children

It's very, very difficult. You have to strike a balance. You must assess the situation in terms of each child.

(Male, 50s, self-made/professional)

Education plus a modest home and £³/₄ million each in a trust.

(Male, 60s, self-made/professional)

A comfortable cushion of £5m to £10m each. The rest probably to our foundation.

(Female, 50s, married wealth)

My son doesn't need help but I wouldn't rest in peace if it didn't go to my son, and grandchildren, when they are in their mid-twenties, but my views are mixed and changing.

(Female, 70s, self-made/entrepreneur)

It was apparent that the question of how much to transfer to children caused the most difficulties for many people. It is a matter of major concern across a range of backgrounds, irrespective of the origin of the wealth.

Even those who had thought they had clear ideas were reforming their approach in the light of changing attitudes in society to the traditions of inheritance, their observations of the perceived adverse effect (in some cases) of inheriting major wealth, the different characters and career choices of their children, and understanding that children may not wish to go into the family business. Many recognised a tension between their principles, their perceptions of the dangers of wealth and their family commitments and expectations.

Traditions of family inheritance

We are rethinking all this. Our conditioning by upbringing is to transfer wealth within the family. I used to think that the law of gravity applied to inheritance. Perhaps after educating them they will make their own way and, ideally, the rest will go to the foundation. I want to discuss this with the children and make a decision. They are stakeholders.

(Male, 50s, self-made/entrepreneur)

Many people were clearly trying to strike a balance between leaving an "appropriate" amount for their children and for other, particularly charitable, purposes. This was partly so that children would have an incentive to work. But for some of the respondents it also raises fairly profound questions about wealth transfer between generations.

One should give enough so the children will be comfortable but we will also leave a lot to charity. Are we breaking down the concept of being a trustee for the next generation? What about the tradition of primogeniture?

(Male, 60s, inherited)

Passing a "moderate" amount to children

The largest category of people included those who intend to pass a "moderate" amount to their children. What might be considered moderate is entirely subjective and relative but for most people the essence was a first class education (nearly everyone mentioned this), a step up the housing ladder (essential for many) and the creation of a trust which will provide for the education of grandchildren (in some cases) or other income support.

One of the most succinct, but typical responses, was quoted at the start of this section:

Education plus a modest home and £³/₄million each in a trust.

(Male, 60s, self-made/professional).

Many, particularly self-made entrepreneurs, made it clear that as well as education, housing and a small trust, they may help with a business venture.

Too much is a disadvantage

As an extension to the above argument, some felt that too great an inheritance would be a disadvantage.

I have seen too many ruined by a large inheritance. I don't want to leave large sums. I will make sure they have property and a decent education and encourage them to get jobs.

(Female, 50s, married wealth)

It was not only a question of the adverse consequences of inheritance; many, particularly those who had created their own wealth, wanted their children to enjoy the satisfaction and self-esteem of making their own way – albeit with a helping hand – such as the parent themselves had experienced.

However, while wanting children to "do what they want", many who did not want to leave "too much" to their children struggled with the idea that children should not have to choose high-earning careers in order to enjoy the standard of living which their parents had achieved.

> *I plan to leave them well educated and well prepared for life and with enough means to get them started. I hate to think of the different pressure if one became a banker and one a teacher. I would want to equalise the two. In my commercial existence I earn lots. I would want to leave enough so that my children could live well and educate their children.*
>
> (Male, 40s, self-made/entrepreneur)

The concept of "equalising" was important for several. People wanted to feel that a child would not be penalised for going into a caring or low-paying profession which benefits society as against a sibling who might choose a high-earning career.

The importance of the family

Some reported responsibilities of overriding importance in supporting the family. These included looking after the extended family as well as less able members of the core family unit.

> *It's very cultural. You must trust the family. It wouldn't occur to me that you couldn't. Every Friday the family comes together, children and grandchildren. We plan inheritance on: a) the most cost-effective way; and b) the principle that the weakest must be taken care of. There are different starting points. Education and health must be guaranteed by the family. You must be able to provide a safety net if people can't support themselves and then people should add to it* [the family wealth]. *Charitable giving is part of the process... They must inherit all in order to deal with the extended family and the charitable obligations.*
>
> (Male, 70s, self-made/entrepreneur)

Such feelings were particularly powerful among Asian interviewees, as in this case, and some of those from the Jewish community.

Family expectations

The reverse side of this is anticipation by family members. No-one found it easy to deal with this.

> *We had an exhausting, but mainly good-hearted discussion when we set up the trust – the trustees, my wife and the four children. One son resented it because he had worked with me and saw himself as having helped to build up the business.*
>
> (Male, 80s, self-made/entrepreneur)

Not everyone had discussed it with their children, and some appeared to wish that the subject would go away. But a few had taken an assertively tough line:

> *I am a locally public person so it's well known how much I have. I have told them they won't inherit lots so they will have to make their own way. My position has hardened over time.*
>
> (Male, 40s, self-made/entrepreneur)

Delaying the decision

Several had not thought about it "yet", and hoped that they could wait until the children were older.

> *It's tricky. Later rather than earlier. Sometimes I don't want to pass on the tricky side of wealth but I want to pass on the benefits! It's a very difficult area.*
>
> (Female, 30s, inherited)

Many expressed the wish that they would live long enough not only to assess the adult choices of their children – whether they had done "useful things" – but for them to have had to make a living. At that point money could be safely left, when, as parents saw it, their characters would be formed and they would have had the satisfaction of making their own way.

Family businesses

Others with family businesses felt differently. While only a very small number of interviewees said they intended to give all or most of their money to their children, including taking over the family responsibilities, the majority of those involved in family businesses had few or no qualms about passing the bulk of the assets to the children, with associated family values.

> *They will inherit the lot and will, I hope, continue to do what we do. If you love your kids you want them to have money, lead nice lives and want the business to continue.*
>
> (Male, 30s, self-made/entrepreneur)

One or two had made this decision almost in defiance of their own rational analysis – as if their heart was ruling their head. But even in these cases the situation was fluid as this quote again shows:

> *My son doesn't need help but I wouldn't rest in peace if it didn't go to my son, and grandchildren, when they are in their mid-twenties, but my views are mixed and changing.*
>
> (Female, 70s, self-made/entrepreneur)

A few people made the point that having already set up a charitable trust with a significant endowment, the bulk of the estate which would be left when they died would go to their wife and children, with some to the charitable trust. Others, particularly with relatively less wealth, were concerned with maintaining their standard of living in retirement.

The benefits of inheritance

Some people expressed the view that inheritance may be beneficial to society but may be harmful to the interests of individual children. Several quoted personal experience of observing both good and bad effects. Others disliked it more for society in general than for their own children. Intergenerational transfers not only underpin family businesses, as we have seen; they were felt to provide incomes to people with leisure who may contribute to society in various ways, from being "lilies of the field" to becoming artists, explorers or volunteers.

There was also what might be called the "heritage" argument. Everyone recognised that great houses and estates were a vital part of the national heritage, culture and local community. They felt it was inappropriate for them to be a drain on the taxpayer, but more importantly, that the family link ensures greater care. This stance was taken even by those who disagreed with the principle of inheritance but firmly believed that individual family commitment is essential to sustaining the communities which surround such estates.

> *Stately homes etc are better off in private hands or the National Trust than being a drain on the public purse. There is always a degree of stewardship and care from the family.*
>
> (Female, 50s, married wealth)

I see maintaining traditions as the only way of maintaining communities.
(Male, 40s, self-made/entrepreneur)

This research was undertaken before the work of the Goodison Review into saving art for the nation but there was some comment on the perceived absence of effective forms of planning for donations of large capital assets such as works of art.

I find it deplorable that there are appeals to save works of art for the nation because otherwise they will be sold abroad to save or pay death duties.
(Male, 30s, self-made/professional)

Inheritance tax and the consequences of inheritance

People should be allowed to decide. But people should be educated to decide properly.

(Female, 50s, self-made/entrepreneur)

Views about inheritance tax (IHT) and the impact of the intergenerational transfer of wealth were, like the subjects themselves, complex to unravel. There was division of opinion about whether IHT was beneficial to society, although there was a widely held view that people should be allowed to decide what happens to their wealth on their death. There was also widespread criticism of inheritance tax as currently designed with people seeing it as a disincentive, inefficient and avoidable.

Most respondents thought that people should have choice over what happened to their money on their death. It was felt that inheritance tax undermined that choice. But perhaps more crucially, it was seen as an unjust form of double taxation and an ineffectual mechanism to redistribute wealth.

Double taxation

I have already paid tax. Double taxation should be illegal. Why should one have to lose the family home because of inheritance tax? It's iniquitous and the same applies to businesses. It shouldn't have to pass out of the family.
(Male, 50s, self-made/entrepreneur)

Many people saw inheritance tax as an infringement of their rights to do as they wished with money on which they had already paid tax. There were strong feelings about this, particularly among those whose asset base was built up as a result of their professional career.

> *Usually wealth is created these days by working and therefore effectively from sources which have been subject to tax already. It therefore feels like penalty taxation to suffer inheritance tax as well.*
>
> (Male, 50s, self-made/professional)

For some, the feeling of unfairness added a moral dimension, and was also the basis of justification for avoidance.

> *I intend to minimise IHT. It's already taxed. You must be able to decide what to do with it. It should be none at all. It's morally wrong, using the occasion of death to tax money which has already been taxed.*
>
> (Female, 60s, self-made/entrepreneur)

On this topic as elsewhere there was resentment of those with non-domiciled status and others who may have avoided taxes.

> *It seems to me we should only be taxed once. Provided someone has been a UK resident and paid taxes throughout their life they should not be re-taxed at death. It's more debatable if someone has taken steps to avoid tax in their lifetime. Maybe there could be some sort of formula. Overall though I don't feel too strongly either way.*
>
> (Male, 50s, self-made/professional)

The impact on families, family businesses and family estates

Much opposition was based on the perceived inconsistency between policy and implementation – on the one hand encouraging entrepreneurs and family businesses to develop and generate wealth, and on the other undermining a basis for their continuity, particularly in certain sectors such as property development.

> *I feel very strongly about this. I have a company I can't pass on without paying 40% tax. Friends can pass on* [their businesses] *but I have no way out. It's a long-term business. The business would have to be broken up because the property is an asset. They don't see it separately.*
>
> (Male, 60s, self-made/entrepreneur)

Because such businesses face this threat, assets which would otherwise be invested to grow the company are transferred to trust accounts and other mechanisms to avoid tax.

> *I will start transferring assets to the children's trust accounts but this means that the business won't grow at the same rate. They think they are taxing death but in fact they are taxing growth.*
> (Male, 40s, self-made/entrepreneur)

Others saw themselves as holding family assets for the next generation. Some have already devised a trust structure to deal with this, but not all.

> *It's a current issue for me. Some aspects are iniquitous. I hold part of my father's estate in moral trust. It should be passed on. I am still learning about it all to make the right decision.*
> (Female, 30s, inherited)

These ideas, associated with the concept of holding assets in trust, were not confined to those who have inherited estates in the UK.

> *I feel strongly that wealth should be taxed when it is created. Once taxed, wealth should remain untaxed thereafter. Where and how it is used should be unfettered by public policy. It's double taxation. I am better able to decide what to do with my money. In our culture* [Asian] *it's like the Patek Philippe ad: you never actually own the assets but hold them in trust for the next generation. You can leave enough for the next generation and ensure there is some to execute tasks for the greater good with them having the responsibility to distribute it.*
> (Male, 40s, self-made/entrepreneur)

An ineffectual mechanism

Several of those who derided the tax supported the concept of a welfare state and the principle of those with more paying more.

> *The government should take a healthy slug for redistribution purposes if people themselves won't. I have no problem with high taxes for big earners.*
> (Male, 60s, self-made/professional)

Moreover, not everyone was completely against the concept of some kind of capital transfer tax but warned against raising the rate to inappropriate levels.

The band is too low. The level at which it kicks in is too low... but I don't know. I can see both sides of the argument. Why should my children have a better chance? Everyone should start the race level but then if I look at it from a personal position...

(Male, 40s, self-made/professional)

It should be 100% tax over a fixed sum – say £2m or £5m. An individual has the right to ensure the financial security of their children but not the next x generations. For example, look at Bill Gates – I am offended by his approach. You should pay for your child's education and give the rest to charity.

(Male, 30s, self-made/professional)

But, almost irrespective of views on such matters, interviewees suggested that the government was attempting tax-raising under the guise of wealth distribution and were contemptuous of what they saw as a twin failure. Indeed, it was argued by some that IHT could have potential adverse consequences for the economy.

Punitive estate taxes cause capital flight as the UK learnt all too well in years past. ARK is trying to tell the industry it should self-tax.

(Female, 30s, self-made/professional)

For many, an antipathy to IHT was linked to the recurring belief that the individual is better placed than the government to decide what to do with their money. In some cases such a stance was tempered by the view that the tax might be acceptable if "well spent".

People should be allowed to decide. It's part of a free society. You should only have inheritance tax if you can guarantee that the money will be well spent.

(Male, 50s, self-made/professional)

The tax is largely avoidable
A key part of the argument that IHT is ineffectual, as well as inequitable, was that it is effectively "voluntary" or avoidable. Indeed, for some, the ease of avoidance made it an acceptable or irrelevant tax

A smart man never owns anything when he dies.

(Male, 40s, self-made and inherited)

IHT is such a voluntary tax that it doesn't really matter.

(Male, 30s, self-made/professional)

[The tax is] largely voluntary, inefficient and stupid.
(Male, 60s, self-made/professional)

For people unwilling to make major gifts in their lifetime, and wishing to make charitable bequests, proper planning enables them to avoid IHT.

I loathe IHT. It creates an industry to get round it. We should be taxed properly in the course of our life, but I can see that it assists charitable legacies.
(Male, 30s, self-made/entrepreneur)

Many, including advisers, made the point that the rich and well advised can avoid the tax, which adds to its inequity.

Yes. I have very little time for IHT. An argument for scrapping it would be seeing a greater sense of philanthropy in society. I don't like the way it can decimate fortunes but the mega-rich can avoid it, so the tax is falling unfairly on the less well advised. Other taxes are more equal.
(Male, 30s, self-made/professional)

Several, including advisers, observed that the potential penalties and the complexities of the current regulations provide great opportunities for the creation of schemes to avoid IHT.

The problem with IHT is that it ends up making lawyers richer because the wealthy can avoid it. The people hit by it most are those who shouldn't be.
(Female, 50s, married wealth)

Several pointed out that the tax can be avoided by the "seven-year rule", which provides that no tax is payable on gifts of money or assets if the donor has lived for seven years from the date of the gift.

In the discussions of IHT, there were several references to the benefits of the US approach to planned giving discussed in Chapter Fourteen. The essence of the US scheme which is relevant here is that tax relief can be obtained on an irrevocable capital gift to a charity at the time of the gift, even if the beneficiary cannot use the capital for a period of years. The donor retains and can allocate the income from the capital until the end of the specified period, or death, at which point the recipient has the use of the capital. This is very attractive for those who are asset rich and cash poor, and for those who do not feel secure enough to give capital or forego the income on their capital. The only option for such people in the UK is to leave a legacy, in which they themselves enjoy neither the tax relief on the gift nor the rewards of the relationship with the beneficiary. Such relationships, well handled, may dispose the donor to further gifts or a bequest.

Benefits of inheritance tax

In contrast to the anti-entrepreneurial argument so strongly expressed earlier, a few favoured inheritance taxes (at some level) over higher income and capital gains taxes. This was in the context of a preference for a low tax/low public expenditure society.

> *The risk is that it becomes irrelevant over time. The incentives to create foundations are separate from telling them where the tax £ can go. Income tax and capital gains tax should be kept low. There are weaker arguments for saying that wealth should pass through generations untouched. I would rather pay inheritance tax and be left alone in my lifetime because that's where job creation comes from.*
> (Male, 40s, self-made/entrepreneur)
> [American-born]

Many of those who said they did not want to leave large sums to their children do intend to avoid IHT. Some have, or plan to, set up charitable trusts; it was suggested by one that it might be easier to persuade the children that a trust is being established to "outwit the tax regime" than to explain that they did not wish the children to inherit. Others had not yet decided their approach.

> *My parents were very generous. Each child received £1m which was put to good use, I like to think. My mother still has substantial wealth. We don't talk about it. If a percentage goes to the government it's fine. You can tie up the money too much. A charitable trust may come.*
> (Male, 50s, self-made/entrepreneur)

While some people, as we have seen, appear to believe that abolishing the tax would encourage philanthropy ("an argument for scrapping it would be seeing a greater sense of philanthropy in society"), others think it favours charitable giving because people set up trusts to avoid it; anything is better than the money going to the government.

Even when such tax was placed in the context of a philosophical approach analogous to tithing, the voluntary nature of the arrangement was identified. Indeed, it was that very characteristic of elective commitment which made the comparison with a religious undertaking or tradition appropriate.

> *Tax is part of modern society. Inheritance tax is largely voluntary with good tax planning but the principle should apply. In many faiths there are two types of 'tax': a) on income; and b) each year we pay a bit of capital to charitable causes. You could give part of your wealth to charity, for example in shares, and that perpetuates your giving after your death.*
> (Male, 70s, self-made/entrepreneur)

Suggested alternatives

Other than taking money from income tax (or of course reducing the tax take) there were few other suggestions. One person identified a possible alternative basis for calculation:

> *IHT is a voluntary tax so basically it should increase. It should be difficult to leave one's children millionaires. I favour James Mead, the Cambridge economist who suggested that capital transfers should be taxed in proportion to the difference in age between donor and recipient. The bigger the gap, the bigger the tax.*
> (Male, 80s, self-made/entrepreneur)

A small number (not those with family businesses) suggested that it should be the recipient and not the giver who is taxed.

> *On the whole, I am in favour of the tax system but capital taxes act as a disincentive to effort and wealth creation. It distorts things. It's fairly voluntary. The socialist in me says you should tax the recipient and not the giver.*
> (Male, 60s, self-made/professional)

Wealth and responsibility

Having considered the question of financial security, wealth, family and inheritance, we turn to wider issues of the allocation of accumulated assets, the opportunities provided by being wealthy, what people feel about the social obligations of wealth and to whom they have might have these obligations. There is some discussion about the concept of tithing.

We then look at aspects of the application of funds for the benefit of others. We explore the extent to which, if at all, there is an interest in forms of investment which produce a social benefit as well as achieving a financial return. Interviewees were also asked about how they would like to see their trust, if established, develop after their death, and their plans and ideas for leaving money to charities.

Opportunities provided by wealth

Interviewees were asked about the allocation of their disposable income, and what they considered to be the opportunities provided by their prosperity. Most people were well aware of the options they enjoyed because of their wealth. They identified a variety of activities and interests, ranging from altruistic initiatives to the creation of collections (themselves a valuable asset) and engagement in enjoyable pursuits. A brief review of these is given here.

Trusts and other charitable activity

As we have seen, about 50% of interviewees have a charitable foundation. For some people, particularly those who have sold their businesses, having a trust is a major source of occupation and interest while allowing expression of personal values and concerns.

In running trusts and other philanthropic activity there were recurrent references to having time, opening doors and gaining enjoyment through self-fulfilment – all concepts which foster and reinforce charitable giving, as we see in Chapter Six. This freedom to do good, to be creative, to develop projects and to influence events was a common theme. There was also the bonus of being recognised for it.

> I have time to do other things: for example be a school governor, being on a charity development board. I have an ambition to spend some part of my working life doing something to improve the quality of life for others. I am developing an idea about inner city sport.
>
> (Male, 40s, self-made/entrepreneur)

Setting up or running businesses

Just over 40% are involved in the start-up or running of a business. This included both those for whom it is a main occupation and those who have retired and invest as venture capitalists or other supporters of start-up businesses. In the latter case this can be almost a hobby, to validate their investment and entrepreneurial judgement and expertise and to increase their wealth.

Politically related activities or causes

Only around a fifth of those interviewed gave financial support to political parties or causes and almost all said this giving was at a very low level. It appears that many of those who said they supported politically related activities were involved with socio-political "organisations" or "causes" rather than "parties". Examples include those who support overseas development charities, Amnesty International or various think-tanks.

Others who are working to influence social change are aware that their wealth gives them the opportunity to influence political direction in the broadest sense of the word. More than one referred to having a "place at the table", or as one person put it, his wealth gives him a "voice".

Personal support of family members

A few people mentioned the opportunity to support their family – in one case a brother with disabilities. It was apparent from other answers that many people provide support to less affluent members of their extended family. However, this was not a question which was asked specifically and it is not possible to provide any gauge of its extent.

Supporting "the arts"

Given the significant support of the arts, reported earlier, it is not surprising to find that artistic pursuits were frequently mentioned among the activities in which having wealth allowed interviewees to engage. Some, and particularly older people, were collectors, primarily of paintings and sculpture. Others mentioned a variety of interests in music, opera, theatre, dance and the fine arts.

Other personal interests and pastimes

Many of those interviewed identified a range of interests which they felt having wealth enabled them to enjoy fully. These included travel and holidays, sport and fitness, gardening, good food and wine and having a second home.

> *I like motorbikes, good wine, opera, and real tennis. It's exclusive but not expensive.*
>
> (Male, 50s, self-made/entrepreneur)

> *Flying and personal development programmes. I am planning two weeks in a Buddhist monastery in the Nepalese mountains.*
>
> (Male, 40s, self-made/entrepreneur)

> *We enjoy good hotels, first class travel, cars. The biggest constraint is time.*
>
> (Male, 30s, self-made/professional)

Time and money

As we have noted before, time is a major constraint. More than one, particularly in the younger age groups, added that they were aware of the apparent paradox: on the one hand money buys time and yet they have no leisure time because they are spending all of it making and managing their money. Younger people also talked about time spent raising children. One person made the point that time for friends was crucially important. Some linked these questions of time, choice and enjoyment of work, and in different ways many people made the point that one of the benefits of wealth is freedom.

> *I enjoy the freedom to be with who I want to be, to mix with people*
> *I want to mix with, to travel, to achieve spiritual growth and wisdom, to*
> *have business activities I can maximise everyday.*
>
> (Male, 40s, self-made/entrepreneur)

The concept of freedom together with the absence of worry afforded by wealth may be something desired by those who do not enjoy significant wealth, but it was only explicitly mentioned by a minority of those interviewed. But some developed this theme from the absence of worry to independence and the freedom to speak your mind. Wealth, and a record of giving and some knowledge of the cause, gives a platform and status.

> *Travel, and I indulge my passions such as opera and ballet. I like beautiful*
> *houses with beautiful things, the power to do things for people and*
> *institutions that no-one else can do, to make things happen that otherwise*
> *wouldn't happen, to give my children the best education and health.*
>
> (Female, 50s, inherited)

Social obligations of wealth

Interviewees were asked for their response to the view that for wealthier members of society, philanthropy is not only a matter of personal choice but is an obligation. People were also asked, if they felt responsibilities and obligations about the use of wealth, how constrained they felt and to whom they felt obligations.

> *Decent rich people should want to give money away.*
>
> (Male, 60s, self-made/professional)

Yes and no. People have a right to decide what to do with their money. You need to create a climate where people think it is a good idea.

(Female, 50s, married wealth)

I strongly disagree: you can't dictate an obligation. We live in a welfare democracy. I don't use the NHS or state education. I pay taxes to educate and medicate my fellow man – why give more? I don't think like that but I understand the expectation that it's the job of the state. People shouldn't need to fund these things.

(Male, 40s, self-made/entrepreneur)

I strongly disagree. You can't dictate to others. You should encourage and inspire by example. I am willing to be a role model in giving time but not money.

(Male, 40s, self-made/entrepreneur)

Views ranged across the spectrum, with about a third agreeing strongly that charitable giving should be part of life and an equal number disagreeing strongly, with a further third somewhere between the two. Reactions were linked to the opportunities people felt were provided by wealth – the possibility of allocation or choice between family commitments, individual pleasures and obligations to a wider society. However, many of those who felt it should be seen as an obligation also emphasised that it was a personal choice. In essence, this was the position of most interviewees. The following illustrates the spread of attitudes.

Philanthropy is an obligation

Even within the group of those who agreed strongly that philanthropy is an obligation, there was a range of views and explanations for such a stance. Some referred to their religion, and certain moral obligations this brought; others linked their perception of their social duty to their view of the nature of society and even the purpose of life – "we are here to do good". Such attitudes were strongly linked to people's motivations for giving, and were shared particularly by those with a sense of obligation to "put something back".

I strongly agree and think it is a moral obligation to give and to teach one's children the importance of giving. People who can afford it should make real donations. We are here to do good. If you want to participate in society, you should contribute.

(Female, 30s, self-made/professional)

For some the sense of obligation is strongly linked to their sense that their assets should be seen as a kind of legacy to society. There was felt to be some responsibility attached to this, particularly by older people. For some this was associated with a commitment to and responsibility for their local community – something which, as we see in Chapter Three, is much stronger away from London, and mirrors the ideas of those who inherit estates.

The better-off should accept some individual responsibility for the local community. With the opportunity to create wealth comes an obligation not just to earn it but also to deserve it and make good use of it.

(Male, 60s, self-made/entrepreneur)

Another person, from a strong Quaker tradition, endorsed the point that the rich should see themselves as trustees of wealth for the benefit of society. But he also emphasised the importance of balance and of the need to provide for both family and personal needs as well. Indeed, many people felt that part of their responsibility was to hold assets in trust for the next generation of their own family and this had to be considered alongside any wider obligations attached to wealth.

Others said it was important not to be categorical about the obligations of the rich. For example, some felt it was easier for those who obtain money in a lump sum – for example, by selling a business. – to give it to charitable causes, probably via their own trust, before they had become accustomed to the idea of wealth.

Others, while agreeing with the principle of social obligation, noted how hard it was.

I agree but it's tough.

(Male, 40s, self-made and inherited)

Several also made the point that people's attitudes to what they should contribute to society might be different if they had no children, or were not influenced by a desire for current or posthumous esteem.

A personal choice – to be encouraged

You can't oblige people to give. I give because it is a spiritual concept. The more I give, the more I get back. The core belief is being open and seeing giving as both financial and emotional.

(Male, 40s, self-made/entrepreneur)

There was a distinction between those cited above and those, an equal number, who agreed with the proposition for themselves (if not strongly) but took the view that charitable giving must be a matter of individual choice for the rich as for everyone else. This applied even if those who did not give were viewed with some disapproval.

I like to feel that obligation is a personal choice. To pass through the world and not give anything back... I am not enamoured with them. It's terrible to judge but... I admire people who give.

(Male, 50s, self-made/entrepreneur)

Many reflected feelings of ambivalence, and here as elsewhere there was the suggestion of the need to set standards, make people aware of what might be "the right amount to give" and encourage people to see contributions to society as an appropriate component of their wealth allocation. They should be encouraged by pointing out the rewards of giving – by example, by honouring role models, by demonstrating the benefits in terms of personal development or social prestige, by showing that it is fun, and a matter for celebration. There was also a need for encouragement so that people would be ready to give at the right time.

It's not an obligation. People should make their own decision in the context of being part of a decent society. We should publicise the fact that the poor give disproportionately more. When I was earning I gave virtually nothing (money or time). I was 100% tied up with the family and business but I was focusing on getting to the point of where I could give.

(Male, 40s, self-made/entrepreneur)

Here again, as elsewhere, some made the point that serious commitment to giving is not something which can be expected at the same time as people are building a business, including giving employment to others. The time constraints, demands of younger families and lack of security inherent in the lifestyles of younger entrepreneurs are not seen as compatible with major giving.

A personal choice – no pressure

If people create wealth they should be totally free to do what they want.
(Male, 50s, self-made/professional)

At the other end of the spectrum are those for whom the decision to give is entirely personal, and this view is allied with their whole philosophy of life. Some felt that "just because I have made money" was not a sufficient reason to feel any sense of obligation, either to society in general or to a specific cause. Others believed their contributions to society are largely met through taxation – or at least suggested that others think like that and it is a perfectly tenable position. Many also made the point that they do not use the services which their taxes pay for.

I strongly disagree. In order to be wealthy I have contributed via taxes. I don't get it back because I don't use the services. So there is no obligation. I am not sure if the state is trying to encourage people to give money because that's what the state does. I have never had the message from government that it thinks that private giving is a good thing. There is the necessary evil of middle class do-gooders.
(Male, 50s, self-made/professional)

This was not the only person to express cynicism about the role of the state in encouraging the wealthy to pay for services which should be covered by tax revenues. But he was the only one to say that government had never suggested that private philanthropy was a good thing in itself – or indeed that it would be appropriate for the government to make that point.

Where do obligations lie?

It is difficult to define precisely. The disadvantaged people in genuine need – there needs to be a link one can relate to.
(Male, 60s, inherited and grew family business)

I feel no obligation to give but like doing so because I have more than I need. Helping friends is part of philanthropy.
(Male, 50s, self-made/professional)

Following the discussion about the obligations of wealth, people were asked for their views on those groups in society which would merit their interest or attention. The groups of people identified as the appropriate focus of obligations did not necessarily match those who are the recipients of funds in terms of priority and size of allocation. However, it is not possible to present a detailed comparative analysis since the response to this question was not analytical nor collected in measurable form, whereas most people were able at least to some extent to quantify their actual giving.

On this topic, as on others, views were not always consistent. Many people were exploring these ideas for the first time, and sometimes were surprised at their own opinions. There was a range of ideas and perceptions about the causes and groups which were perceived to have insufficient – and sufficient – resources. Sometimes this, as well as lack of connection, was used as a reason not to support a particular sector.

> *No group in particular. The institutions which helped me and the institutions which are important to the children. The underprivileged – but I have strong views about people I don't identify with e.g. AIDS – they've got enough money. You can't help everything.*
> (Male, 30s, self-made/professional)

In this context as elsewhere people mentioned the local community as an area to which they had particular responsibilities, although almost without exception these were outside London – in the North East, the North West and Wales or Scotland (as the community of origin). For many who had created businesses, the "putting back" was closely linked to the source of their wealth, and to their whole philosophy of life and values.

> *I agree strongly for all sorts of reasons – not least that our wealth was created not only by our own hard work, but also by that of the people of [area of the UK] and so we should repay that by investing in good causes and projects which benefit the [X community]. I feel somewhat constrained. Wealth does bring freedom but that automatically brings responsibilities. We want not to lose friends through our lifestyle change, nor to gain them(!), to teach our children about the importance of relationships over and above any financial/economic considerations.*
> (Male, 50s, self-made/professional)

While few saw their obligations to society as confined to the UK, undoubtedly there was a feeling that UK society as a whole, plus other areas if possible, was a proper focus of people's obligations to society.

While nobody used the phrase "charity begins at home", the local community and UK society are a major focus. There was a tiny minority whose social focus was the developing world.

Tithing

Interviewees were asked their response to tithing – the idea that they should give a regular percentage of their income each year. The number of people who were positive about the concept in principle far exceeded the number of those who actually allocate a calculated percentage of their income to giving.

Each should give according to their means. I strongly agree.

(Female, 50s, married wealth)

It is to be encouraged. I don't like the idea of a percentage target but people should know and think about it.

(Male, 50s, self-made/professional)

Anything that encourages people to give responsibly should be encouraged. But how?

(Male, 30s, self-made/entrepreneur)

A very, very good idea but I didn't have the discipline.

(Male, 50s, self-made/entrepreneur)

Formulaic things don't work well. It was invented as a way to twist people's arms. People must be allowed to be eccentric. It's not like taxation.

(Male, 60s, self-made/professional)

Arguments in favour

Nearly all of those who thought it was a good idea and practised it, at least to some extent, come from a Muslim, Jewish or strong Christian tradition such as the Quakers. However, within religious groups there were differing ideas about the appropriate level. But as already indicated, most of those who thought it a good idea in principle did not practise it to the level they advocated. Many people emphasised that it must be a voluntary decision. Several commented on their perception of how much they could afford to give – the value of their "portfolio", "net worth" or "overall wealth"; concepts associated with feelings of security.

> *I feel very positive about it. It is right that people should budget their giving and then should give away sensibly. I support the Quakers' concept of 10% and to undertaking the Rosenberg calculation.*
>
> (Male, 60s, self-made/ professional)

This refers to Claude Rosenberg Jr, who had been a very successful investment manager in the US and published *Wealthy and Wise* in 1998. In essence, it is a guide for individual donors which respects people's desire for financial security while giving them confidence that they might be able to give more. It helps people to decide how much they can afford, how to allocate donations to causes which match their areas of interest, and how to be sure that the money will be well spent. It is based on a method of calculating a financial profile which enables people to view their general spending patterns in a particular way. The approach is described in more detail in Appendix Two.

Several of those who approved of the idea of tithing in principle suggested 10% as a starting point, but also pointed to the need for flexibility, depending on means and circumstances. The advantages of a target or an ideal were recognised by many, either as part of "training" to give, or as a means of earmarking a source of income or making a specific arrangement which would somehow ensure compliance with the aspiration.

> *It's a useful concept. It gives a target. What I did was to identify a particular source of income (rent on property) and have always given from that. It was really useful because it worked straight through like having a trust.*
>
> (Female, 50s, self-made/entrepreneur)

While some saw tithing as applicable to all levels and types of wealth, others thought it "no bad thing once people have reached a certain affluence". A few younger people were thinking about the idea as a framework for planning their charitable activities. And while approving the concept, most did not want to establish a benchmark, and were unsure as to how it could work in practice, even with media encouragement and workplace schemes such as payroll giving.

Arguments against

Those who were less enthusiastic about the idea said they gave in relation to the opportunities available rather than having any notion of a fixed quota. Several made the point that tithing is analogous to tax.

> *It is hallowed by tradition. It's to be encouraged but it must not be compulsory. The concept is analogous to taxation and the rich should be encouraged to give more.*
>
> (Male, 70s, self-made and inherited)

This reference to tax was made by several who put tithing into a historical context, and essentially positioned it as a pre-welfare state device to sustain society.

> *It's a very noble concept. In those societies where historically governments didn't deliver it was the only way the worse-off could survive.*
>
> (Male, 40s, self-made/professional)

But for others, the compact with the state in a social democracy has removed the need for tithing.

> *In principle it's a good idea. We could all manage with 10% less. But we pay tax according to our capabilities; in a sense we delegate responsibility for social welfare to the state so no-one has to give.*
>
> (Female, 60s, self-made/entrepreneur)

Others referred to the need for "fun and spontaneity" in giving and, more exceptionally, to it only "counting" if people were making a "real sacrifice". Many emphasised the essentially personal and private nature of the decision about how much to give and the need for privacy. Several, including major donors, pointed out that:

> *Cash isn't the only way of contributing to charitable causes.*
>
> (Male, 60s, inherited and grew family business)

In summary, far more people – the majority of those who addressed this question – felt that some form or concept of tithing was a good idea, but very few actually do it. For others, the analogy with tax, the idea of coercion and the lack of spontaneity were all seen as negative features.

Socially Responsible Investment

It's a load of rubbish! We are trying to be too much of a politically correct society.

(Male, 50s, self-made/entrepreneur)

*I wouldn't invest in pornography. I'm happy with weaponry, dams...
it's not an issue.*

(Male, 50s, self-made/professional)

I feel ambivalent about this. Defining criteria is difficult. It is in the interests of business to be corporately responsible but I don't give advice to asset managers to avoid certain areas. I don't think this will change.

(Male, 50s, self-made/professional)

I am not against it but I don't do it myself. I'm all for the social audit of companies but it's not part of my horizon.

(Male, 60s, inherited)

The study provided an opportunity to explore the extent to which people of substantial means, including some who have long experience of thinking strategically about philanthropy and the impact of their giving on society, make any link between their giving decisions and their investment priorities. Several schemes and ideas can be grouped under the heading "socially responsible investment" (SRI). SRI combines investors' financial objectives with their concerns about social, environmental and ethical issues. SRI usually involves two approaches – screening and involvement.

Screening, which can be negative or positive, refers to including or leaving out assets because of the effect they may have on society from a social, environmental or ethical point of view. It is an approach used by many individual investors, but also by some organisations, such as trade unions, charities and pension funds. Some investors become more involved, and want to improve the performance of companies by taking an active part (for example, by trying to influence policy and voting at annual general meetings). Usually, it is institutional investors who take this approach, as well as some campaigning organisations, churches and some individuals.

There was a limited discussion on what is included in the concept of "socially responsible investment". Undoubtedly for some it meant no more than "not investing in arms". For some the complexity of making investment choices on social criteria, and the impossibility of being "pure" about it, were sufficient reasons not to try. For them, if one eschews tobacco, but not tobacco retailers, including leading supermarket chains, it is a meaningless exercise.

Unfavourable responses

A sizeable majority was adamantly against the idea. The highest possible return on their capital was the major criterion for their investment strategy. Any diluting of that benchmark for asset managers would be dangerous.

For most people the term SRI was associated with specific products (tobacco, arms, pornography). Even when the concept of social investment was more fully understood, it was felt a complex issue that needed time for consideration. Some were more ambivalent, but the perceived complexity was a deterrent – and perhaps the excuse.

> *I haven't got time to follow this. My instructions are to avoid tobacco etc. It's a tiny percentage of my portfolio. I am interested in growth rather than return.*
>
> (Male, 50s, self-made/entrepreneur)

The most negative reactions were from those who equated encouragement to make socially responsible investments with political correctness. They see it as a pointless distraction, and believe that the worlds of business and charity should remain completely separate. Furthermore, any attempt to make them overlap, and hence reduce the return on the business investment, would diminish the amount available for charitable giving. In this group there was no appreciation of the concept at the heart of social investment – that money invested, albeit with a lower return than a high-yielding financial product, could be recycled and make a change to an entire disadvantaged community.

Some thought it difficult to be consistent, and therefore not worth bothering. However, for the large majority it is seen as muddling two separate ideas.

The duty of investment managers is to maximise the return for the benefit of the investor. There are confusing aims if one is effectively subsidising another charity.

(Male, 50s, self-made/professional)

Money has no conscience. One should make money and pay one's dues to society.

(Male, 40s, self-made and inherited)

Implicit in this is the idea that the highest possible return on one's own investment maximises the amount available for charitable distribution under one's own control and choice – not for "another charity". "Another charity" in this context might include social regeneration projects which benefit from targeted investment in disadvantaged areas.

For many it was not an issue that was thought about at all, either because of antipathy towards the idea or because of lack of time – or knowledge – to give it appropriate consideration.

I don't think about it. It doesn't come in to my consciousness. If I invest money I do so to make the maximum return and with the maximum return I hope to do good. I wouldn't consciously invest in bad things like arms. I might get out of something if it was controversial. I hand the whole process over to investment managers.

(Male, 40s, self-made/entrepreneur)

Some added that as long as companies are operating legally it is not for the individual investor to judge.

People are entitled to operate how they like within the law.

(Male, 60s, inherited and grew family business)

Many of these also make the point that in their view successful companies are those which operate with socially responsible principles and this practice will become more widespread.

It is part and parcel of any decent company's activities.

(Male, 60s, inherited and grew family business)

Others with their own companies pointed out that the question might have limited application for them.

I like the idea of employment bonds and ethical trusts but it's not for widows. None of my assets are invested like that! I'm unlikely to do anything since most of my assets are in [my company] shares. I have less than £1m in other shares. I am not interested. It must be managed well. I don't want to put restrictions. I have no time. I accept they may be polluting rivers and I accept the inconsistency. It is difficult to work out what is socially responsible and what is not.

(Male, 60s, self-made/entrepreneur)

This was by no means the only example of people who are thoughtful in their giving (this person supports river conservation projects), who recognise the contradictions in their position, but who do not want to allocate the time they think would be required to manage or oversee a genuinely socially responsible portfolio.

More favourable responses

A few were receptive to the concept of social investment, when it was explained. But even for most of those supporting organisations such as The Prince's Trust, with a major focus on investing in young people and their businesses, the holistic approach implicit in social investment was a step too far – at this stage.

In one exceptional case, with the highest level of assets devoted to SRI, the donor is very actively involved in the voluntary sector.

I was involved in the fair trade start-up. I try to ensure ethical investment. It accounts for 30% of our assets. For example, we own a care home as a business. We must be happy for our own mothers to go there. We will get round to making changes and doing more.

(Female, 50s, self-made/entrepreneur)

A very small number were just embarking on exploring social investment, of which almost all are women. But even for these, with one exception, it represents under 5% of their portfolio. Others recognised the higher risks involved but were considering some possibilities.

I am looking at a fund in the Caribbean right now. It would help Caribbean nations with investment possibilities. It's a high risk punt with a low return but the added spin is the reason to do it.

(Male, 50s, self-made/professional)

Some people, mostly women, were actively striving to link their investments to their charitable interests. In the example below, the donor allocates a major part of their giving and operational activities to encouraging environmentally friendly projects and has initiated an awards scheme to celebrate innovations and encourage replication.

> *My trust is looking into social investment and my personal portfolio. I have just started putting money in to environmentally linked investments. I would do more if the government backed renewable energy – for example windmill farms and solar panels. It's approximately 3% of my portfolio. This is low because I am just starting; I can imagine it going up to 10% maximum. There are new opportunities in project related investment which are very exciting. One can do this without going through bureaucracy. It's a great way to help charities and small organisations.*
>
> (Female, 30s, inherited)

> *Yes – we have personal investments in various smaller local businesses to encourage real employment alongside giving to organisations that are bordering on trading as distinct from purely charitable voluntary organisations. It's less than 10% of our assets.*
>
> (Male, 50s, self-made/entrepreneur)

In the second example, we see awareness of the links between supporting disadvantaged communities in the North East, the focus of the trust set up with 20% of the proceeds from the sale of his company, and investing in "real employment".

Some people with more favourable responses to SRI saw it as something they might consider at some stage – a "not now but probably later" approach. And others were thinking about cause related investment.

> *I pay some attention to the moral issues in what I invest in. I invest in BP not Esso but I don't worry about tobacco shares unless it comes to my notice. I am interested in new ideas, for example, to take the capital reserves of charities and invest them in cause related investments such as Centrepoint.*
>
> (Male, 40s, self-made/entrepreneur)

There is not a complete distinction between those who are not interested at all and those who support the idea of SRI. Rather there is a continuous range of ideas, with some feeling more positive about the concept, and perhaps defensive about the fact that they have done nothing about it. Over a quarter of respondents say that it is a good idea and that they have, in some cases, thought about it but for various reasons, including complexity, cost and inertia, they do not want to take it further, or it is a minimal part of their concern. More than one made the point that there may be a sizeable cost in changing a mature portfolio because of potential capital gains tax liabilities. The following person is a major supporter of social causes and devotes most of his time to voluntary sector activities.

> *It's a good idea but my portfolio is not designed around it. The assets devoted to SRI are very small but I exclude tobacco, arms etc. If I was starting again I would consider it because I could invest it and leave it and wouldn't have to use my judgment. But now if I move my investments there would be a big capital gain. Now I give shares enough to eliminate the CGT charge.*
>
> (Male, 60s, self-made/professional)

What would change attitudes?

Respondents were then asked what, if anything, might make them increase the amount of assets devoted to SRI. They were offered six possible developments, of which they could choose any or all. These were:

- ◆ Large financial institutions begin supporting the concept.
- ◆ Investment returns become more competitive.
- ◆ Causes covered by SRI become more diverse.
- ◆ Increased validation of the good done by SRI.
- ◆ Positive recommendation from your investment adviser.
- ◆ A trusted friend becomes involved and recommends.

About a third of respondents said that none of these changes would make any difference. The rest said that one or more of the changes would be likely or very likely to make a difference. Of the responses, there were two overwhelming deciding factors, mentioned by over a quarter in this category. These were:

- ◆ Investment returns become more competitive.
- ◆ Positive recommendation from your investment adviser.

In over half the cases the same interviewee cited both possibilities. No other factor was remotely influential.

Clearly, there is a profound lack of understanding of the nature of SRI, and the range of opportunities which come under this broad category. Those who are interested are few, a very low proportion of anyone's portfolio is devoted to SRI (with one exception) and even those who are well disposed to consider it are struggling to find the best way to address what all agree is very complex issue.

Leaving money to charity

Shrouds don't have pockets.

(Male, 50s, self-made/entrepreneur)

I don't plan to die for a while yet.

(Male, 50s, self-made/professional)

By 2012 I will have given it all [the money in the foundation] away. I don't want to leave it to my executors to enjoy my giving.

(Female, 60s, self-made/entrepreneur)

Interviewees were asked what their views and plans were for leaving money to charity. There was a wide range of responses, starting from those, particularly without children, who say they will leave it all to their foundation or to charities they have supported, to those who plan only to give in their lifetime, have already endowed their charitable trust, or are undecided. Another group, small but not insignificant, said that they would leave most of their money – more than 50% – to an existing trust or charities that they have supported.

> *I plan to leave 75% to 80% to my own trust (if I were to die now). It's difficult to give all in one's lifetime because one may live longer than planned. I'd rather create things that last, for example a foundation.*
> (Male, 50s, self-made/entrepreneur)

Among those who plan to give significant amounts to charities there is a wide spectrum, from those who plan to give most as legacies to those who will give part or all in their lifetime. As we know, about half the respondents had established a trust, some with substantial endowments. Those, and others, expressed a preference for lifetime giving from these trusts. Some are already very structured about their estate planning, with trusts established to look after the interests of surviving family members.

> *We are mainly giving in our lifetime. We are leaving a third to the surviving partner, a third to our sons and a third to charities. We have left a letter of wishes as to which charities with our will.*
>
> (Female, 50s, self-made/entrepreneur)

This group includes some with children who they think already have sufficient or who have been provided for – for example by grandparents setting up a trust.

For some, as we have seen, the decision is as much about control as about uncertainty. Posthumous giving removes the difficulties of planning for old age but also takes away the power of allocation and the enjoyment of philanthropy. The pleasure of involvement which is a key motivator reinforces the tendency to lifetime giving, particularly for those who have established sizeable trusts with a significant proportion of their realised capital.

Some people were open to professional advice but others were more inclined to trust their own judgment.

> *I expect to leave more to my daughters. I will be guided by my lawyers but expect to leave 10% to charity unless I win the lottery.* [His trust is already very large in proportion to his other assets]. *Some will go to the trust and some directly to charities.*
>
> (Male, 70s, self-made and inherited)

> *I am not planning to leave anything to the trust. My accountant is encouraging me to but I think it's got enough.*
>
> (Male, 60s, inherited and grew family business)

The group which is undecided or thinking about it is about the same size as those who are fairly clear about their intentions. The undecided cover a range of age groups, and several are contemplating establishing a trust. Most are postponing the decision – to retirement, in some cases.

> *I have not decided. I will think about it when I retire. I would rather give in my lifetime and see people enjoy it. How much I leave to charity*

depends on ensuring that the children are indeed self-sufficient,
although I feel they have had their inheritance.

(Male, 30s, self-made/professional)

Others who had thought they might leave more to charitable causes were open to changing their mind. Several advisers noted this tendency for people to change their minds, particularly in relation to how much they give to their children.

I haven't thought about it yet. The RSPB is currently the residuary
recipient. I am thinking about it. I had thought I would leave all to my own
trust. Now it probably won't work like that. Also, I have set up a trust for
the grandchildren so I have made a commitment to the next generation
which is sheltered.

(Male, 60s, self-made and inherited)

Many commented on the difficulty of planning, and several will pass the decision to the surviving partner.

It's terrifying because of not knowing how long one person will survive
and because of the terrifying changes in financial parameters. The
percentage depends on the order of events. If we both go in a car crash
70% will go to charities; if I go first it will be 5%. It will go to institutions
I've supported in the past.

(Male, 50s, self-made/professional)

This corresponds with the comment of an adviser who said that it is the second death that matters. Some couples arrange for the survivor to decide, while others create a mechanism through which the survivor benefits in their lifetime, but the commitment to charitable beneficiaries is established at the first death.

I have set up a major trust. At the moment I have a cascading will.
Everything goes to my wife and then it all goes to the foundation.
The children are already accounted for but this might change.
I worry about it.

(Male, 50s, self-made/entrepreneur)

The evidence suggests that there is great uncertainty about leaving money – or more money – to charity. This exists across the range of ages, levels of net worth and sources of wealth. People want to enjoy giving in their lifetime. They feel constrained about giving too much capital because of the uncertainties of the future, and want to leave the surviving partner with sufficient capital.

People who have endowed foundations with significant capital feel they have allocated wealth in their lifetime. They may allocate a further small percentage of their assets to their trust, particularly if advised by their lawyer, but are more likely to leave the bulk of their assets to the surviving spouse and children.

Those without children to take over as trustees plan to spend the capital in their trust. Others may also adopt this strategy if they believe their children do not want the burden and responsibility of managing a major trust. However, most hope their children will continue the family trust, and adopt the same values in allocating the income to charitable causes. Most reiterated their concerns not to give too much to their children, but many were ambivalent about their ideas.

How people would like to see their trusts develop after death

People who had established trusts were asked about their plans for the trust after their death. Just over half had already planned that their trust will be administered by their wife and/or children and a small group said the other trustees will continue to administer it. A similar number have decided that that their trusts will be transferred to another trust to administer. About 10% have decided to spend all their capital in their lifetime. Half of these are childless. About a fifth have not yet decided.

The options are seen as:

◆ Continuing the trust in perpetuity, or at least for the next generation.
◆ Bequeathing all the assets in the trust to the charities supported by the donor.
◆ Giving the capital of the trust during the lifetime of the donor.

For those who have decided that their trust will continue to be administered through their children, this is seen as the obvious course. Some have already strengthened their foundation through the involvement of an outsider as a board member. Those who are not yet sure or have not yet decided are usually quite thoughtful about the options.

I am thinking about it. The children have shares in the company so they are wealthy, but my wife doesn't think we should plan for them to take over the trust. The need is there now. I like the idea of continuing to be a donor for some time, but we are now committed to over £100,000 a year so it will eat into the capital.

(Male, 60s, self-made and inherited)

This was not the only case in which the interviewee reported a difference of views with their partner. In some cases, particularly younger people, they are not yet sure whether their children will be interested in carrying on the responsibility of a major foundation.

It would appear that the overwhelming majority intend their trusts to be continued by their families or to transfer the responsibility for administering and dispersing the funds to other organisations sharing the same concerns. Clearly, the establishment of the trust has not only been important during their lifetime but for creating a permanent endowment which will continue to do good after their death.

10

The state, the media and perceptions of wealth and philanthropy

I n this chapter we explore what interviewees think about the relationship between private giving and government funding, the proper role of the state and the response of the state to philanthropy. We consider wider public responses to philanthropy and by extension to the creation of wealth that makes charitable giving by the wealthy possible. We also discuss cases where donations have been criticised, and explore what might be done to create a more positive environment in which to foster a stronger culture of giving.

While the media may be harnessed for lobbying for change, most people were of the view that the attitudes of the media and some key opinion formers to philanthropy and making money were negative and unhelpful. Perhaps in reaction to the perceived cynical attitude, many people prefer to do good by stealth. This can become a vicious circle: the rich who do give are not talking about it; there is a general perception that wealthy people don't give and there are few role models, increasing the negativity about the rich; some of the perceived cynicism is linked to political donations.

In any case, it is thought vulgar to talk about money and to give is not a defining characteristic of the social elite. This issue overlaps with the question of recognition discussed in Chapter Six, and contrasts strongly with the approach in the US, explored in Chapter Fourteen.

The role of the state

There was a range of views about the proper extent of the role of the state, but virtually universal agreement that the state should pay for "basics", including health and education, that the public sector cannot do everything and that private philanthropy should lever rather than substitute for government funding. Charities were seen as more effective and more likely to be able to be pioneering – creating models of best practice not always taken up by the public sector. For some the potential of change on a macro scale justified and indeed required advocacy and lobbying to multiply the impact of a successful initiative or to address root causes.

In discussions about the role of the state a number of distinct issues were raised.

Paying for the basics

> *Public money should provide a decent basic infrastructure.*
> *Private philanthropy should increase it to the best.*
>
> (Male, 50s, self-made/professional)

In one way or another nearly everyone expressed the view that the state should pay for what might be regarded as the cornerstones of the welfare state – health and education. Housing was also mentioned, as were hospices (not currently publicly funded). For many it included some aspects of the arts. The following quotes are typical examples, although not everyone would agree about the choice of boundaries between state and private responsibility.

> *The state should pay for the basics. Private philanthropy can turn good hospitals into great hospitals. London should be ashamed if it doesn't have a world-class children's hospital – people, facilities, research. The state should fund basic research. Public money should provide a decent basic infrastructure. Private philanthropy should increase it to the best. In the arts it can turn a good museum in to a great museum. The state will never provide enough. The British Museum receives £30m of public money but the Great Court couldn't have been done with public money.*

Real dependency is when the people depend on the state – that is pernicious. It creates a dependency culture. Institutions which get private philanthropy are not dependent. Public expenditure is so inefficient. The cost of bureaucracy is enormous.

(Male, 50s, self-made/professional)

In an ideal world the state should provide across a whole range of needs which should be matched and the state should take responsibility for finding other partners – it's about leverage. But education, health and housing are basic human needs which should be available. The arts too. The UK is a rich country but there will never be enough. It's a bottomless pit. The problem about the arts is that a small amount of money would make a huge difference.

(Female, 50s, married wealth)

Several themes are captured in these examples which reflect the views of a majority of respondents. Apart from the focus on health and infrastructure, we note the leverage effect of public money, and the idea of public and private money working in partnership, with added value – from basic to best – provided by private money. There was recognition that the state will never be able to provide for all demands. Indeed, some suggested that attitudes in this area are changing, and perhaps becoming more like those in the US. The start of the change was dated to the Thatcher era.

Does anyone now believe that government should do it all? Do they really say 'I pay tax so it's up to them to solve problems such as the homeless and so on'?

(Male, 40s, self-made/professional)

Some felt that the state is not funding its core responsibilities, and that the private donor, via charities, is picking up what should be state-funded activities. Within certain fields knowledgeable donors were fairly specific about what the government should fund – buildings and basic equipment or research for hospitals being a major area of agreement.

Charities exist to supply what the state can't supply. But it (charity) has become the middle of the cake, not the icing. I don't like funding hospitals; I prefer hospices or Macmillan [1] to big capital projects. It's the duty of the state to provide the NHS, not to fund the arts. It's the absolute duty of the government to do health and education.

(Female, 50s, inherited, and a major funder of the arts, among other causes)

[1] Macmillan Cancer Relief – providing advice and services to people living with cancer.

Core education was seen as the role of the state but extra investment – for talented or disadvantaged children, for example – was seen as a proper, or inevitable, role of private individuals.

Views differed about the role of government in the provision of state benefits and pensions with some suggesting the focus should be on those who "can't afford it".

> *Some social services should be paid for by government, and basic healthcare. There should be some level of protection for the mentally ill and disabled but the government does not owe people a pension. This is a thing that bothers me. My father had a low income but saved for his pension but also gets some state money. It's crazy for the state to pay. My generation won't see the benefit from social security.*
>
> (Male, 50s, self-made/professional)

There was a range of views, including among arts donors, about the extent to which the state should continue to support the arts. Those giving substantial sums to the arts were among the most vocal about the need for the government either to do more or at least be more honest and direct about what it is up to. Several made the point that if the government wishes to support free entry as a matter of state policy, or promote "accessibility", the museums and galleries and theatre and opera houses to which this applies should be fully funded to provide this service.

> *They can't have it both ways.*
>
> (Male, 60s, self-made/entrepreneur)

People also noted that, in terms of the national budget, relatively small amounts of money could have a major impact in the cultural sector, and expressed anger at what they saw as the government "raiding the lottery for health[2]".

[2] This refers to the recasting of the lottery beneficiary structure in 1998 from five "good causes" to six, so that each of the original sectors, including the arts, receive proportionately less. One is The New Opportunities Fund, which included health service related projects. It has since merged with the Community Fund.

More exceptionally, some people, including those who do not support the arts, disapproved of any government support of the arts, believing that it "distorts the market, especially the major national assets". It was suggested that the government should recognise that the funding of the arts is not a priority.

> *They should allow and encourage arts organisations to become more independent. The same goes for higher education.*
>
> (Male, 50s, self-made/entrepreneur)

Interviewees were asked what changes they would like to see in government funding. In terms of the allocation or re-allocation of state provision, there was a fairly even spread across the board. There were many references to the NHS and the massive demands on its resources, and strong feelings, particularly outside London, about the importance of local support for local causes.

> Generally I would say no to hospitals. It's what the NHS is for, but for example I might support cancer scanners in the local community because of the funding shortage and the fact that technology is available. With hospices, there is a lot of value in seeing these created from the ground by the local community.
>
> (Male, 30s, self-made/professional)

Also within the health field, hospices were frequently mentioned as an appropriate focus of government funding. People also wanted more money to the elderly, education, transport, the homeless, drug dependency and overseas aid. There was also a reference to the need for state support for the architectural fabric of parish churches.

It is noticeable that there are major areas of government expenditure which are absent from this list, including social security, the criminal justice service and defence. Interviewees were not prompted in this or any other area of the interview, but it might be reasonable to assume that the absence of reference to these sectors is because there is not thought to be a role within them for individual private funding.

A small group felt there should be as little as possible from the state in a range of sectors. There was a reference to societies such as Hong Kong, where:

> The government supports the needy but relies on families clubbing together. My view is that as little as possible should come from the state and as much as possible charged to those using the services.
>
> (Male, 60s, self-made/professional)

Undermining government responsibilities

Interviewees voiced a great reluctance to "let the government off the hook", or to "undermine the obligation of the state". This was directly linked to individual perceptions about where government responsibility stops and that of private individuals starts. There is a tension between the understanding that the state cannot provide for all needs and the reluctance of people to give if they feel the impact will immediately be diminished by an equivalent reduction in government or other public sector support. One way or another, many people made this point about a range of sectors.

> *It would be bad if, as result of [a donation], the government would reduce funding. It lets the government off the hook. One can't generalise. The government can't and won't pay for everything. Most things should be a mix of private and public funding.*
>
> (Male, 70s, self-made and inherited)

Perceived inefficiency of government

There was extensive comment on the perceived inefficient bureaucracy and inflated costs of management of public expenditure. Everybody who expressed a view felt that the private sector and charities would spend it much more effectively. Again the approach was seen as pragmatic rather than ideological.

> *I don't have a doctrinaire view. There will never be a clear distinction about what the state should or should not pay for. By and large I prefer private organisations which at least in theory should be more agile and efficient.*
>
> (Male, 50s, self-made/professional)

Apart from avoiding overstaffed administrative infrastructures, several were of the view that the personal involvement of private donors made for more effective organisations "because people are more committed".

The necessity and limits of public/private partnerships

While there was a range of views about the proper focus of government funding, and a common desire to hold the government to its responsibilities, a growing gap was perceived between requirements or expectations and what can be provided from public funding.

> *If I think it is a hard core obligation of government such as the NHS I would be sceptical about allocating my resources. However, the government can increase its expenditure by between 1% to 3% per annum; the needs of causes grow in a double figure percentage. The gap will have to be closed by private sector philanthropy.*
>
> (Male, 60s, inherited)

Most people supported the idea of some form of partnership between state support and private philanthropy in some situations, and for the majority this was a seen as a practical necessity rather than a political ideology.

> *The government has limited resources. It will never satisfy all the needs of the health service, education and the arts so it must manage with what it gets and get the balance elsewhere. It's a practical rather than an ideological view.*
>
> (Male, 50s, self-made/professional)

Some suggested that the government should activate such partnerships by offering an incentive for private contributions by identifying the public funds which would be unlocked. Examples cited included City Academies.

> *I don't have a problem if organisations get lots of public money. For example, youth improvement programmes are a good idea and the private sector can add to what government is doing. Kids' Company is an example: I gave money when I heard the government was going to support it – it's the leverage effect.*
>
> (Male, 40s, self-made/professional)

However, others felt that private funding in partnership with government support was less attractive or appropriate in areas seen as the basic responsibility of the state. This position was substantiated with the views of the inefficiencies in the state system already discussed and the conviction that more could be achieved with existing budgets. This position was reinforced with the suggestion that where the government contributed significantly the donors would pay less.

> *The state has a bigger role in paying for health and education. This is not a role for individual trusts. Current public expenditure could be spent more effectively. I don't generally support big causes [which receive major state support]. If there's a special health interest I would research it.*
>
> (Female, 30s, inherited)

> *If it's government money, there is one less thing I will give to. If my money equals 'their' money then they can pay for it. If there are large amounts of public money I think 'hang on, I am giving twice to this'. If Clare Short[3] is giving my money to overseas causes, why should I give to Christian Aid? It's more and more difficult to know.*
>
> (Male, 60s, inherited and grew family business)

[3] At the time of the interview, Secretary of State for International Development.

Communal responsibility

Another reason cited for a mixed funding approach was the lack of ownership and the risk of detachment from a sense of corporate or community responsibility that can arise if the state is too prescriptive. Many criticised what they saw as the increasingly controlling nature of the government, and the adverse impact on self-help, volunteering, opportunities for the poor and local community spirit.

In these contexts, it was observed that private giving is a manifestation of commitment and involvement by a wider community, sharing responsibility and demonstrating mutual support.

> *Communal organisations are very important. Once they are institutionalised then people think that their small donation means nothing, and there is a great risk. I also think that government wants to be everywhere. This can be a turn-off from giving. One must see giving as enabling, creating a service for a client or customer. For example, the government sets standards in care homes. If you are too authoritative, people say 'sod it! you take the responsibility'. Charities rely on volunteers. If the government takes control, why should I give my time? We want the capitalist system with a heart.*

> *From the capitalist point of view, money in the NHS is well spent for the benefit of the country; I would pay more in tax if I was confident it was going to infrastructure. Another good example is with the problems in the pensions industry. It started with the Pensions Act 1995. Companies are now saying 'sod the employee, the government has made it so difficult, let it sort it out', which is leading to them stopping final salary schemes. The government shouldn't interfere. The poor lose out when it takes over.*
> (Male, 50s, self-made/entrepreneur)

> *I don't think there are things that only the state should pay for. If the state is not involved individuals must be or society collapses. The state cannot do everything. Tower Hamlets would sink if individuals were not involved.*
> (Male, 50s, self-made/professional)

The perceived benefits of proximity to the grass roots are not confined to the UK; those supporting overseas development strongly advocated "operating at ground level".

Charities as pioneers

It was recognised that even where an area of work generally might be part of the role of the state, charities might initiate and pilot new ideas. With private funding and donor agreement, risks can be taken.

> *The line is blurred because some non-profits might have a different approach from governments. I might support a charity because it has a pioneering approach. If it also has state support it doesn't affect my giving.*
> (Female, 50s, self-made/entrepreneur)

However, some had found that even when they had supported a successful charitable pilot scheme, the government or local authority had not scaled up or replicated the initiative.

> *Four funders set up a project in the [XYZ area] for £90,000 a year, to help hard-to-reach children. They were really tough truants. We then agreed to run courses based in [XYZ] but the schools and LEAs are not paying their share, even though they recognise how good it is.*
> (Male, 60s, self-made/entrepreneur)

The point was made that this apparent unwillingness to build on successful non-profit projects is not only frustrating for the donor and a disincentive to further giving, but suggests the lack of a coherent strategy by government.

Giving and advocacy

For some the charitable role had to go hand in hand with lobbying the government for change.

> *You have to take political action to improve people's lives and respond to charitable requests. In the short term you can help through charity. So for example you help poor students and also lobby on grants.*
> (Male, 50s, self-made/creative)

For a few the possibility of achieving systemic change was the major impetus.

> *To change society you need to pass an act saying that charities must get involved in politics. I tend to put resources where I can get the greatest change. When change is achieved, I then withdraw.*
> (Male, 40s, self-made/entrepreneur)

Key points

While there was a range of views about the extent to which the government should fund public services, and on the definition of such services, there was broad agreement on the desirability of central NHS provision, education, transport infrastructure and some element of social services. There was significant support for government funding of some other health and medical services, in particular hospices, and core funding for the arts. However, particularly in the NHS, there was a prevailing view that it would be better to subsidise and support the users of the services, and enable them to choose from a range of providers. Many resisted supporting what they saw as the role of the government in the NHS, because it is seen as a major call on the tax budget and the NHS is believed a very inefficient provider. They believed that rather than the NHS needing more money, it needed far less bureaucracy and better managed budgets. As we see in Chapter Seven, the least satisfactory experiences for donors had been with NHS related projects.

However, the advantages for communities and individuals of taking local and individual responsibilities for projects such as hospices were well attested, and everyone saw a role for private philanthropy to work in partnership with public funders. Opportunities to leverage government funding in a range of sectors were appreciated. While success stories were celebrated, there was also evidence of irritation at the apparent unwillingness of the public sector to replicate and build on pioneering initiatives which have been supported by private donors and had been shown to be effective. This was particularly the case with projects dealing with difficult or truanting children, or after-school activities, where it was felt that early and appropriate investment could transform lives.

Criticism of such decisions was seen as inconsistent and demonstrating "lack of joined-up thinking", and this view applied to arts funding as well as social welfare.

Attitudes to wealth, wealth creation and the status of philanthropy

Philanthropy is not something we talk about in the UK. It's not high status, it goes against the English type who doesn't like to talk about money and how much they have given.

(Female, 30s, inherited)

Wealth and the accumulation of wealth are not honoured. This is partly because journalists and academics are very badly paid and those are two origins of opinion formers. Society doesn't appreciate private donors, there is an assumption that rich people don't deserve sympathy and are not admirable. This is pernicious. It is at the heart of what is wrong with society. If that attitude changed, we would achieve an increase in philanthropy because we could show how the money has been made and that we are happy to provide for other people. It's disgraceful that people can despise philanthropy. It's completely at odds with the things I believe in. They despise the people they write about.

(Male, 50s, self-made/professional)

We will never win until we fundamentally change the culture. In the US I would feel embarrassed if I don't give, but here I would be embarrassed if I give 'too much'. We don't celebrate success in the same way.

(Male, 40s, self-made/entrepreneur)

There was a widespread feeling of unhappiness about the status and respect accorded to philanthropy in the UK. Such perspectives were supported by all with experience in asking for money. For many, the status of philanthropy was linked to the perceived complexity of the attitudes of the English to money and wealth creation, and to class, and the absence of role models or indeed expectations that people in a position to give will do so. An additional facet is the perceived reluctance of the English to talk about money.

Some people have become members of networks which provide opportunities for issues relating to ownership of wealth to be discussed.

Talking about it is not truly respected. I am surprised that people are reticent about the causes they support. It is not talked about. This is a pity. You find out more often if people give time. It is considered indelicate and vulgar to talk about money. One of the attractions of the Network for Social Change is that you can talk about money.

(Female, 50s, self-made/entrepreneur)

The role of the media

The media have negative attitudes to success. It's a cultural thing. You can't be seen to be trying too hard. US culture is completely different. The media don't respect the success of entrepreneurs so they don't respect philanthropy.

(Male, 40s, self-made/entrepreneur)

Journalists decry giving. They enjoy digging the dirt. The press can be very hurtful.

(Asker, politician)

There is a responsibility on the part of the press media to do more. It would be a better society and a better world if good causes were celebrated in the main media. It will bring in new people. Of course many people would feel embarrassed if a public fuss was made but it is nice if someone notices.

(Male, 70s, self-made/entrepreneur)

Several people spoke of the role of the media in generating or perpetuating negative attitudes to wealth and charitable giving. A range of reasons were suggested for this, including envy and resentment of the rich, a lack of understanding of wealth creation and scepticism about motives, linked but not confined to political giving. Several people made the general point that in this area, as in others, the media look for negative stories, especially about "heroes", with the more or less cynical assumption that this approach will sell papers.

> *Why are the media nasty? They don't do good news, they are snide, and they pander to jealousy. The obituaries of philanthropists are nice but during their lifetime journalists dig. There's nothing to be done; perhaps if more people do it then there would be more respect. Most people hate getting publicity.*
>
> (Male, 70s, self-made/entrepreneur)

Such views were echoed by many and several referred to examples of papers and articles they saw as pernicious or damaging. Particular reference was made to "the scurrility of *The Guardian*" and several mentioned the negative article in that paper in mid-2002 about the wealth of the Rausing family and its contributions to British society.

It's portrayed as a way of tax evasion rather than doing what the
government wants – look at the Rausing article. It is so disappointing
because we don't want to discourage giving. The media behave as
though they do.

(Male, 40s, self-made/professional)

Not only was it taken for granted that the press is there to present those
who give in a negative light, but there was puzzlement and resentment that
this stance was adopted by those who ought to be "on the side" of those
who are giving. Again, in this context, *The Guardian* attracted criticism
because it is thought to have an intelligent interest in the non-profit sector.
Negative articles were seen as a particular betrayal by those active in the
voluntary sector.

Papers such as The Independent *and the* FT *report it neutrally. The*
Network for Social Change decided to recruit a few more members and
spoke to a Guardian *reporter. The NSC was very open but this led to a*
very snide article. They can be very negative.

(Female, 50s, self-made/entrepreneur)

Indeed, several people contrasted the way giving is reported with the
actual situation of those who pay taxes and give substantially to charities.

I am afraid of the media. It's always negative, especially about property.
The reporting standards of the press cause lots of problems. They have
great power and there is no right of reply. People don't want to hear
good things about our family such as that we pay taxes and give to
charity. We almost have a country now where you want to hide success.

(Male, 30s, self-made/entrepreneur)

Many people suggested that this led to a desire to give discreetly and,
more crucially, discourages a culture of giving.

We have a terrible attitude about knocking wealth. That's why there is
lots of anonymous giving; it's not reported with graciousness. There is
such snide reporting: for example the Posh and Becks party for the
NSPCC [4]. It's why people don't give as much as they could. If it were
different people might come out of their shells.

(Female, 50s, married wealth)

[4] In May 2002,
England football
team captain David
Beckham and his
wife Victoria, former
singer "Posh Spice",
gave a party for the
England team in aid
of the National
Society for the
Prevention of Cruelty
to Children (NSPCC).

But many were resigned to the situation and thought that nothing could be
done about it.

> *Reforming the press is a hopeless cause. We won't be able to change their negative approach. You need to accept from the outset that whatever you do will be rubbished in newspapers because that's what they're there for. If you are giving money away people will think you are doing it for self-aggrandisement.*
>
> (Male, 50s, self-made)

A number of specific features of media reporting particularly aggrieved those interviewed.

Attributing despicable motives

> *Only very big gifts are reported. The media often look for a hook as to why they are giving. I don't believe every political donation or gift is done with an ulterior motive. The press believe they are – they tar everyone with same brush. There is not much press coverage locally for donations.*
>
> (Male, 50s, self-made/entrepreneur)

Media perceptions and reports about philanthropic giving are felt to be tinged with suspicion about motives, particularly for gaining social or political access. As we see in Chapter Five, people are inspired to give by a range of motivations. Prominent among these are the nature of the cause, wanting to make a difference and a sense of "social responsibility". Although social aspirations, broadening the circles of acquaintance and obtaining privileged access to tickets and exhibitions were sometimes noted, particularly at modest levels of giving, they were more often seen as rewards rather than influencing factors. So media misrepresentation of the motives of philanthropists was deeply resented by many of those interviewed – and for some was quite distressing.

> *Sadly, it is usually reported negatively. There is jealousy and quite a lot of sniping. This is particularly for political giving but in the eyes of the public they may not see much difference between the Labour Party and the Tate.*
>
> (Female, 50s, inherited)

There was a specific reaction to reports of political giving; many interviewees shared the suspicion that such giving may be improperly motivated, although the tiny number who support political parties sought no influence or position for themselves. Although very few people had direct experience of criticism of their own donations, personal examples mentioned included a significant donation to the Labour Party.

*It was very unfair. I gave because they had been in the wilderness
for so long. I wanted a better society; there is more social justice
with Labour. It was given with a sense of social responsibility,
there was no personal interest.*

(Male, 70s, self-made/entrepreneur)

Hostility to specific causes

· It was felt that giving to certain causes generated particular hostility in the press – for example, when people see big gifts going to an Oxford college. It was thought that the arts came in for particular attack, with the Royal Opera House singled out for specific attention.

*The media are heavily biased; some of the reporting on the Royal Opera
House is very biased. Look at Wembley: there's nothing like the attack
on the Opera House. I know a lot of people who when they give,
do so anonymously. People don't trumpet because they don't want
the media after them.*

(Female, 30s, inherited)

In more exceptional cases people had been criticised for funding more challenging social causes: "*for example gay/lesbian support groups.
It was a 10-minute fluster*". Another was not criticised in public but received "*private letters saying we should be giving to prostate cancer,
not breast cancer*".

As we saw when considering anonymous giving, fear of criticism, including public disapproval, was a spur to confidentiality; particular examples included the funding by Jewish donors of Palestinian groups seeking reconciliation.

Attacks on sources of wealth

Media hostility was also associated with the source of wealth of donors, whether self-made or inherited. There were several references to and examples of individual cases, with the property sector featuring more than once.

People don't like the rich, especially property dealers.

(Male, 30s, self-made/entrepreneur)

An additional element is the stance taken in some coverage, which is nearly always linked to specific cases, that apart from the undesirable origins of the wealth, the donor may have a disproportionate influence on the recipient and how the money is spent. This is often reported irrespective of the actual views of the beneficiary, who may have carefully considered the issues and negotiated detailed arrangements with the benefactor.

> *With bigger gifts and things more visible the paradox is that people who make large donations may be seen to have undue influence on the donee. This is always a problem, even in the US. In some cases 'journalism is the enemy of philanthropy'; examples are Mr Said with the Oxford Business School [5] and Mr Vilar with the Royal Opera House [6].*
>
> (Male, 50s, self-made/entrepreneur)

Often such criticism achieves a double insult: it questions the motives and probity of the donor and at the same time implicates the recipient in collusion or naivety. The situation is complicated by what a large number perceived as the unhelpful approach of many in the higher education sector, which they linked to a disdain by academics for activities associated with making and raising money.

Linked to this was criticism of wealth generally. One person who set up a substantial trust after selling his business was unprepared for the impact of *The Times* front-page article about him. He was concerned not so much for the actual content but the tone.

> *"It was puerile – unlike in the US the language is objectionable: for example 'tycoon'. The way the press deals with it is unhelpful.*
>
> (Male, 50s, self-made/entrepreneur)

Other examples reflected what was perceived to be a deliberate confusion between corporate and personal wealth. In some cases this was a question of timing, particularly if there had been a period between donation and announcement. Someone who was giving from his long-established trust but also running a company was sympathetic to the concerns of his fellow directors because of how and when his significant personal contribution to a project had been presented.

> *When my gift was mentioned, I felt it inappropriate to be seen to be splashing wealth when we were cost-cutting. It was not quite right. Some of my colleagues thought this too.*
>
> (Male, 50s, self-made/professional)

[5] The Said Business School was established in 1996. It was made possible by a donation of £20m from international businessman Wafic Said.

[6] International businessman Alberto Vilar has given or pledged well over $200m to the arts in the US and Europe, including £10m for the Vilar Floral Hall at the Royal Opera House.

Apart from business and the City, "celebrities" were seen to be regarded as fair game. We noted earlier the reference to the "Posh and Becks party". An asker with in-depth knowledge of the entertainment industry observed:

> *You get cynical reports on certain artists. Journalists say they are doing it [helping high profile charities] to shore up failing careers, but it's not how it works. People do it to help.*
>
> (Asker, entrepreneur in the creative/entertainment sector)

He went on to point out that in this sector as elsewhere there were sometimes unrealistic media (and charity) expectations.

> *There is a misconception about how rich people are in the entertainment industry. There are few people earning more than £^{1}/2m with a capital base. I have only one client earning more than £1m. They are perceived to be wealthy but that is only a few rock stars. They live to their means. It's not Goldman Sachs type stuff. There are no major profitable TV production companies. There is an obscene risk:reward ratio in the City. When there is the perception that they are richer than they are, people are disappointed if they 'only' send £1,000 instead of £5,000.*

Is criticism ever justified?

Notwithstanding what is seen as the often unhelpful approach of the media, many recognise that on occasion motives may at best be mixed, and as we have seen in Chapters Five and Six, there is often a range of factors influencing major gifts. Several observed that cynicism may be justified in some cases.

> *They should do away with gongs. It's blatant in some places and all mixed up with political giving. Average people don't know what the rich do and the majority of the truly rich don't fulfil their responsibilities so perhaps the man on the Clapham omnibus is right. I am not sure how to tackle the issue of kudos for doing right. It's healthier for the 'haves' to be seen to doing something.*
>
> (Male, 30s, self-made/entrepreneur)

It was recognised by many interviewees that a large number of people do not give.

It is sad if there are snide remarks such as 'he can afford it'. But not all who can afford it, give.

(Female, 50s, inherited and grew family business)

The attitude of government

As well as some public negativity, reflected and reinforced by the media, there was some comment about the ambivalence of the apparent attitudes of the current Labour government to philanthropy. It was seen as wanting the wealthy to give but at the same time sending out messages of "a bias against the rich". The interviews were conducted in 2002, during a period when there was much discussion on the issue of "fat cats", senior executive pay, share options and bonuses. It was, however, recognised that such market "distortions" have a negative impact.

Attitudes to wealth creation should be more constructive. There should be more recognition that those who achieve will be rewarded but there are distortions at the upper end which cause harm with public perceptions of wealth.

(Male, 40s, self-made/entrepreneur)

In the next sections we explore what interviewees thought might be done to address some of the negative attitudes to philanthropy reported here.

How to change attitudes

Role models and league tables

I agree with the need for role models. It would be the heart of a moral society.

(Male, 40s, self-made/professional)

I would welcome more publicity generally. It would encourage others. We might get embarrassed but it's a price you have to pay. I am in favour of a display of competitive giving. There must be league tables.

(Male, 60s, self-made/professional)

Transparency has gone barmy. Unless the donor particularly wants publicity, giving should be a relationship between donor and recipient.

(Male, 50s, self-made/professional)

Giving shouldn't create heroes.

(Male, 30s, self-made/professional)

A lot of people like to be in The Rich List. I think it's ghastly.

(Female, 70s, self-made/entrepreneur)

The problem in the UK is that several people don't want to advertise their giving. If we want to change the culture we need to have examples.

(Male, 60s, self-made/ professional)

The question of how best to recognise outstanding philanthropy and encourage people to be role models was seen as difficult and complex. Some people talked of league tables, such as those being developed by *The Rich List*. Others spoke of the importance of giving being seen as the thing to do.

It was recognised that in some cases reported philanthropy can enhance a hero status although, as we have seen, it is more often thought that the media seek opportunities to knock people down. It was suggested that one way of addressing such negativity is to recognise the need for a range of role models, both as entrepreneurs and as philanthropists.

We don't celebrate wealth or philanthropic achievement. The problem of recent years is that the only icon of entrepreneurial success is Richard Branson [7]. This is sad because others could be in the limelight. There are lots of successful people in the UK and they know how to handle wealth but they haven't been icons. So we don't really value entrepreneurs, and there's a problem for entrepreneurs because everyone wants their money. I agree with the need for role models. It would be the heart of a moral society but would the government be interested? In the UK we build up and knock down. The press is waiting for Beckham to fall. Sportspeople do amazing things but don't get the credit.

(Male, 40s, self-made/professional)

[7] Richard Branson, flamboyant entrepreneur, creator of the Virgin group of 150 companies, including travel, retail, financial services, cola and entertainment operations.

It was suggested that if people are happy to be public about their philanthropy then it should be reported to encourage others. This approach was much more popular than the idea of Rich List league tables and "naming and shaming", not least because of the inaccuracy of such tables and analyses. But a very small minority felt that publicity was necessary to encourage philanthropy, even if a few of those cited were unhappy about it, and that competition and league tables would be a positive development.

> *I don't like* The Rich List *but if it is there, it should show what everyone has done. I have made money in IT and I know others who have done it. New money being created has a strong element of philanthropy.*
>
> (Male, 50s, self-made/entrepreneur)

It was recognised that this is a difficult area: virtually everyone saw the benefits of presenting role models, but one or two were doubtful as to whether this approach will work in the UK, because the press would be interested in other aspects of their lives, not just the giving.

> *There is the knowledge that if you go public you open yourself up to criticism. The prospect of people intruding in your lives rather than getting kudos is a great deterrent. There is a need for role models, as in the US, but I fear all that you would achieve is to expose the people concerned to a media spotlight. The media would assume that people are doing it because they want the publicity and are fair game. I wonder if it would work in the UK?*
>
> (Male, 50s, inherited and grew family business)

Furthermore, as some pointed out, there is the question of the inaccuracy of *The Rich List* and similar tables, and the difficulty of comparing like with like, as discussed in Chapter Two.

A small minority believed that the media are supportive, particularly local papers, and that it is the lack of willing role models which is the constraint.

> *There was good coverage for Niall Quinn[8]. It raises issues. There is much more that could be done to celebrate philanthropy with role models, especially in the field of sports.*
>
> (Asker, entrepreneur in the creative/entertainment sector)

The research was undertaken before the establishment of the Beacon Awards[9], first announced in 2003.

[8] Niall Quinn MBE, the international footballer who in May 2002 donated the proceeds of his testimonial match to charitable projects for children.
[9] The first annual Beacon Prizes were awarded in 2003. They were created to celebrate role models and promote a culture of giving. Niall Quinn was one of the award winners.

Other ways of changing attitudes

> *Gordon Brown has changed the rules but he hasn't changed society's attitude.*
>
> (Male, 50s, self-made/entrepreneur)

> *We need to find a way to encourage those with money to see themselves as partners in creating a better society.*
>
> (Female, 50s, married wealth)

There have been several references in this chapter and elsewhere to the need to change attitudes of the press (and eventually the public), potential donors and indeed potential beneficiaries. Role models and even league tables may be one approach, but several observed that this would not be sufficient, and pointed to what they saw as the lack of a tradition or culture of giving among some people with wealth. The City is a key constituency for this, and the following quote encapsulates a range of advice and suggestions, with a focus on the workplace and the role and responsibility of employers.

> *There is not a tradition of giving so people don't see an obligation to give. The newly wealthy don't have a background which supports philanthropy in the UK. It's not yet part of the culture. The challenge is to address this. Fundraising is focused on the subset of those able to help. Widening that net is part of the way to improve philanthropy. The government has overcomplicated it. It should be made much simpler. It would help the basic task of getting this community [the City] to be involved. Also they don't have time to be involved and are not exposed to the same environment that others are. Employers have a huge responsibility here. Many fail in this. They need to encourage their employees to develop an understanding of other areas of society.*
>
> (Male, 40s, self-made/entrepreneur)

In Chapter Four, when discussing early experiences of giving, we see the importance for some of workplace example – sometimes pressure – to give. This was particularly prominent among those with experience of working in the US, and is also discussed in Chapter Fourteen.

Several made the point that those who are seeking funds need to be more effective at soliciting support from this group of new rich, who experience very sophisticated approaches from others trying to part them from their money.

It's more to do with the fact that people who have made money don't come from a culture of giving and don't know how to be giving. The process of giving hasn't caught up with the sophistication of other marketing techniques thrown at the rich.

(Male, 40s, self-made/entrepreneur)

Key points

There is a consistent view that, on the whole, the way that philanthropy is reported reflects antipathy and cynicism about wealth and wealth creation. This may be based on complex attitudes to class and money among the general population, which some sections of the media reflect rather than lead. But the views are reinforced by opinion formers among journalists. By extension, suspicion of the motives of those who support political parties is transferred to those who support charities. Some reports appear to imply that the motives of donors are mainly self-seeking, particularly for social advancement. This is at odds with the view that philanthropy is not a characteristic of the social elite. A minority noted the value of an organisation where issues relating to wealth and giving can be aired.

Other factors attributed to scepticism or negativity about giving include jealousy of the recipient, sometimes together with contempt for apparently putting themselves at risk of inappropriate influence by the donor. The source of wealth of the donor is occasionally an element in the disapproval. In some cases the nature of the cause itself has provoked criticism.

Nearly all agreed that to a greater or lesser extent some criticism of the wealthy is justified. Not all the rich give, and something should be done to encourage a culture of giving. The promotion of role models was widely endorsed, with very limited support for league tables. In the City in particular, workplace backing was advocated. Those seeking funding should become more expert in working with this category of people.

At the very least it is felt that a more positive and constructive approach to wealth, entrepreneurs and philanthropy would be less discouraging, would promote the idea of the wealthy as partners in creating a better society and celebrate the humanitarian impulse which creates strong communities.

11

The experience of asking for money

In the Talmud we are told that asking for money for someone else is the highest good deed[1].

(Chair of a separate fundraising board and board member of the main institution)

Among the interviewees were 10 people with in-depth experience of asking for money. Many others are also askers to some extent, including a few who have leadership experience of major campaigns. The characteristics of this group are:

◆ All have extensive experience of major fundraising activities.

◆ That experience covers a range of sectors and sizes and maturity of organisation. They include the NHS, cathedrals, art galleries, museums, performing arts venues and companies, educational institutions, disability and social welfare charities operating in the UK and overseas, and political parties. Campaign targets ranged from £1m to £150m, and from major capital projects to long-term recurring revenue support.

◆ Although respondents in this group were asked about their own backgrounds, attitudes and experience of giving, the main focus of the discussion was asking for money.

[1] An interpretation of Maimonides' Eight Degrees of Charity.

The age of those interviewed ranged from the forties to late seventies. Two of the 10 were women, and the female partner of one of the male interviewees participated in the discussion. The two women are involved in public service, one in the House of Lords and one as chair of a major hospital trust. Two others are involved in the creative and entertainment industries. One man has a very distinguished record in public life and one in the City. One is a prominent corporate leader, and three others hold or have held senior positions in finance or the professions. Some are major donors but the majority are not. They give but, although well-off, do not as a group enjoy a level of net worth comparable with the majority of interviewees. Their commitment of time and expertise is, for them, a way of giving. Nearly all currently hold or have held chair or board membership positions of a range of organisations, including major national charities or institutions.

Interviewees were asked how much time they spent on fundraising activity. The average was fairly consistent at about 10% of their time. The two who spent significantly more – between 1.5 and at least three days a week – were retired. One or two commented that it was quality of input that mattered.

> *10 minutes of focused time can produce more than 10 hours.*
> (Self-made entrepreneur, has chaired a range of major and smaller
> organisations in a number of sectors)

People were asked about their involvement and relationship with the organisations they help. They were questioned on how they became involved, how they managed the balance between directing the strategy for the fundraising and actually cultivating prospects and asking for money. We also discussed how they saw the relationship with the organisations they supported in this way and whether they thought their perceived status in an organisation was important for effective fundraising.

Origins and history of their fundraising activity

The askers were drawn into fundraising either because the organisation with which they were involved needed support – sometimes desperately – or because they were the chair or senior board member of an organisation embarking on a major project. Others found themselves involved, often reluctantly.

> *I got involved with activities which resulted in being an advocate and therefore raising money.*
> (Former banker, involved with organisations in more than one sector, often as chair)

The interviewees selected were identified because of their in-depth experience, so most were serial askers: over the years they had been involved in many campaigns. Indeed, their association with a successful appeal would guarantee a flood of requests to lead other fundraising operations, often unrelated to the passions of the asker.

Interviewees were asked whether there was something in the family tradition which had led them to fundraising. Most said not, but in some cases there was experience of voluntary work. The majority said that they undertook the work because "it is interesting and challenging", and because if they cannot give large sums themselves, they can help organisations raise such sums through their efforts.

> *My upbringing was in a family successful in running other people's affairs. There was money in the family. My parents had an estate and 1,200 acres in [X county] but no money. They tried to do their bit by giving time and commitment and bred it into all of us. We are not in position to give large sums but enjoy helping others.*
> (Formerly in City, chair and board member of a range of institutions)

Most askers were of the view that wealth carried obligations.

> *Noblesse oblige. If you have lots you should give a significant percentage away.*
> (Self-made entrepreneur, has chaired a range of major and smaller organisations in a number of sectors)

It may be that these opinions were a latent factor in influencing their willingness to take on a fundraising role. However, all said that their views had no impact on how they raised money.

Although members of this group were motivated by a desire to help, and to respond to a challenge, they also said that they disliked asking for money – but "you must be prepared to get your hands dirty". Many denied any interest in recognition for these efforts and most were already well known in their fields and beyond. It is not surprising that the reported rewards echo those mentioned by other interviewees who give time, which are not dissimilar to those for giving money. These include respect for their business or financial expertise and the relationship with the organisation for which they are soliciting support. As we see in Chapter Five, people's use of their commercial or professional expertise in a very different field proves very satisfying.

Seriously participating in something different to commercial life, making a necessary and useful contribution and helping to get things done. Recognition is irrelevant.

(Entrepreneur, has led and guided campaigns in a number of arts organisations)

For all, the "buzz comes from the link with the charity and the people who run it". A few made the point that they worked behind the scenes.

Visible people must get all the credit.

(Chair of major charity, entrepreneur)

The role of the fundraiser

There was a range of views as to the importance of the perceived status of the person asking for money, from irrelevant to crucial. Some observed that the status need not last beyond the campaign.

It's not a problem for me because of my own street cred and brand values. My own endorsement enhances the value of a project.

(Former chair of national institution with very successful record in fundraising, business and public life)

How much status matters is for the individual. I have just identified my successor as chair of appeal who will give and get. I never give to people I don't know and it's true of others, but I am not sure that prospects mind about my status.

(Chair of the institution and also of the appeal; contributed but not a major giver; on the board of several charities in a range of sectors.)

My status is very important vis-à-vis the donor. I can speak as the head. I used to think that being a trustee was only marginally important to the donor but important within the [institution] as one of their bosses. I know I command respect. No-one owes a penny to [the institution]. I am asking a favour but not for myself.

(Chair of a separate fundraising board and board member of the main institution)

Views varied about the extent to which the asker should be involved in details of the strategy for the fundraising campaign. This was partly related to personal style and inclination, and partly to the maturity of the organisation and experience of the in-house team.

I deal with both strategy and fundraising. I write a huge number of letters. It doesn't matter if you are involved in strategy if there is a well organised fundraising office. It's 80% perspiration, 20% inspiration. The relationship with the organisation is based on performance. I don't want to be embarrassed by incompetence or trivial administration cock-ups.
(Chair of the institution and also of the appeal; contributed but not a lead giver)

For most people it was a false distinction: as a leader they had to be involved in both strategy and implementation. The quality of implementation depends on the professional team, and several pointed to the need to be "serviced and supported". There is also a need to balance delegation and being prepared to take responsibility for asking. The following example draws together a number of the issues in a thoughtful comment:

The question of the support of the institution is interesting. The skill sets needed are related to money and my involvement is a proxy for my money which is tied up in my business. So it's about the organisation and the people running it. There is no business benefit for me. It's an opportunity to contribute and an opportunity to meet interesting people. It's about the people, the mission and the skills set. The usefulness of this is in the eye of the beholder. I need to feel needed. As CEO of my business, my expertise is in business management and funding. It's about unbundling cash. There are gradations of approach. I would like to be chair because I could deal with the management issues I see. I expect nothing from the organisation but any adviser should leave if their advice is comprehensively rejected over a period. I like to get my involvement and information flow into an efficient form. To be effective I need to know.
(Instrumentally involved in several successful fundraising campaigns but not as a chair of the institutions or in a very public role)

Because people put so much effort into asking for money, and since they are in a sense "professional", some take rejections as a personal failure.

I feel I have failed if you warm someone up and then they don't make the effort. I also think 'mean bastard'.
(Entrepreneur, has been involved with campaigns in a number of organisations)

However, most askers are more phlegmatic, and all recognise that they have to move on to the next prospect. Several mentioned the feeling of achievement after what is always a long haul over several years. This is not surprising, as apart from the success for an institution they care about, part of the satisfaction is relief at completion.

Achieving the impossible – for example [a difficult capital campaign]. I don't expect much recognition but a lot of people do. There is no trouble for some causes, for example [a family charity] but mental health is different.

(On the board of several charities in a range of sectors)

Several made the point that fundraising staff are undervalued and – associated with this – many do not stay long with the charities for which they work. This reduces the likelihood of effective long-term relationship management which askers – and donors – see as crucial to recurring giving.

People have other commitments so you have to put in time to get to know them. If you take money from people you must keep in touch with them. You must thank them. Fundraisers are paid badly and treated badly. They keep moving on so institutions don't look after past donors. It's all about interpersonal skills. Training for fundraising is bad. The chief executive should line manage this directly.

(Has had board and fundraising experience in a number of sectors; also a major donor)

Effective asking for money

There are four questions they consider: 1. Do they know and respect and trust you? 2. Is the cause competent, careful, well managed? 3. Will their money be lost in a huge pool? 4. Is the cause one for which they have sympathy? It would be assumed that I had contributed and it turns off the fundraising department if you haven't.

(On the board of several charities in a range of sectors)

The core of the discussion was related to the experience of asking for money. Issues explored included some of those reviewed with the main body of interviewees. People were also asked about whether it mattered if they themselves have made a financial contribution. In most cases the experience of askers echoes and reinforces the views of other respondents, not only as they described their own knowledge of fundraising but, more importantly perhaps, in their reports of their own reactions and responses to solicitations for support.

There must be respect, trust and belief in who asks. Some people are largely influenced by the cause and hardly influenced at all by what it will do for them. Others are interested in the particular place and determined that it will succeed. 50% more often than not are interested in what it will do for them. No-one has asked whether I have given. So the cause is first, and what it will do for them, including naming, is important for some.

> (Chair of a separate fundraising board and board member of the main institution; distinguished record in public life; not wealthy)

What matters is the personal relationship, the social implications of being involved, the nature of the cause, the intellectual pitch, the quid pro quo in terms of social recognition, involvement, seeing behind the scenes. Knowing whether I have given can make a difference.

> (Former chair of national institution with very successful record in fundraising, business and public life)

The project is key. There is unbelievable competition. The project must be exceptional. You should have a small team. Four or five volunteer leaders and four or five key staff in the office. Does it matter if I have given? – No, not one jot. In the US it does matter and would be expected from someone wealthy. Donors want to see the top two or three people that they would expect to see as givers.

> (Formerly in City; highly respected, not regarded as significantly wealthy)

The most striking thing is that one does very little cold calling: a) I don't like it; and b) it doesn't work. What works is getting people involved and making them feel that they are part of the party.

> (Former banker, chair and involved with organisations in more than one sector)

Everyone is prepared to give me 20 minutes of their time. What I have learned is that one-to-one is the only way to raise big money. It's important to be seen to be in control. They know that I am taking it very seriously. It's going to be a tight ship and well run.

> (Formerly in City, chair and board member of a range of institutions)

These extracts exemplify and cover many of the key factors to successful solicitation from the wealthy. The sources of these ideas cover the widest range of fundraising challenges and sectors. There is unanimity on the importance of respect for and a personal link to the asker, belief in the cause, confidence that their money will make a difference, and a sincere and effective form of involvement, so that donors feel they are part of the team creating the project. That team should include volunteer and professional staff working together. The exact nature of the involvement and benefits, including recognition, vary depending on the interests and personality of the donor.

A key element cited was the quality and nature of the support from the organisation for which money is being raised. Aspects mentioned included attention to detail, comprehensive research briefings about the prospects, a professional and well regarded fundraising team with appropriate standing within the organisation, and the involvement of staff who deliver the mission, whether senior social workers, professors, artists or specialist experts. In order to sustain the relationships and prepare the ground for further giving, some askers identified the importance of structures which offered opportunities for major donor involvement in governance.

> *There needs to be more of a link between the serious fundraisers and sources of serious wealth. ABC has treated raising money as a business. Compare it with others who don't. It's about management, poverty of ambition, the selection of people invited as leaders and the attitude to fundraising staff. At ABC getting the involvement of the [specialist staff] was crucial. You need a culture where fundraising or development is part of the ethos.*
> (Entrepreneur, has led and guided campaigns in a number of arts organisations)

There is also some endorsement of the value of having certain donors on a list of contributors, particularly if this might be expected for projects in specific areas such as the arts. This may pose a challenge if the donor wishes their contribution to be private. But we see a divergence of views on the importance of the asker also being a donor. In a tiny constituency this was definitely age-related. Those in their seventies believed it not to matter – perhaps their august status and reputation made it less important for them. Furthermore, neither of these people was known to possess significant private means.

The value of persistence was also emphasised by some.

> *The key thing is to ask. That's what people don't like doing. If you believe in something enough you should ask and go on asking and endure embarrassment until they give.*
> (Former chair of national institution with very successful record
> in fundraising, business and public life)

Attention was focused on some of the issues of detail explored in Chapters Five and Six.

Networks and constituencies of givers

Askers were questioned about the existence of clubs or networks of givers. There was a range of views. Some, including askers who were Jewish and those who were not, identified the strong Jewish network, and within that network certain people who were key influencers. However, with the exception of "a small group of the very rich" and associations of institutional foundations, most thought the networks were socially driven rather than being about membership of a circle of donors.

> *There is a network of social climbers but the tradition of elite philanthropy doesn't work here. There is no concept of emotional or physical tithing except perhaps among wealthy Jewish people. Turning up for a gala at the Almeida [2] isn't about fundraising.*
> (Entrepreneur, has led and guided campaigns in a number of arts organisations)

It was suggested that current "vogue" has a part to play, with campaigns or organisations in a range of sectors being fashionable. Others observed the emergence of corporate circles in the City which now include people with significant net worth. However, it was also noted that these display different characteristics, not least because they are still building their careers and wealth, albeit already substantial.

> *High earning people are younger and wealthier but time poor. Look in the City: there is an order of magnitude difference between people in the City and the rest of the country (in terms of wealth).*
> (Formerly in City, chair and board member of a range of institutions)

Some askers were wary of younger prospects and the "new rich". It was difficult to know how to reach them, and all believe that on the whole "they are not ready to give. There are a few under 45 who give". As one said "*they are illiquid, and probably lack ethos.*" However, the same person, and others, recognised that this is a crucial constituency for the future.

> *Building up support in the young is important. We are very research-active in the office. Occasionally, we find new donors in their forties. Research is essential. One in 10 become hooked after an initial introduction at a breakfast, lunch or dinner.*
> (Chair of a separate fundraising board and board member of the main institution; distinguished record in public life; not wealthy)

---

[2] A theatre in Islington, north London, which has attracted fashionable support.

Those with experience in working with "celebrities" had a particular perspective. There was an emphasis on making it fun, and on asking for time and involvement as a way into longer-term engagement. It was also felt important to tell such people how much they have helped to raise. The leverage effect of major celebrity participation can be considerable and some find it easier to ask for this than for money.

> *It is usually easier to ask for talent than a big donation. I would be uncomfortable about these people making a personal donation but I don't mind using moral pressure to encourage them to participate. Exposing them to the issues rather than taking it for granted that they will understand is a very important part of the process. This leads to them being motivated and changes the way they think and to people appreciating their lot in life. You must never trivialise the need but must be clear about the issues and messages. There is so much injustice. You can show them that by doing a little, they can make a significant difference. They can get an extraordinary result for a manageable commitment.*
>
> (Entrepreneur, chair of major national charity)

Some suggested that there was not enough effective social pressure to give, compared with the US. Those with long memories in the City thought that the impact of such pressure had declined, along with a sense of social responsibility. However, others thought that people do feel a sense of obligation. This was stronger for causes concerned with children and, perhaps for different reasons, for the arts and heritage. As an asker, the task is to identify those to whom it matters and manage the relationship accordingly. Presenting the cause as fashionable may be part of the strategy, particularly for younger people and the newly wealthy.

Special access

Most askers approved of providing special services to those who want them. Just as social aspirations vary, so does the level of interest in privileged access. Most askers made the point that here as elsewhere it must be a case of individual assessment and discussion. While it is important to respect the passions and anticipated fun and enjoyment which underlie any possible donation, "few people give just to have a private dinner".

> *As a generalisation, it's not vital. The approach must vary. You must ascertain how people want to be involved. With serious money, the fun is explaining the artistic mission, who is the chief executive and so on, and in*

*the process you will be able to assess what they want. Listen and give it
to them. It's a process of selling and not insulting the donor's intelligence.
It's about creativity, but management doesn't always implement effectively
what they have learned. There is a cost of after-sales service.*
> (Entrepreneur, has led and guided campaigns in a number of arts organisations)

Recognition

*It's surprising: sometimes those who you think would care desperately don't and
vice versa. I have come across no-one to whom it is repugnant, although some are
embarrassed. People who part with their own money deserve recognition.*
> (Chair of a separate fundraising board and board member of the main institution)

*Few will give only because of recognition, but people like to be remembered
and recognised. I don't mind my own name on lists. It is helpful to the
charity. The honours list matters to some but it is more blatant.*
> (Formerly in City, chair and board member of a range of institutions)

These quotes encapsulate the views of most askers. Only one of those
interviewed had ever experienced in many years of fundraising someone
seeking a knighthood as a precondition for a major gift. As it could not be
promised, the donor withdrew from the discussions.

Some donors who were raising money expressed concern about their
inability to offer public recognition for certain causes. Given the views of most
donors described earlier, this may not be as crucial a factor as they assume.

Anonymity

Half the askers had some experience of anonymity or requests for
discretion. In a few cases it was the usual practice of the donor being "a
modest understated man". Other donors dislike the limelight or they do
not wish to alert others to their wealth. In other cases it was a tactical
move. Some major gifts had been anonymous at the time, but announced
later. Another tactic was to be seen to give generously but not excessively.

> *One trustee gave £25,000 as a challenge but he didn't want to be seen to be overdoing it because he had already given.*
>> (Formerly in City, chair and board member of a range of institutions)

The idea that a trustee would be "overdoing it" by adding to their gift raises some of the issues about perceptions of philanthropy explored in Chapter Ten.

Sector of fundraising

Most askers had raised money across a range of sectors, although one or two were mainly concerned with arts and education. They thought it likely that the attitudes and response of donors would be similar regardless of whether they might benefit from a gift (for example in the arts) or there was no direct advantage (for example, the homeless). The constant theme was the importance of commitment to the cause.

But there was a sense in which raising money for sectors other than those with which they were currently engaged was perceived to be easier. Those involved in social welfare suggested that raising money for arts and education might be less difficult, whereas those with a primary focus on cultural causes thought otherwise.

> *You don't get a better reception in heaven for supporting the arts. There is more self-esteem if you support the homeless or social problems than if you support the arts, and the government is not interested in the arts.*
>> (Chair of a separate fundraising board and board member of the main institution; distinguished record in public life; not wealthy)

Tax mechanisms

> *At the highest level most gifts are through a charitable trust. At lower levels one grinds away at Gift Aid but it's not in the culture. We have a few who have given shares.*
>> (Chair of a separate fundraising board and board member of the main institution; distinguished record in public life)

Do mechanisms make a difference? People who are going to give will give anyway. It has a marginal effect on the amount. But share giving is a real change. It's a bonus.

(Entrepreneur, has led and guided campaigns in a number of arts organisations)

All askers believed that tax mechanisms were not a deciding factor in the focus of a specific gift but very helpful in determining the level of donation. Where a charitable trust already exists it would be a question of meeting the predetermined aims of the trust.

Share giving was regarded as "very good news", but at the time of the interviews there has been limited experience. All complained about the lack of awareness among donors and charities about Gift Aid and share giving. There was also criticism of the unnecessary complexity of the Gift Aid mechanism, with the benefit split between donor and recipient.

Tax benefits are not a decider but I am amazed at the ignorance about Gift Aid and giving shares. It's difficult and complicated for charities to explain. We need to make it attractive for people to give. Charities are not good at giving recognition for the gross amount received.

(Former banker, chair and involved with organisations in more than one sector)

Several observed that some charities are slow to credit the donor with the total sum they receive as the result of a Gift Aided donation. There was recognition that the government had improved the position in recent years by removing the ceiling for Gift Aid and generally raising awareness of tax-efficient giving. However, the situation was contrasted with that in the US, where there is the possibility of obtaining current tax relief for an irrevocable pledge to give in the future.

It is helpful that the government is raising awareness. It's getting better but it would be nice to get an immediate credit for a future gift.

(Formerly in City, chair and board member of a range of institutions)

It was pointed out that the absence of such products, together with what were perceived as the over-cautious investment strategies of trustees, largely inhibited the amassing of planned endowments. This was a particular concern for those involved in higher education and cultural institutions, but not confined to those sectors.

The worst is endowment because of charity law in this country requiring conservative husbandry of resources, and the lack of mechanisms allowing capital gifts whilst enjoying the income. It's much more flexible in the US.
(Entrepreneur, has led and guided campaigns in a number of arts organisations)

Rejection

Notwithstanding their years of practice and understanding of factors which increase the chances of success, all of these askers have experienced refusals. All had received small gifts from someone known to be very wealthy. And all professed to be disappointed, but not surprised. They cited a range of excuses.

I have a long and distinguished list of refusals. Sometimes it's genuine, sometimes people say they are giving all to X. You have to live with the competitive nature of fundraising. Others will say they don't like the particular project. It's quite mysterious. Then there are those who delay.
(Chair of a separate fundraising board and board member of the main institution; experience in many campaigns)

In some cases the refusal is linked to attitudes to money, having wealth and financial security, which are explored in Chapter Eight.

Key points

The askers suggested a range of factors which create and support a commitment to make a major donation. They echo and reinforce the views of others with experience in asking reported in Chapter Six and, more importantly, highlight the same features which the donor interviewees identified as important influences on their giving. The same messages are being received, with some subtleties of emphasis, about the key elements in the management and nature of any involvement with the recipient organisation.

All recognise that a passion for the cause is vital. This may exist already, or might be created through effective introduction to the activities of the organisation, and the particular project, but without this there will be no major donation. However, a concern for the cause is a necessary but not sufficient condition for a regular and serious commitment.

Any approaches must be carefully researched and planned. The level of gift must be identified and the volunteer fundraiser supported by a first class professional team which has high internal status within the recipient organisation. That team must also operate within a corporate culture in which those who deliver the mission see the nurturing of relationships with major donors as part of their role and essential to creating the partnerships which will sustain their organisation. Such partnerships will be based on mutual respect, and this will be reflected in the nature and style of communications and feedback, and the way in which donors are involved in the leadership and governance of the institution.

12

The experience of professional advisers

Many of the issues related to having and managing wealth were also discussed with the 14 professional advisers who took part in the study, some of whom introduced one or more clients as interviewees. Ten were partners in professional legal firms, two were partners in accounting practices and two were senior bankers providing private wealth management services to high net worth individuals. There was a wide range of levels of net worth represented in the client base.

> *£5m to £10m. They don't have a mortgage, tend to be in their fifties, have paid the school fees and sorted out their lives.*
>
> (Banker)

> *£20m to £50m. It's commonplace in the City to find people worth £20m-plus as a function of being lucky with their bank – for example Goldman Sachs. Even those who are not partners do well. Senior MDs have had £3m to £5m in bonus payments for the last three years. Young people in hedge funds are making tens of millions – stratospheric sums of money.*
>
> (Solicitor)

> *£5m to £100m and up to £500m.*
>
> (Accountant)

£25m-plus with many over £500m.

(Solicitor)

One banker, with a client base with net worth between £20m and £50m, added that 70% of their business was related to sales of private companies.

In this chapter we explore advisers' feelings about the financial security of their clients and their perceptions of clients' attitudes to passing money to children and to inheritance tax. We also explore the extent to which they think their clients feel a sense of social obligation and how they perceive their attitudes to giving to charity, whether in the lifetime of the donor or as a legacy. There is also a section on the advisers' views of the main concerns of their clients and on giving as part of asset management.

Financial security

Advisers' views about how secure they thought their clients felt were gauged using the same basis and scale (of 0 to 10, where 0 is least secure) as given to the donor interviewees (see Chapter Eight). In general, their perceptions mirrored those reported by donors. In particular, all were confident that their clients' feelings of security would be independent of actual levels of wealth. Some suggested it was linked to their age and the stage of their business development. Those whose clients were building businesses suggested that they would feel low to medium security – an assessment consistent with the findings of the donor research.

Four to six. They are entrepreneurs and therefore risk aware and conscious that money can be lost.

(Solicitor)

Others thought to have a medium sense of security were self-made professionals.

The question of confidence was seen as crucial. Many advisers gave an unprompted opinion about the link between feelings of security and likely levels of giving. Most believed that their clients would not give significant capital unless they were absolutely confident that they had more than they needed for the rest of their lives as well as sufficient to provide for their families. This in turn depended on lifestyle, perceived needs and leisure activities.

In general, high feelings of security were seen as a necessary but not a sufficient condition for significant giving.

> *My clients would be 10 on the scale [highest sense of security].*
> *People who have made money give, people who have inherited don't*
> *because they have no ability to make money. They are mean and*
> *they have no self-confidence. They lack courage, they don't even add*
> *to their assets in terms of art, furniture and so on. Their houses don't*
> *reflect themselves, they don't commission modern art. People who have*
> *made large sums believe they can make it again and are more amenable*
> *to thinking about charitable causes. They are less likely to make*
> *significant donations to charity after they have retired. They are*
> *frightened of their children.*
>
> (Solicitor)

It was suggested that some of those who inherited wealth lacked courage and generosity, although it was recognised that those who have inherited land, a great house and art may spend large sums in maintaining it for the next generation, for whom they see themselves as holding it in trust.

The discussion turned to how financially secure they perceived people like their clients need to feel. Some looked at it from the perspective of income requirements, suggesting that an income of £1m a year plus a house was a likely starting point.

> *As an example, I know an extremely wealthy widow who needs £1m a*
> *year to live as she is accustomed with four establishments. What is*
> *the minimum yield on a broad range of investments? Say 2% per*
> *annum, so she would need £50m, plus something for a disaster, on a*
> *total return basis. But if you want to live on the income but are*
> *prepared to raid the capital as well, you could look for 5% return on*
> *investment to generate 3% for income and 2% for capital. If you want*
> *to maintain the real value of capital and your portfolio has gone up*
> *15% with inflation at 5%, so capital growth was 10%, you can safely*
> *raid the appreciated capital. So £50m would give you £1.5m gross of*
> *tax at 3%.*
>
> (Solicitor)

As we see, this adviser suggested a net worth of £50m. Looking at capital or net worth, assessments ranged from £10m upwards as the minimum for their clients to £30m as the lowest threshold.

Passing money to children

Most advisers confirmed that the question which most concerned their clients was how much should be left to their children.

> *There is concern about leaving too much to the children. It's usual that the children should have £x then the wives and mistresses.*
>
> (Solicitor)

But as with the client constituency, there was a range of views:

> *People don't want them to be too rich (or not all of them do). The interesting issue is the age at which people want their kids to get their hands on capital. It's rare for parents not to put money into a trust for their children. It's not possible for technical reasons for the parents to be trustees. They have to choose relations or the bank or similar. Physically, capital can be advanced at any age: for example at 25 when they want to buy a flat, but at what age are they under a duty to make capital available? It varies from parent to parent and child to child.*
>
> (Solicitor)

A desire not to "ruin" the children or give them so much they are "spoilt", as illustrated above, is perceived to be shared across a wide range of clients. In some cases this was seen to vary with the source of wealth.

> *People often feel they have done enough for their children. If a capital transfer tax is brought in it may prompt people to leave more money to charity. If people have inherited money, the view is that it should be passed on to the next generation. If they made it themselves, they are not so keen on giving their children too much.*
>
> (Banker)

Some advisers believe that some of their clients may be slightly in fear of their children and this explains why intentions to give less money to children are not always implemented. For others there may be an element of distrust.

> *Fear. They don't bring in their children early enough. They think 'I appreciate money because I make it.' There is fear of destroying the relationship. Paranoia. 'How can I tell what they will be like after university?' They need to trust their kids more. It restricts the decision-making on the allocation of charitable pot.*
>
> (Accountant)

However, one adviser, who was generally dismissive about the charitable impulses of his clients, believed that in the end blood is thicker than water.

> *Most people have dynastic desires. It's an exception not to want to pass on wealth to your children.*
>
> (Accountant)

He, and others, pointed out that in the end people often leave more to their children than they might initially have planned. Various reasons were suggested for this. They may be persuaded to change their mind by the children, may want to "reward" the child or children in some way or compensate them for a career choice or disappointment. Alternatively, they may see it as a choice between that and paying tax since gifts made to children and grandchildren seven years before the death of the donor avoid tax.

> *Some people – very few – are aware of the dangerous effect of inherited wealth but most are concerned to save tax.*
>
> (Solicitor)

Inheritance tax

There was a consistent view that all their clients wished to avoid inheritance tax (IHT) if possible. As the donor interviewees say, this comes from a combination of believing that they have already contributed their share and that the government will not spend it well.

> *Every one hates taxes. They think they should keep 100%. They have paid enough tax in their lifetime and they think the government will only waste it.*
>
> (Solicitor)

We note in Chapter Eight that there is some resentment among donors that it is the lawyers and accountants who benefit from the present position regarding IHT and most professional advisers were conscious of that.

> *IHT is the big ogre. Most clients see it as iniquitous and want to avoid paying it. In dealing with new wealth, they feel they have created it and already paid tax on it. It's an iniquitous burden. They can avoid it because of the seven-year rule.*
>
> (Solicitor)

Because of the seven-year rule, people are advised to establish the necessary structures when they are confident that they will live at least that long. But as several advisers pointed out, it is human nature not to wish to consider one's own mortality, and those who are creating wealth in businesses or City careers have limited time. Unless they are realising their assets earlier, and look at tax planning as part of an overall approach to the management of their estate, they "don't think about this until they are middle-aged".

> The flow-through of money to charities by people like [well-known entrepreneurs] won't happen until they think they need to start thinking about the seven-year rule. Thinking about the middle-aged, the pressure of the hereafter will only start to bite when their advisers say they must now take advantage of the seven-year rule. Their minds will only get focused at that age.
>
> (Solicitor)

Several observed that even when consideration is given to these issues there is not often a major interest in charitable giving.

> There is a universal wish to avoid IHT. They want to get money to the next generation. Charity is not part of the deal. People have charity in mind but not enough.
>
> (Accountant)

Social obligations of wealth

Advisers were asked whether they thought their clients felt that wealth carried any social obligation. On the whole, advisers were rather sceptical about the levels of obligation felt.

> It's very, very low. Charity begins with your own family.
> An increase in wealth leads to worry about the tax bill,
> not about putting something back.
>
> (Solicitor)

Several saw the key concern of their clients as tax minimisation. This may be a reflection of the agenda defined by the client, and reinforced by the advisers' perceptions of their own role and specialist knowledge. The client may already have decided to allocate a certain amount to charitable giving and to focus discussions with their advisers on seeking the expertise they need, rather than taking time for a more philosophical analysis of motivations. However, it was certainly the case that avoiding tax was seen as a key requirement.

> *Some clients have socialist beliefs but are paranoid about paying taxes. It's a strange combination but I have seen it more than once. I have yet to meet a rich socialist who wanted to pay taxes. They are socialist because they have chips on their shoulders.*
>
> (Accountant)

But one banker, whose organisation would expect to discuss philanthropic commitment and allocation with its clients, suggested that changes in the constituencies who have wealth may bring greater philanthropic giving for a range of reasons.

> *There have been changes. There have been huge amounts of wealth created through the sale of private companies over the past 10 years. There's been at least £27bn raised in UK. For some of them it's about evening up the score. 'I have been lucky.' With old money it is about service and looking after estates. With people of Jewish and Asian origin it's not a question of being honourable but something one does.*
>
> (Banker)

All the advisers, including those who were most sceptical about their clients' interest in philanthropy, reported exceptions among their Jewish clients and those from Hindu and Islamic backgrounds. As we have seen, these views, if oversimplified, are consistent with the analysis of the experience of interviewees. Few of them reported discussing such issues with their advisers, other than as part of estate planning. Some advisers pointed out that individual ideas about responsibility and allocation evolve over time, and speculated that apart from businesses associates, as one accountant suggested: "*Clients develop their ideas – from family, religion, friends*".

Advisers who see the encouragement of charitable giving as part of their role were more positive about the likely interest among their client base, including younger entrepreneurs. It is not possible to say from this study whether this is the result of the selection (often by recommendation) of a particular style of adviser which will suit the values and interests of the client. However, there may be at least a limited indication that those who position philanthropy as part of the asset management mix may meet a positive response with certain clients.

Giving in lifetime or bequests

As we have seen, most people give something, and all advisers had donors among their client base. Advisers were asked for their views on the preferences of their clients between giving in their lifetime or making charitable bequests.

There was a range of expertise and advice, from a preference for lifetime giving to legacies.

> *Our advice is that it's more fun to give money away while you're alive. It's about being strategic for the family's future. International people tend to give anonymously because they don't want everyone knocking on their door. Some just give to whoever asks.*
>
> (Banker)

> *I try to encourage both. If people have given away a lot in their lifetime there is less need to do so on their death, except they can leave money to their charitable foundation.*
>
> (Solicitor)

If people do not have a trust (mostly younger people), the adviser will probably not be aware of the giving commitments of their clients. More than one adviser with clients who had assets in the US (for example American bankers based in the UK) referred to the opportunities provided by the US approach to planned giving, with split interest trusts.

> *40% of US giving by major donors is planned giving. For example, this can apply to people who have a second home. They could pledge the house and would obtain tax relief on the discounted value of their house on an actuarial basis of their life expectancy. There is a high probability of this kind of thing happening. There is a resistance to endowment because of a lack of trust in investments.*
>
> (Solicitor)

There were different perceptions about the popularity of charitable bequests, perhaps not surprisingly in view of the wide range of attitudes expressed by interviewees.

> *Only the older Anglo-Saxon clients give principally through legacies.*
>
> (Solicitor)

There's a huge range, but perhaps an increasing number of legacies.

(Accountant)

There was also a variety of opinions about the amount that people actually leave to charities.

10% to 15%. It comes back to absolute amounts and depends on what they did in their lifetime.

(Accountant)

It's usually less than 5%. For example, you might have an estate worth £3m of which some legacies will go to godchildren and say £50,000 to charities, with the balance to the spouse and on her death to the children.

(Solicitor)

That person added:

It depends on the family situation. Sometimes the main incentive is negative – for example, when there are no children or dependants. Charitable giving comes at the second death.

(Solicitor)

Several reported that people leave money to their surviving spouse, with the proviso that on their death it will go to their trust or charities.

Less than 1%. For many people with estates in the £1m to £5m range a legacy of £500 is a fortune!

(Solicitor)

Concerns of their clients

Tax, saving, succession planning, monitoring, confidentiality. Passing money to their children, inheritance. Most clients think that some of their money is surplus. At that stage they need a strategy and a structure. Preservation of the pot.

(Solicitor)

Professional advisers were asked what they consider to be the main concerns of their clients. The answer above was one of the most succinct and the most comprehensive. All advisers mentioned tax and succession planning which, for a business or management of family assets, is seen as a key issue, particularly for older clients. Tied into this is concern about the volatility of the stock market and family security, particularly that of the surviving spouse.

Younger people making significant sums wish primarily to hold on to their assets.

> *Estate planning. The UK is still a relatively low tax area. They are young so IHT is not in the forefront. Offshore trusts are legal, giving long-term capital appreciation and security. They already have three houses. They come to us because we are the market leader. They want to know how they can keep as much as possible. It's only later on that issues of how they devolve it to their children, IHT, even philanthropy come up. When the kids are nearly grown up, parents start thinking carefully about them.*
> (Solicitor)

As people get older, or if a business is sold, there may be a more comprehensive approach. Some advisers thought that younger people were also interested in strategic planning – for example, arrangements for school fees.

> *It's a package of family and business. They want a strategy for family wealth, planning for kids' schooling, their old age. It's about equilibrium, quality of life and use of financial assets. The more money you have, the less likely you are to get there. 95% of family problems are caused by money.*
> (Accountant)

Questions surrounding how much to leave to children were central concerns, as described earlier. The process of "equalising" between children, already described by interviewees, also causes difficulty, particularly if one child has contributed to the success of the family business. We note that some people try to address these tensions through family meetings and involving their children in the family foundation. As we note in Chapter Eight, those with family trusts who include their children see this as crucial to imparting values and maintaining good links with their children. Some advisers recognise this and try actively to encourage it.

> *We try to flush out what they want to do including establishing some idea of the sort of charitable interests. Over the past 10 years we have seen strategies come to fruition. The relationship with the children is key. They want to build bridges and formulate a strategy to do so. Philanthropy is a core part of that.*
> (Banker)

Advice on structuring philanthropy

Advisers were also asked whether, when and in what form they recommend their clients to structure their giving. Few advisers (two or three out of the 14) saw it as an integral part of their role actively to promote the idea of philanthropy, either on the basis of duty or social obligation, or as a means of strengthening the family. But most of the solicitors, one of the bankers and one of the accountants would include as part of their responsibility the capacity to give advice (and even encouragement, if they felt there was interest) on charitable giving. They believed that they have a professional duty to be aware of the range of tax mechanisms, and to alert their clients to the options, structures and benefits (fiscal and personal). This is particularly the case at times of major change or decision, such as the sale of a family business or making wills. It was apparent that the nature and depth of the discussion would depend on the intimacy, understanding and trust between adviser and client.

> *I would say that most advisers ask clients if they want to give.*
>
> (Solicitor)

It was suggested by some that people do not necessarily understand how wealthy they are or have knowledge of how to give.

> *My experience is in dealing with high net worth individuals on the soft side. The suggestion is that there are a lot of people who are very wealthy who would like to get a grip on their money to structure, organise, manage and give properly, but because they haven't found any way to work out a coherent strategy and don't know whom to trust and don't know how to give properly, there is apathy. My vision is to build a strategy on the basis of what is important for them.*

> *I always have a trust in mind. People at this level want to give but they don't know if they have enough because they don't have a grip on their wealth. If they did they would be happy to allocate a percentage. People are out of their depth with their own wealth even if they are very, very wealthy and financially secure. Also, they don't know how to give effectively. This twin ignorance leads to apathy. Setting up a trust is not a real problem because the Charity Commission is good. It has to be bureaucratic to an extent and the Commission must set a standard. There's a risk if you try to set up a trust with not enough money and then you can't afford it... If you want recognition without bureaucracy there is CAF.*
>
> (Solicitor)

Some advisers do not take an active role in proposing charitable giving, but observe that there might be more of an incentive if there were greater tax benefits to making major gifts in the lifetime of the client.

> *I don't. Clients have their own mind but perhaps there should be an incentive, the incentive should be to do it now. We need a US-type approach.*
>
> (Solicitor)

Charitable trusts

Several of the advisers said they suggest a charitable trust to their clients at some point.

> *I suggest putting money into a trust because control is important. With a trust they are settlors and trustees. They can have their cake and eat it. It is flexible, there are tax advantages, they have control, the trust can continue indefinitely, they can pass it on to their wife and children as part of the inheritance and they can pass on their values. As long as the settlor is alive, it is he who determines where 95% of the money goes.*
>
> (Solicitor)

Others pointed out the benefit of a charitable trust as a mechanism for passing on family values and interests. But it was suggested that such arrangements were more likely to succeed in that aim if there was a genuine underlying concern with a cause.

> *We recommend setting up a trust with professional trustees – not the children because of the control issue but with children on a committee. It should have wide ranging objectives but you must agree the primary purpose. If the purpose is to make the children more responsible then you should set up something which will make that happen. The strategy of the holding structure is determined by the goals. It is usually bad to set up the structure specifically for tax reasons. Where there is a passionate interest in something it is much easier.*
>
> (Banker)

Estimates of the level of assets needed to endow a charitable trust ranged from £100,000 to £10m.

> *Trusts are still the favoured route because of ownership of philanthropy. The younger generation still needs to be educated in philanthropy and*

the best way to do that is get them involved. It inculcates stewardship and a responsible attitude to money in people who are at risk of going off the deep end because they have more money than they need. I suggest a trust if they're willing to put in £100,000 capital or a CAF account if it's less. There may be a diverse set of circumstances leading to setting up a trust. An example might be someone who has made money himself, is interested in reviving his community, is serious about what he wants to achieve and thinks too much money is not good for the children. I bring it up in the context of discussing wills and mention it as a possibility when considering overall planning.

(Solicitor)

We created a charitable trust for a client who wanted fun in old age, for another with gifts of shares. We don't bother for less than £¹/₂m capital.

(Solicitor)

There was one adviser who was dismissive of the entire concept.

I would never suggest but I know them well enough to know what they want to do. I would describe it as a damn nuisance. It's a difficult thing to work with trustees obliged by law to take a view of charitable interest. It's a foolish thing to do. It restricts your options.

(Accountant)

One adviser suggested that trusts can be considered after death, when the beneficiaries agree to establish a foundation as an alternative to paying tax.

It's not just about charitable matters but as a general commercial lawyer I have the opportunity to suggest that they put something into a charitable trust. I usually do this. There are occasions when people can be most attracted to giving. People must feel comfortable and secure before they start to give money away. a) If you are about to float a company or sell off a part and can see that real money is coming in for the first time, and that it will be a lot of money, at that time you can be talked into putting a part of the shareholding into a charitable trust, and it escapes tax and you still have control. People haven't mentioned the importance of the name association with the trust. They are interested in planning the future on the basis that they will be there. b) Another occasion is death when there are various inheritors. You can explain to them that they can have their cake and eat it. They can have a deed of family arrangement whereby they can re-write the will. All the beneficiaries under the will can agree that say 20% will go to 'x foundation' which will escape inheritance tax. Do you want to give the government 40%? It's an opportunity for charities; they don't do enough going after relatives.

(Solicitor)

Gifts of shares

Unlike the adviser above, others were less enthusiastic about the idea of share giving.

You would need a sum of money which is surplus to your ambitions. Also you need at least £10m. I would give no consideration to allocating the shares of any business to charity. They never bring it up.

(Accountant)

Gift Aid

Some advisers suggest Gift Aid, particularly but not only for smaller amounts or levels of giving. This is because of its simplicity, lack of need for long-term commitment, confidentiality and anonymity if desired, with no likelihood of being overwhelmed by appeals and criticism.

I suggest it when I can. If it's in their will, I will suggest they give while they are alive and can enjoy it. Sometimes people use Gift Aid because they don't want the responsibility of a trust or a CAF trust.

(Accountant)

Responses to the advice

Advisers were asked about the reactions to their advice, and the extent to which giving is seen as part of estate management and planning. Responses were very consistent.

Jewish clients 5/10. Non Jewish 1/10. For many Jewish clients it is in their will and 'you ain't nobody unless you give'.

(Solicitor)

The estimate that at least 50% of Jewish clients might respond positively was linked by some to their understanding of the traditions of that community and to some extent social pressure. This analysis is supported by the reports of the Jewish interviewees themselves. It was suggested that the main focus of giving of Jewish donors was Jewish charities, communities and causes, and this is consistent with the findings reported in Chapter Three that giving by faith communities, of all persuasions, starts with that community.

The other faith category which was reported to respond more positively to advice on giving was the Hindu community.

> *It varies enormously. Probably 20% decline. The key is the client feeling that he can afford to divert some of the capital. It's a question of feelings of security and background. There is a much stronger charitable instinct with people from Jewish and Hindu backgrounds. I don't think this is to do with age. I've been involved with fundraising and have been successful in targeting a newer generation. This is in the Jewish community. Some people are influenced to give because they are flattered by the invitation from someone they would like to meet – for example the Chief Rabbi, or someone senior in the same line of business.*
>
> (Solicitor)

Here as elsewhere many commented on the differences they perceived between those who have inherited wealth and the self-made professional or entrepreneur, who is thought more likely to propose or be interested in philanthropy.

> *Most do when they have made their own money but not when they have inherited money. People who have made their own way want to help others. People who are really rich can do a great deal of good or a great deal of harm. Most start thinking about it in their forties or fifties. It is higher in the Jewish community; characteristically, they are enthusiasts. They understand they have been lucky and they can be persuaded. There is a link between charitable giving and enterprise. You need to have the habit of charitable giving instilled by your fifties, perhaps through involvement in giving time.*
>
> (Solicitor)

Again, this was a consistent view from all who responded to the question, with some further distinguishing between new and old wealth. Some observed that many in the younger generation, including those who have inherited wealth, have more generous impulses.

It is very difficult and varied. The main influence is families and examples from previous generations. There is a split between old and new money. Some new boys do if they get into a charitable club or they decide to do something because they have avoided tax or want a knighthood. Someone who has just sold a company may give to be part of The Prince's Trust network. With older money – more than two generations – there is more likely to be a charitable trust, but if there is a mean tradition, that will be continued and they won't add to the trust. There is a good record where there is a history of philanthropy in the family and children will add to the charity if they are successful.

(Accountant)

It was observed that there may be various reasons why people do not choose to undertake any serious charitable giving. These include feelings of financial insecurity, decisions related to their children's inheritance, or assessments about further investments needed to develop their businesses, as described earlier. But some advisers clearly saw a serious need for education in the area of charitable giving.

It varies. You have to be emotionally rugged. In the Jewish community, it is part of the tradition and religion, and it is more likely to be positive with old wealth where there is a tradition and people feel solid. With new money, some want to put something back. There should be a parity of education about charity and philanthropy. Religions have neglected this. The discussion of citizenship in the curriculum is a good idea.

(Accountant)

Key points

The experience and perceptions of advisers reflect and are consistent with the range of attitudes and concerns reported by wealthy people themselves.

On the whole, advisers believed that the factors which made an allocation to charitable giving more likely were being self-made/ entrepreneurial, aged at least in their 40s or 50s and coming from a strong faith tradition. They felt that some who have inherited wealth and come from a family with a tradition of philanthropy may also give, but this is less likely when there is the responsibility and maintenance cost of a great estate and collection, which is seen as being held for the next generation.

Other elements which are felt to encourage charitable giving are a desire to avoid tax, a reluctance to pass on too much to the children and a desire for involvement in a cause of interest with accompanying recognition.

However, feelings of financial security are a necessary if not sufficient condition for people to make a significant and strategic commitment to philanthropy. Advisers report that such feelings are unrelated to actual levels of wealth, but are linked to a lack of confidence that lost or diminished assets could be replaced. Having such confidence is more likely among entrepreneurs. However, those running family businesses feel least secure.

Some advisers were aware of the theories of Claude Rosenberg (see Appendix Two), and advocated their application, as part of a general programme of awareness-raising, in the UK. Estimates of the level of wealth needed for financial security varied, but the most common range (reflecting client actuality) was £30m to £50m.

Some advisers observed that attitudes to leaving money to children may change; a combination of pressure by the children themselves, a realisation that the children are able to handle wealth and a sense that "blood is thicker than water" may account for this. However, all were aware that the "current generation of entrepreneurs" may be different.

Few advisers saw the active promotion of philanthropy, as an end in itself, as part of their role, but nearly all saw themselves as having a responsibility to advise their clients of the options, mechanisms and benefits, both in terms of tax and for the family. Some observed that a lack of understanding of the real level of wealth combined with the absence of tradition or expectation of giving and, in some cases, perceived complexity of "form filling", led to inactivity. This was reinforced by uncertainty as to how much to give and lack of time to devote to the question, particularly while building a business or career.

Advisers had a range of views about the minimum level required to set up a charitable trust, from £100,000 to £10m. No-one suggested using a trust as a mechanism through which regular transfers of income could flow, even with the incentive then in place of 10% added to the value of donations if made through payroll giving. However, there were comments about the absence of tax incentives to encourage gifts of capital in the lifetime of the donor, such as exist in the US.

13

The UK context – estimating the value of private gifts in the UK

By Cathy Pharoah, *Charities Aid Foundation (CAF)*[1]

This chapter reviews the information available on the value of private donations to charity, with a particular focus on the contributions of wealthy donors.

Measuring monetary contributions to charity is sometimes seen as a rather arid business. This is because a gift derives its worth not only from its financial value, but also from the context in which it is given – from its meaning to donor and recipient and from the myriad gifts of time, relationships, social connections and expertise which may accompany the gift. Yet the finance is extremely important, as John Manser, former chairman, Robert Fleming Holdings, put it[2]:

> *I suppose a business leader contributes a unique mixture of skills and money: you can't get away, in charities, from money.*

Precisely because the work of voluntary and community organisations is so dependent on the willingness of individuals to provide funds and on the ultimate levels of money raised, it is important to place any review of charitable involvement within the context of its financial value.

[1] The charity CAF provides specialist services to support every aspect of planned giving, from trust and foundation administration to investment management, grant-making and research..
[2] C Walker and C Pharoah. *Making time for Charity: A survey of top UK business leaders' involvement with voluntary organisations.* CAF Kent 2000.

Unfortunately, there is little systematic data on giving by particular groups within the UK population such as the wealthy. The best that can be done is to try to piece a picture together using information from different sources. We look at three tiers of giving, from the broad picture to the small group of very wealthy donors:

◆ Total giving by the general population.
◆ The giving of the mass affluent.
◆ The giving of the very wealthy.

Total giving by the general UK population

In trying to estimate the contribution of wealthy donors to charity, it is important to think about gifts from individuals, charitable trusts and companies, as major donors may contribute in all three areas. The total current private giving in the UK is in the region of £10.2bn. This is calculated on the basis of the following considerations.

Individual giving

The key sources of information on giving by the general public are the annual individual giving surveys now carried out jointly by CAF with the National Council of Voluntary Organisations. Figures from this survey for 2001-02 estimated total annual giving at £7.3bn. Legacies account for about another £1.5bn of giving[3]. Legacy giving is one of the most important forms of major giving, with average legacy gift value at £13,000.

Charitable trust donations

Many wealthy donors give through charitable trusts, but there are no precise figures in the UK for what this giving is worth. Private CAF research suggests that the assets of family trusts in the UK are likely to be around £8bn, but this includes trusts that were set up in previous centuries.

Corporate gifts

Corporate cash giving is worth about £300m, although corporate donors increasingly prefer to publish a total corporate support value for their charitable giving which includes the value of gifts in kind and other types of help. In addition to the above totals, we can add a possible £200-300m per annum of gifts derived from earnings on the endowments of family trusts, and a further £800m of tax reliefs provided by government on individual giving to reach the total of £10.2bn. This represents just over 1% of GDP.

[3] See Richard Radcliffe in *A Lot of Give*, with reference to statistics collated by Smee and Ford.

Giving by the "mass affluent"

Before focusing in on the giving of the very wealthy, a small group in terms of numbers, it is worth looking at how much of total giving is contributed by the mass affluent. There is no single definition of "mass affluent", as approaches shown in this chapter will show. One useful approach is to think of them as higher rate taxpayers – this is a category used in national data such as that provided by the Inland Revenue, and it is possible to use that data for information on their tax and income levels.

There are just 3.1 million higher rate taxpayers in the UK, 11% of all taxpayers. Not all of these people give to charity. CAF has estimated that the level of total individual giving among this group (ie excluding corporate or trust giving) is about £1.2bn per annum, or 17% of all individual giving. The average giving of this group is about £500 a year.

This is twice the £226 annual average annual given by the general population. The average amount given by higher rate taxpayers rises steeply with income. For example, CAF research[4] suggests that those earning £100,000 per year may be giving on average around £1,600 per annum.

Since the absolute amount given is related above all to the amount people earn, it is not surprising that that the average gift of the wealthier segments of society is several times higher than that of the population as a whole. Although absolute amounts given by the wealthy are higher, it is salutary to note that the poorest 10% of people by income give away about 3% of their income, while the richest 10% barely give away 1%[5]. The data presented below, however, suggest that the very wealthy among the richest 10% are giving away more than 1% of their wealth.

Giving by the wealthy

Data on giving by the top earners in the UK is very patchy. But with imaginative leaps it is possible to make an estimate. Surveys of individual giving among the general population tend to under-represent major gifts by the very wealthy because the survey sample numbers are small and major donors are spread thinly in the population. *The Sunday Times Rich List* is one source of data specifically on levels of wealth and giving by the rich.

The Rich List 2004 reported the gifts of the most generous 30 donors by proportion of wealth given to charity; together they amounted to £297m.

4 Using data from the Family Expenditure Surveys and the Individual Giving Surveys, unpublished.
5 J Banks and S Tanner. *State of Donation.* Institute of Fiscal Studies. London 1997.

This includes a mix of giving as individuals, from family trusts and from companies and represents 2.3% of their wealth, a figure much lower than that of the very wealthiest people in the US who donate an average of as much as 13% of their annual wealth. It is significantly higher than the 1% of income donated by the higher tax rate group as a whole, but is confined to the few wealthy donors at the top of the list.

It should be noted, however, that the figure of £297m is skewed by one very large gift of £105m by Tom Hunter which is unlikely to be spent in one year. If this gift were excluded, the giving of the rest of the top 30 would represent about 1.2% of their wealth[6].

Causes supported by wealthy donors
Wealthy donors favour very different causes from poorer donors. Broadly, richer donors favour education and the arts, which receive little support from the general population. The study of giving carried out by the Institute of Fiscal Studies[7] showed the richest donors giving to culture and the arts, recreation and leisure and the environment, while the poorest donors preferred international aid and animal charities. *The Sunday Times Rich List* confirmed that the arts and the environment were popular causes for the rich. However, it showed that health and medical causes and education were mentioned more than twice as often as the arts and the environment. Education as a cause receives little support from the general population, and its popularity among the rich no doubt reflects gifts to universities and private schools from a group who have enormously benefited from them[8]. Generally, health and medical causes are well supported by all population groups alike, revealing that while wealth divides people, health is a great leveller.

Tax-efficient giving among wealthier donors
Unsurprisingly, for wealthy givers the existence of tax reliefs on charitable gifts is more important than for other donors. This probably reflects both the tax advice such donors receive from their financial advisors, and also that the more tax is paid, the more valuable the tax relief. In one research study[9], one half of all donors in the top AB social class group said they rated the tax relief paid back to charities as important, compared with 39% in the bottom DE social classes.

However, the fact that 50% of wealthier donors did not see the tax paid back to charities as important suggests that awareness of the value of tax reliefs is not as widespread as it might be. There is further evidence that this might be the case from the Lloyds TSB survey, which reported that one-third of its wealthy donors (defined as having a salary of £100,000 or

[6] Theresa Lloyd has major reservations about the accuracy of this data, for reasons discussed in Chapter Two.
[7] J Banks and S Tanner. *State of Donation*. Institute of Fiscal Studies. London 1997.
[8] But see also evidence in the *Philanthropy* UK research for support of talented individuals.
[9] Annual CAF/NCVO giving survey 2000.

more) did not make use of tax-efficient giving schemes. This represents a significant loss to charities, and some loss to higher rate taxpayers themselves who could benefit from the donor tax breaks.

Levels of participation in giving by the wealthy

Several studies of giving including the work of Banks and Tanner in looking at the Family Expenditure Surveys and the CAF/NCVO individual giving surveys have consistently shown that there is a decreasing level of participation in giving and that the total amount of giving has only increased because of bigger gifts among those who do give. More recent analysis of the Family Expenditure Survey 2003[10] confirms that the wealthiest groups are more than four times as likely to give to charity as the poorest groups. It seems then that charities in the UK are increasingly dependent on the support of the wealthier groups in the UK. This is as true of the giving of money as of the giving of time.

The giving of time by the wealthy

There is some evidence that the wealthy are more generous with their time than other groups. The recent *Wealth Watch 2004*, published by Lloyds TSB Private Banking, reported that the wealthy were twice as likely as the average member of the UK population to commit time to charity as well as money. CAF's survey of business leaders[11] showed a similar trend. Two-thirds of the senior executives in the survey said they gave time to charity, and the giving of time was particularly common among chief executives of companies. About one-third of the senior executives noted that their gifts of money were important to charities, and this rose to 50% among company chairs.

Key points

The *Sunday Times Rich List* indicates that only a handful of very wealthy people contribute more than the average UK population of 1% of income to charity. The – admittedly patchy – evidence available on giving by the wealthy in the UK shows that the gifts of major donors are extremely valuable to charities. It would need only a small number of other wealthy people to follow their example to make a significant difference to the resources of UK charities.

Until the research published in this report, there has been little information about how donors decide on the actual level of the gifts they make, and it is notoriously hard to model or predict donor behaviour because it is

[10] Unpublished study, commissioned by CAF.
[11] C Walker and C Pharoah. Making time for Charity: *A survey of top UK business leaders' involvement with voluntary organisations* CAF Kent 2000.

influenced by so many different factors[12]. It is clear, however, that there is a wide range of behaviour. At one end are the people, rich or poor, who understand the real costs of meeting needs, calculate how much they can realistically afford to give and are aware of the impact of their contribution. At the other are those whose decisions about charitable giving largely lie outside the realm of economics. Charities, however, do not have the luxury of ignoring economic reality.

While giving in the UK has grown in absolute terms over the last decade, it has not grown as a proportion of total expenditure[13]. The challenge for the next decade is to raise the proportion of the nation's wealth which is dedicated to the essential work of voluntary and community organisations.

[12] See, for example, chapters by Catherine Walker and by Adrian Sargeant in *A Lot of Give* (ed C Walker and C Pharoah, CAF Kent 2002).
[13] Stephen Ainger, address at CAF conference November 2003.

14

Major philanthropy – how do we compare with the US?

The purpose of this chapter is to explore what we know about major philanthropy in the US, and the key differences in culture and practice which emerge from this UK research. For this analysis the main sources have been *Why the Wealthy Give,* by Francie Ostrower, published in 1995, and *The Mind of the Millionaire*, which presents findings from a national survey on *Wealth with Responsibility*, published by Paul Schervish and John Havens in January 2002. In the UK, apart from the interviews conducted for this research, we have had informal discussions with half a dozen US citizens now based in London with extensive fundraising experience on both sides of the Atlantic.

Why the Wealthy Give was based on interviews conducted in 1987 and 1988 with 99 wealthy donors in New York and contributing to New York institutions. The sample base was drawn from donor records. Although the interviewees were selected on the basis of donation rather than wealth *per se*, the study captured 82% of New Yorkers from the Forbes list of wealthiest Americans. Francie Ostrower observes that the fact that the percentage is so high testifies that the organisations used in the sampling procedure do attract donations from a large proportion of New York's wealthy. In the year preceding the interviews, a quarter of respondents had contributed $500,000 or more to charities, almost half had given $100,000 or more, over three-quarters had contributed over $20,000 and the remainder between $5,000 and $20,000.

The Mind of The Millionaire is based on research carried out between 1998 and 2000. 112 people completed questionnaires sent and returned by post. The base was drawn from a sample with wealth at or above $5m, including 30 households with net worth of at least $50m. In the preceding year, 97% had contributed to charitable causes and 65% to political causes. Interestingly, a quarter of respondents had contributed $500,000 or more to charitable or political causes in 1997. Of the average contribution of $1.2m, the largest amount, over $750,000, went to trusts, gift funds and foundations – the focus of planned giving allocations. Those with family net worth under $20m contributed about 10% of income. This increased substantially at higher levels, possibly affected by the significant impact of one-off major gifts of capital to gift funds.

In the first section of this chapter we look at general attitudes and broad themes relating to the nature of society, as perceived and reported by the interviewees. We also consider the tax structure. In the second part specific topics related to giving practices are explored.

What do we know about major philanthropy in the US?

Attitudes of the wealthy

Values, attitudes to the state and community responsibility

A major part of US giving is linked to community. People with wealth feel that they have a responsibility to embellish their community and indeed that a range of high quality local amenities reflects well on their own success in business or enterprise. As one person said, "*Every city has certain institutions which make it the city it is... they give the colour, substance of a civilised aggregation of people.*"

So wealthy people who do not contribute risk being perceived as not "doing their share" while benefiting from other people's support. Someone referred to these people as "free riders".

In the Francie Ostrower research almost everyone (over 90%) rejected the idea of reducing or even eliminating the tax incentive for giving and having the government/state use the increased revenue to support the types of welfare and cultural activities which have benefited from philanthropy.

Comments on the alternatives included *"that's socialism"* and *"if I wanted to live that way I'd move to Sweden."*

Part of the reason for giving, and for giving the maximum for which they received a tax reduction, was a marked antagonism to the idea of any extension of government expenditure, and the proposition that their taxes would otherwise be contributing to the growth and maintenance of a welfare state. Creating a foundation is seen as a way of "not giving all your money to the government in taxes". *"Instead of a Congressman telling me where my dollars are going to go, I am telling them where their dollars can go[1]."*

There was also scepticism about the ability of government to provide an effective substitute for private philanthropy. But beyond the perceived impracticality of the idea is a stronger view that a vital aspect of philanthropy is that it allows individuals to support the causes they value. Linked to that is the question of influence, or even control. *"If government took over, then unless I become a legislator, how can I have a say?"* And there was a fear about an "official line". *"This country is about freedom of choice."*

As we see, donors argue that it is desirable that philanthropy places a significant level of the funding of welfare and other activities in private hands and outside the government domain. They value the individualism in terms of the choice, initiative and impact which they believe the current system represents. For these reasons, philanthropy represents more to donors than a mechanism for channelling money to worthy causes. It is seen as representing some of the most valuable and even defining elements of American society. For one woman in the Ostrower research, philanthropy is *"the idea of giving and citizen participation – and I think that's what America's all about"*. One man talked about *"the whole difference between our system* [that is, the American approach] *and the European system, where the government fills the gap and the people don't do anything"*. Philanthropy not only sustains a set of organisations; it sustains a set of values.

Philanthropy as a characteristic of the elite

Equally important in the US, philanthropy is an integral and defining element of elite culture. It is crucially linked to the nature and functioning of upper class culture in American society. The US lacks the aristocratic and sharply defined class distinctions and social traditions which still persist in the UK, but the analysis of philanthropy in the US shows that

[1] Quotes from *America's Wealthy and the Future of Foundations* by Dr Teresa Odendahl, published by the Foundation Center in 1987.

American elites do fashion a separate cultural world for themselves by drawing on and refining elements and values from the broader society. Philanthropy becomes a mark of class status that contributes to defining and maintaining the culture and organisational boundaries of elite life. As donors put it, philanthropy becomes a *"way of being part of society"*, and *"one of the avenues by which society makes its connections"*.

Philanthropy and altruism

It is important to distinguish between philanthropy and the more general issue of altruism. Philanthropy in the US is as much about the idea that individuals should "do their share" to support the organisations from which they benefit as it is about giving to others. Although instances of giving to support causes used by wealthy donors have been criticised as an abuse of philanthropy, such giving is typical, and not only among the very wealthy. Of course, donors give to organisations they use, as well as wanting to help others to enjoy them too. At the same time, as the donors in the US research recognised, philanthropy can occur in the absence of generosity or a desire to help. A desire for prestige, or to enter a certain social circle, can play a part. Indeed, affluent individuals who are deeply committed to particular causes are often expert at appealing to such motives to elicit donations.

Giving as a norm

Characteristic of the people who formed the basis of the US research is that they live in an environment in which giving is a norm, and regard philanthropy as an obligation that is part of their privileged position. It is seen as a responsibility that goes with success. This is particularly strong in the Jewish community, and as we see in Chapter Four is a feature of those interviewed from that community in the UK too.

Encouraging the practice of giving – the workplace experience

As we see in Chapter Four, those who had worked in the US, or for US employers, referred to their experience of workplace encouragement, or indeed pressure, as an important influence in their learning process. While some initially resented "undue pressure" in what they regarded as a private area of their life, in the end all were positive about the effect of workplace persuasion and example. An element of competition between departments added to the impact. Those whose employers organise and support programmes of community engagement spoke positively about them. Others referred to the practice of encouraging and publishing donations by senior directors – in one example all earning over $\$^1/2$m a year are expected to give 3% of their income.

The broader picture

Philanthropy in the US is a social institution that takes on meaning in the context of a cultural emphasis on individualism and private initiative and a mistrust of government power and large scale bureaucracy. (These themes are not confined to the elite, but are found more generally in American society.) These underlying values provide a framework in terms of which philanthropy as a social institution makes sense. The existence of such a framework is important, as it is not obvious nor necessary that philanthropy would be valued by elites, or anyone else. It would appear that the introduction of tax incentives for giving in other countries, including the UK, has not automatically resulted in fostering comparable levels of philanthropy. At the very least, it argues that for a culture of giving to flourish, tax incentives are not enough; there must be clear expectations of the role of individuals and a belief that the wealthy must take responsibility for certain aspects of society, associated with an ethos of respect for the values of individualism and enterprise which underpin wealth creation.

The UK approach

We need to find a way to encourage those with money as seeing themselves as partners in creating a better society.

(Female, 50s, married entrepreneur)

There is not a tradition of giving so people don't see an obligation to give. Gordon Brown has changed the rules but he hasn't changed society's attitude.

(Male, 50s, self-made/entrepreneur)

The idea that philanthropy in the US is not just about giving, but is about engagement, was expressed by several interviewees in our research. The point was made that although tax incentives are important, philanthropy in the US is a reflection of a whole set of values and attitudes; US-style philanthropy will not flourish with the completely different set of values, class structure and view of the role of the state that exists in the UK.

> *Harvard Business School says 'if you want to be taken seriously, you have to give'. It's the notion of participation. One has a responsibility to participate, not just write a cheque. It's completely different here. Philanthropy is not particularly highly regarded except by a few. There is an embarrassment about being rich and negative attitudes to wealth, particularly in the chattering classes. Condescension is a tool of class. Inevitably, you have scandals but the US celebrates nouveau riche behaviour which includes displays of generosity. The UK Government doesn't understand how the US works. You can't invent parallel value systems. It's about enterprise and self-reliance which is lacking in the UK. The key is the centralisation of power which couldn't be achieved in the US. In the UK lots of people are taking and few are giving (systemically not charitably).*
>
> (Male, 40s, self-made/entrepreneur, and an American now living in the UK, building a business and bringing up his family)

Others referred to the reticence about money and attitudes to wealth creation discussed in Chapter Ten, and compared this with the transparency in the US. We know that wealth and philanthropy are celebrated in the US. These are linked because, it is suggested, attitudes to the reporting of wealth and the reporting of philanthropy are linked.

> *I find Britain's secrecy and shame over money a block on philanthropy. I think we should publish a list of money given away as a percentage of wealth and see what it looks like. I think there are a lot of generous people in this country but I also think that there are a lot of people for whom it is not part of their personal or national culture to give away money. That is a shame.*
>
> (Male, 40s, self-made/professional)

Not everyone would support the "name and shame" approach, including this writer, not least because of the difficulty of establishing a fair and accurate basis of calculation, as discussed in Chapter Two. However, the principle of encouraging others by setting standards and appealing to a range of motivations and aspirations is endorsed by many.

We see that in the US, philanthropy is not just an option provided by wealth but a defining characteristic of the elite. We know that this is not the case in the UK. Hard though it may be to define the social elite, we know that the extent to which elite philanthropy opens doors to the highest levels of British society is limited[2], and that there are many people who are perceived to be members of the upper levels of the social hierarchy in the UK who are not major donors. Furthermore, those who are perceived to aspire to elite status are sometimes despised for apparently displaying their wealth through giving, and such sentiments can be a disincentive.

Let's have more social snobbery! I can't stand people who criticise others for being generous. This criticism is a stance by people who are mean: 'Ah, but she can afford it'. The status is getting better but there is plenty of room to work on it.

(Male, 50s, self-made/professional)

Philanthropy in the US has developed in the absence of a comprehensive welfare state as we would understand it in the UK, particularly as it relates to health provision, and in an environment which is against the idea that the state has a prominent role to play in the provision of welfare and higher education services, cultural facilities and community assets. Not only does support of people's town or city reinforce local pride; it provides a focus for civic engagement[3]. Some of that sense has developed in the UK in recent years. For example, the renaissance and pride in Birmingham was influenced by, and is now reinforced and exploited by, the rise to prominence of the City of Birmingham Symphony Orchestra, and partnership funding for lottery-funded projects has been strongly linked to civic pride. But that pride is not necessarily underpinned by significant private support for capital projects, and outside the North East, North West and Wales, support for community projects was very limited among those interviewed in the UK study[4].

The lack of any relationship with or knowledge of the recipient which is inherent in the provisions of services by the state also minimises the sense of reciprocal responsibility and commitment which was the hallmark of pre-welfare state philanthropy. For many this awareness of mutual obligation and interdependency is essential for a sense of being part of a community. Although such a sense is regarded as a positive aspect of society, as we see in Chapter Five this is not a major motivator for significant giving in many parts of the UK, although it is stronger in rural areas, among those who have inherited wealth and are further away from

[2] One American fundraiser based in the UK told me that it had taken her some time to realise that the royal patron of the charity for which she worked would certainly not ask an individual for money, and that even a very major gift would not produce a private invitation to the home of the patron.

[3] Furthermore, it is understood that in the US there is more flexibility for an individual who uses a community foundation as an institution for managing funds and donor advisory services in comparison with one who endows a private charitable trust.

[4] It is recognised that there are strong community foundations outside the North East in the UK, but none of the interviewees came from areas where this was apparent.

London. Some not in this position regret the absence of such links of mutual dependence in the UK, whose decline is associated with the advancement of the role of the state.

> *I am in favour of dependency – not to lord it, but links of dependency are one of the major social cements and attempts to abolish it are totally dehumanising. If the links are wholly with the state it would be a very unattractive world. A sense of mutual dependency is very desirable and if brought about voluntarily, even better. The profile is increasing because my impression is that in the last 20 years the number that feel that this is a normal and pleasant thing to do has increased. The tax system is making it possible. The reduction in the top rate to 40% transformed attitudes.*
>
> (Male, 50s, self-made/professional)

In considering the status of philanthropy in the UK, while many see it as playing a "cementing" role in society, one or two suggested that in an ideal world it would not be needed. This is the opposite of the US approach.

> *Philanthropy is a necessary evil. It would be better to have a less unequal society where no-one could afford to be a philanthropist. It sometimes concentrates power in the hands of the wrong people. There have been some excellent philanthropists but I wouldn't want to live in a society dominated by gifts of rich people with the values of rich people.*
>
> (Male, 80s, self-made/entrepreneur)

Having said that, they too suggest that a world without giving would be a poorer society.

> *In an ideal world philanthropy shouldn't be needed. But a society where people do voluntary work and give money to those less fortunate is a better society.*
>
> Male, 70s, self-made/entrepreneur)

The impact of being an immigrant society

One aspect of US society is not echoed in the UK. Most families in the US claim at least one great-grandparent as an immigrant, and the majority count an immigrant grandparent in their family. A strong theme which emerged from US research was the extent to which people feel gratitude for a society which gave refuge and economic opportunity. That motivation has been strong in the Jewish community here, and is emerging in some parts of the Asian community, as we see in Chapter Three. As research by the Institute of Jewish Policy Research showed[5], giving in the UK by those of Jewish origin begins within the Jewish community and extends with wealth. This pattern appears in the Asian community, within the different religions. But without further detailed research in the UK it may be hard to distinguish between the impact of gratitude and "putting something back" and the strong influence of traditions of tithing and charitable community support prevalent in Judaism and Islam, for example.

We have touched on the paradox that "outsiders" (whether new rich, members of ethnic minorities or immigrants) may see charitable giving as a way to become an "insider", although in the UK, unlike in the US, giving is not seen as an attribute of the social elite.

> *People are suspicious. Minorities use charitable giving as a way of buying their way in and are often very disillusioned at the end of it. There is a big difference with the US. There everyone wanted to be involved and support the local museum.*
>
> (Male, 30s, self-made/professional)

The welfare state

The antagonism to the welfare state is far less marked in the UK than in the US. As we see in Chapter Ten, virtually every interviewee thought that the state should pay for "basics", and for most people basics included the NHS and education. No-one advocated the abolition of the NHS, and while the cost of the social services is always a cause for concern, it is unlikely that there is the same impetus to "tell them where their dollars can go".

A corollary of the belief in the importance of the welfare stare is the view that it is the task of government to pay for certain things out of taxes. Certainly hospitals, for example, have to work hard to explain why private individuals should be expected to contribute when they are already paying income tax, national insurance and VAT. However, there is a virtually universal recognition that wealthy individuals will always have to top up what government provides, and that whether for hospitals or opera houses, private support can turn the adequate into the excellent. It is suggested that attitudes to this, and the role of the wealthy individual, are changing rapidly.

[5] *Patterns of Charitable Giving among British Jews* Jacqueline Goldberg and Barry A Kosmin Institute of Jewish Policy Research July 1998.

Current attitudes are a result of society's experiment with socialism and high rates of taxation.

(Male, 50s, self-made/professional)

It might be said that we live in a society in which for many decades, the message has been that the state will take responsibility for health, education, pensions, care of the elderly and social welfare, and that tax rates have risen accordingly. Indeed, generations brought up in the welfare democracy do not regard access to basic services as a matter of charity, but one of rights. Rights are reinforced by government. But as research by the Institute for Public Policy Research published in May 2002 showed[6], the increase in demand and perceived patchy quality of service provision mean that many in the categories they interviewed (affluent rather than wealthy) do have a sense of responsibility, but feel it must first be directed to their own (extended) family. *"We're forced into being selfish in order to cover our own needs"*. Rather than dismiss these concerns as "denials" and just excuses, we might wish to explore further the whole area of what is perceived to be the role of government, linking this to the values and attitudes to wealth creation and enterprise which sustain the US standpoint on philanthropy.

Among our interviewees, some advocated that as well as encouraging a culture of giving among the wealthy by celebrating exemplary givers and creating an appropriate tax regime, the state should gradually reduce support in certain areas (suggestions for which varied with the interviewee).

> *It is very, very complicated. We need to separate day-to-day philanthropy from big gifts. Everyday philanthropy doesn't have a bad name and people can see its merits. The problem is: a) it's not a defining characteristic of the elite in the UK; b) we need the demonstration effect – role models – look at the Jewish community; c) justification for excuses relating to the constraints of the tax system are being removed; d) there has been more surplus money in the US for a generation. We need a productive economy; and e) we have had 50 years of the welfare state. The government must gently put the foot on the brake to create need.*
>
> (Male, 50s, self-made/entrepreneur)

[6] *A Bit Rich? What the wealthy think about giving* Laura Edwards May 2002.

The first three points made by this interviewee have been raised elsewhere, but we find two new ideas. The first is that in order for philanthropy to flourish there must be a productive (and, it could be added, stable) economy in which people feel that they have a surplus and can give significant sums with confidence, and the second, that the government must not be seen to do everything; there must be less interference from the state. This was expressed in other ways.

> *The status is much more institutionalised here. The government should provide some safety net but almost anything is better than government programmes.*
>
> (Male, 50s, self-made/professional)

Several mentioned the idea that the welfare state lets potential donors "off the hook", even though income tax rates are relatively much lower than they have been and the prevalent indirect tax structure falls relatively less heavily on the rich. It is more complex than the idea that "the state will pay", but that is part of it.

> *It has improved in the UK but we still have a huge amount to learn from the tax framework in the US. We need to be more imaginative. Will it be more effective to solve the problems of society if you channel money through non-profit organisations rather than the state? We must make it easier.*
>
> (Male, self-made/professional)

However, some observed that attitudes are changing.

> *If you compare the status with the US, it's in pretty bad shape, but it's changing. Look at Oxbridge compared with US universities. Celebrities and the new rich are writing cheques at the end of an evening, US-style. It's beginning to change.*
>
> (Male, 60s, inherited and grew family business)

Comparing the tax structures

> *There are not as many tax breaks here as in the US, the climate in the UK doesn't make it as possible to be as philanthropic.*
>
> (Female, 50s, inherited)

Essentially, people are seeing the use of the tax system in this way as a form of hypothecation – earmarking taxes for a specific purpose. As is pointed out in *The Millionaire Givers*[7], the belief in the US among many donors interviewed that "a free market system fosters a giving

[7] *The Millionaire Givers Wealth and Philanthropy in Britain* Howard Hurd and Mark Lattimer Directory of Social Change 1994.

environment" coexists rather curiously with the way in which high tax rates function as an incentive to give. The highest number of foundations of all sizes was created during the period of highest tax rates in the US. Nevertheless, no-one is suggesting that tax mechanisms alone create a culture of giving. However, they underpin major philanthropy, just as they encourage donations from the less well-off.

Several people made a link between the US culture of giving and the question of tax incentives. In the US, cuts in direct taxation in the late 80s acted as a disincentive to the act of giving itself[8]. "*If it were not for the savings in taxes – the notion that the government really is participating in a gift – I think there would be an awful lot less giving*".

A fundamental difference between the two tax regimes is that in the US it is possible to make an irrevocable gift of a capital sum, obtain tax relief at the time of making the gift, and still enjoy the benefit of the income (which can be assigned, for example to children) from the capital until a specific date, sometimes the death of the donor. If the income is not needed at any stage it can also be donated, with appropriate tax benefit.

The value of the capital gift, and hence the tax relief, is calculated on an actuarial basis, with a discount depending on the donor's age and other factors. The money is put into an escrow or ring-fenced account. The recipient organisation cannot spend it until the donor is dead, or the term of the trust is reached, but it is an asset on the balance sheet (and can be used as collateral for a loan). Furthermore, if it is invested wisely and the value of the capital increases, so too does the value of the donation credited to the benefactor. An alternative approach enables the donor to retain the capital but give the income for a certain period, and obtain the appropriate tax relief.

In these ways, the donor enjoys the benefit of the tax relief at the time of making the gift decision. This is what is meant by most "planned giving" in the US, and it accounts for a significant proportion of major gifts received, particularly for endowments for cultural and educational institutions.

[8] See an article in *Trust Monitor* in 1990 by Mark Lattimer, based on research by Dr Teresa Odendahl conducted with 135 very wealthy US donors in 1987).

As we have seen, many of our interviewees who had lived in the US and the UK, and those with experience of asking for money from US and UK citizens, advocated the merits of mechanisms such as charity remainder trusts. Some commented on the apparent inconsistency in the position of the government which is wedded to the concept of the beneficial influence of tax reliefs for more modest levels of giving but resists it for the very constituency and type of gift (capital) where the impact of the incentive is likely to have a multiplier effect. At the time of interviewing and writing, tax benefits available in the UK are still not equivalent to those in the US for major gifts of capital in the lifetime of the donor.

Planned tax-efficient giving is much further down the road in the US than the UK, precisely because it allows the type of estate planning that enables the donor to benefit before he or she dies. It provides a large degree of flexibility and is a major feature of most endowment campaigns.

It seems to be more often used by people who are either asset rich/cash poor or extremely rich and want to provide for their family but leave the bulk of their estate to charities. This is the case with one donor to a UK cultural organisation who, along with her siblings, is the beneficiary of a $2billion charitable remainder trust promised to four institutions, each of which has pledged to make annual payments to the children for the remainder of their lives. The ability to pay is based on the institutions taking out loans secured on the eventual promise of the gift.

It should be added that one interviewee expressed scepticism about these products. The income benefit may be lower than expected or obtainable elsewhere.

We have already noted the incentive for an individual to place funds with a community foundation rather than a private trust and this may be one factor in accounting for the greater success of such foundations in the US.

Works of art

In the US, arts organisations are soliciting fractional gifts of works of art, using this approach more frequently (increasingly so in an art market where the value of art is ever rising). If someone gives a 10% share of a $10m painting, they receive a $1m tax deduction (spread over seven years if desired). There is a further bonus: for example if they decide to give another 10% in five years' time, when the painting has increased in value to $20m, they get a tax deduction of 10% of $20m – in this case $2million. This can go on until the whole has been given.

The donor prepares a deed of gift for all fractional gifts which start out with a 10% interest, specifying that the remainder will be given either during their lives or on their death. The approach is very flexible. Donors are allowed to keep their works at home for the same percentage of time as the stake they own. In practice this too is flexible and depends on discussion between the institution and themselves. If they die before they have finished giving the work, the estate gets the balance of the tax relief.

In January 2004 the Goodison Review[9] recommended (among other proposals) tax reforms in the UK for gifts of works of art similar to those available in the US, although the tax relief would be based on the valuation at the time of the initial commitment.

Gifts in kind

Another feature of the US system is that tax relief is available on other gifts in kind, not only works of art. This has a major impact on the apparent level of charitable giving in the US. Gifts of old clothes, obsolete computers, redundant toys and a whole range of second-hand goods, including cars, qualify for tax relief. Recipient and donor have a vested interest in assessing the worth of the donated article at its highest probable value. The recipient adds the value of gifts received to the total annual income and the donor obtains a receipt which can be used in the year-end tax process to claim tax relief. This process reminds the taxpayer of the benefits of tax relief, and reinforces the benefits of giving from an early age. It is one of the practices which underpins a culture of giving.

In the UK such giving, which sustains charity shops, organisations for the homeless and other welfare charities, is not "counted" by the donors, nor does it feature in individual giving statistics, although the shop income, for example, will appear in the accounts of the recipient charity. In recent years gifts in kind, including property, jewellery, shares, works of art, cars and food (from the food industry) have accounted for about 25% of US reported giving[10]. Statistics comparing US and UK giving as a percentage of GDP are not comparing like with like.

Other differentials

There are other ways in which the attitudes to wealth and the approach to philanthropy differ between the US and UK. Probably the most significant is in the realm of volunteer activities.

[9] *Goodison Review – Securing the Best for our Museums: Private Giving and Government Support* January 2004.
[10] As reported by Mike Hudson in *Managing at the Leading Edge*, published in March 2004. He points out that there has been a significant increase in non-cash donations in the US; from 1988 to 1997 they grew from 12% to 28% of all gifts. His source is *The New Profit Almanac and Desk Reference*, Murray Weitzman et al, Independent Sector, 2002.

Board membership and other involvement

Volunteer activities, particularly board membership, turned out to be of major importance for giving among the wealthy in the US. Among the elite, contributions of money are part of an overall involvement with non-profit organisations. In the US elites have played a major role in founding, sustaining and overseeing non-profit organisations.

Francie Ostrower found that 75% of her interviewees served on a non-profit board, and 78% raised funds for various organisations. It should be remembered that the sample selection was based entirely on monetary contributions, with no regard for volunteer activities. With striking frequency the largest gifts went to organisations with which the donor has a relationship other than as a giver. Board membership, being a user of the services and having a close relationship with someone linked to the organisation were key factors. This was true for over 90% of all gifts in the areas of health, education, culture and religion. With the exception of donations to the place of worship, educational institutions and hospitals, board membership was the most frequently cited relationship.

For example, nearly 45% of the largest gifts to cultural organisations went to those where the donor was a board member. The figure was the same in the sector addressing rights, advocacy and policy issues. The figure was about half that for educational institutions and hospitals, for which the key factor was having attended (well over 40%) or the illness of a family member (a third).

These findings were echoed by the Boston-based research, which found that 71% of those interviewed serve on a board, and over 75% engage in fundraising activities. Over half were involved in event planning.

As the US research shows, there are two aspects to the importance of board membership. The first is the fact that personal involvement provides the opportunity for learning about the organisation and its needs and for sharing responsibility for its success. This leads to the second: organisational involvement, in the form of board membership, which entails an obligation to donate. As one said: "*you don't dare go onto a board without being prepared to give*".

Another explained: "*I look at my other board members and whether they contribute. There's pressure to give because you're on the board... and you try to put the bite on them. But... I'd call it community. It's your circle of friends.*"

In our research well under 40% of interviewees were on the board of a charity (apart from their own foundation), compared with over 70% in the US research, and apart from the 10 askers only about 10% engage in fundraising activities. The need to construct creative and credible opportunities for the involvement of major donors features in Chapter Seven, and the reported sense of satisfaction with such involvement was considerable.

More than one US citizen and major donor now based in London compared their experiences of charities in the UK unfavourably with their US counterparts.

> *'The sense of the donor as someone to be exploited simply for their financial resources is a mistake in my view...it is not conducive to charitable giving'.*
>
> (Female, 50s, American)

She, and others, suggested that there should be mixed boards: there should be expertise in child care, or theatre direction, but "*the ideal board member is someone who either has great expertise in a field, is a major donor, an effective fundraiser – or ideally all three*". They recognised that UK boards may have a wider brief than US boards, but more than one described situations in which, as they perceived it, "*board members are sometimes not particularly expert in the given area nor do they give financially*".

In the UK the boards of major educational and cultural institutions, and charities generally, have a far broader responsibility than fundraising, and hence a broader range of people serve on them, many of them not monied. Some interviewees reported concerns expressed by organisations with which they had been associated about what they perceive to be the dangers of a board controlled and driven by major donors. The organisations did not always recognise that donors may have something to contribute, underpinned by a real passion for, and knowledge of, the cause. They may not accept the relevance of commercial experience in corporate governance. The dictum attributed to the role of US board members - "give, get or get off" – was quoted with disdain. But at the same time, few charities have found a means of involving major donors in a way which genuinely respects and harnesses their commitment and expertise – and is therefore likely to enhance their giving.

Financial security
Just under half of the US interviewees in the *Wealth with Responsibility* research, based on 112 wealthy individuals, reported a level of net worth

below $20m. Some 57% of the UK interviewees placed themselves at below £20m. About a quarter of UK respondents assessed their net worth at over £50m, compared with 28% at over $50m in the US. In other words, the samples are broadly comparable. In the US study virtually all respondents placed themselves above the mid point in a self-assessed scale from 0 (not at all secure) to 10 (completely secure).

As we see in Chapter Eight, about three-quarters of UK respondents placed themselves in this position. It will be remembered that the US research relied on the completion of multiple choice questionnaires, dispatched and returned by post, whereas the UK research was based on face-to-face interviews. Nevertheless, notwithstanding the variations in methodology there does appear to be a real difference. It may be partly accounted for by the timing of the interviews in the UK (during 2002) but as has been observed, the age of "new wealth" in the UK is much more recent than in the US.

Satisfaction with giving

Although more satisfied than not with the effectiveness of their donations, the vast majority in the US thought there was room for improvement in their charitable giving, with 40% indicating that risk of mismanagement or corruption in some charities limited the amount they now contribute. This is in sharp contrast to findings of the UK research, reported in Chapters Five and Seven. Here, nearly 60% are very satisfied with the effectiveness of their donations, and a very significant minority would do nothing differently, with many others feeling it was too soon to tell.

It would seem that while some people were concerned about potential mismanagement, particularly in the field of overseas aid, this was a very small proportion of the total. None of the regretted donations were related to financial mismanagement, and most people affirmed that having checked beforehand they gave with confidence.

General factors likely to increase charitable giving

To learn which factors are most likely to lead to increased giving, respondents were asked to rate how likely each of six changes would be to increase their giving. The UK responses are reported in Chapter Five. It can be seen that there are major differences, with the apparent evidence that tax incentives and better information about tax benefits are less important in the UK.

Factors which would increase giving

	UK	US
Interviewees	76	112
Proportion citing factors which would increase giving*	%	%
Increased net worth	75	65
New cause about which care passionately	55	90
Increased tax incentives	35	65
More time to think about philanthropy	25	45
Better information that donations are making a difference	10	65
Better information about the tax benefits	5	20

*Figures rounded

Despite the different base there does seem to be a significant difference: finding a new cause of passionate concern, important for about 55% of UK respondents, was the most important factor in the US Boston-based research: over 90% said it would increase their giving. Increase in net worth, important for 65% of US respondents, was the key factor for over 75% of the UK interviewees. There are of course always several factors at play, and there are different combinations for different people.

A possible interpretation of this data is that many of the UK respondents were in essence saying that unless they had more money they would not be giving more away, however enticing the cause. It will be remembered that half already had a charitable trust, some endowed with capital from the sale of a business. Feelings of financial security are far less pronounced in the UK. While increased net worth is a pre-determinant on both sides of the Atlantic, lack of confidence about giving away capital combined with the absence of a tax incentive for such lifetime giving means that having more money is a relatively more important issue in the UK. In addition, although those who know about the different mechanisms in the US are strong advocates of such incentives as charity remainder trusts, the majority of UK respondents were apparently unaware of these possibilities. Tax reliefs for charitable trusts, gifts of shares and one-off donations have all improved in the UK in recent years, and the 50% of respondents who had already established charitable trusts did not see themselves as increasing their lifetime giving because of further tax incentives.

It is interesting to observe the difference in the approach to the availability of time, particularly given the major commitment to board and committee involvement on the part of US donors. Juxtaposed with the much higher level of confidence in the provision of information by charities in the UK, and less concern about financial mismanagement, it could imply that UK donors do not see themselves as constrained by the absence of easily available high quality financial data.

It is recognised that there are several factors influencing these findings, and each respondent will demonstrate a different picture. Notwithstanding this, there is a significant pattern in both countries: perceptions of and confidence in the level of their wealth together with passionate engagement with a cause are more important than intellectual comprehension, and relatively much more important in the UK than in the US. The wealthy understand and express a combination of material realism and emotional idealism. Increased wealth and improved tax benefits provided the foundation for increasing the supply of charitable dollars or pounds; intensity of emotional engagement activates that substantive resource. Respondents in both countries are virtually unanimous in saying that significant charitable commitment derives from finding a cause to feel passionate about. Fuller information about the allocation and impact of donations, and more time to study a cause are of course important, particularly, it would appear, in the US. As we have seen, an unsatisfactory assessment of financial competence and effectiveness would deter a donor in the UK and, it must be assumed, in the US. But in generating additional generosity, the evaluation process is secondary to a feeling of greater wealth and emotional engagement.

Focus of giving

While the *Wealth with Responsibility* survey did not obtain sufficient information to categorise the various organisations to which the very wealthy contribute time and money, it did ask about the policy issues in which the respondents felt their wealth could have an effective influence. The most frequently mentioned policy issues generally revolve around developing human capital, such as improvement of education, reduction of poverty and hunger, promotion of arts and culture, and strengthening family stability.

Francie Ostrower's research showed that about 70% supported education, 43% culture, 30% hospitals and 29% social services. 15% supported churches or other places of worship. The *Wealth with Responsibility* research showed that although wealthy people support their places of worship at a rate higher than the general population in the US, they are even more likely to contribute to charities in general[11]. This is consistent with a well-known general tendency, namely that the wealthier donors are, the more likely they are to contribute a greater proportion of their total donations to these non-religious organisations. In the UK, for example, the report of the Institute of Jewish Policy Research already cited[12] shows that as people become wealthier their philanthropy extends beyond the synagogue and the welfare services associated with it.

These findings do not mean that American wealthy people are less dedicated to their congregational life than the rest of the population in the US, nor does it mean that they are less committed to religious causes or less motivated by religious impulses than they used to be. It only means that the religious organisation category was defined, as in the UK research, to mean places of worship, such as temples, churches, synagogues, or mosques. Unless there are major capital campaigns, wealthy people are not generally called upon to make large gifts to their places of worship. Requests for major gifts are likely to be infrequent because the operational budgets of congregations are relatively small and will be shared among the congregation as a whole.

In the UK, contributions to place of worship were a negligible interest reported by interviewees. We believe that this disparity is largely cultural, as church attendance is both more common and more frequent in the US than the UK. Even among Jewish and Asian respondents, such donations formed a small proportion of the total giving, for the reasons given above. The main areas of interest, as we see in Chapter Two, were arts and culture, social welfare, education and health and medical research. There was a minority interest in overseas development (perhaps supported by the interest of members of the Asian community) and the environment.

The higher emphasis on education in the US may be attributed in part to the significant level of giving to schools and universities attended by the interviewee or members of their family. Nevertheless, apart from the

---

[11] According to the report, *Giving and Volunteering in the United States: 2001*, published by Independent Sector, 69% of households contributed to religious institutions in 2000, giving over three times as much to these organisations as they did to other charities.

[12] *Patterns of Charitable Giving among British Jews* Jacqueline Goldberg and Barry A. Kosmin Institute of Jewish Policy Research July 1998.

interest in religion, and with some differences in emphasis, we see that on both sides of the Atlantic a major focus of philanthropy seems to be a strategy of investing in and developing individual potential – providing opportunities for those from underprivileged backgrounds and at the same time improving the conditions of the poor and disadvantaged. Interest in the arts was as much about investing in talent and creativity as about improving the venues enjoyed by all.

There is another significant difference between the US and the UK. Americans are more likely to give to political candidates and parties than are Britons. For example, 10% to 15% of Americans donate to political candidates[13]. It is difficult to obtain comparable data, but membership of the main parties in the UK is about 750,000 – well under 4% of adults. A negligible number of our survey participants contributed to political parties. This divergence in campaign donations is due, we believe, to the different structures of the political systems in the two countries, as well as to campaigning practices and fundraising strategies. Furthermore, political parties in the UK are not legal charities, and so our survey participants may have excluded any political contributions when discussing their charitable giving, although the question about support of political activities was asked. However, we also attribute insignificant political contributions to a general ambivalence about political affiliation. When asked to describe their political affiliation, only one-fifth of the UK survey participants indicated a strong alignment with a major political party.

Key points

We have noted the very different attitudes to wealth creation and the role of the state, and we have also observed the importance of philanthropy as an essential behaviour pattern of the social elite. We have commented on the importance of board membership and active volunteer engagement. Changing attitudes and practices in these areas will take time. There are several findings from both the US and UK research which have particular relevance for the Treasury, employers, fundraisers, charity professionals, and others who advise wealthy people about their finances and philanthropy. These are discussed in the Chapter Fifteen.

As the *Wealth with Responsibility* paper puts it, broadly stated, its research reports on the relation between material resources and moral purposes. The findings do not confirm that all people of wealth or affluence will pursue the most intelligent and caring allocation of their

[13] Michael Signer, *Don't Hooverize, Voucherize!: A New Way To Clean-Up American Politics*, www.tompaine.com March 23, 2000.

material assets. The findings do establish however, that the wealthy, like most other people, are asking and responding to the question of how to deploy their assets in the service of values and interests other than those associated with the accumulation of wealth.

The paper quotes Aristotle as stating that the purpose of life is happiness, and that the path to happiness is wise choices. One consistent finding from nearly two decades of research on wealth and philanthropy by the authors of *Wealth and Responsibility* is that a fundamental characteristic of wealth is the latitude it provides for choice. We have seen that this feature is prominent in our UK research too. Although being wealthy does not intrinsically lead to wise choices in regard to oneself or others, it does broaden the range and effect of the choices that are made. The findings of the research studies reported here show how the rich in the US plan and implement the charitable purposes of their vast material resources.

Our UK research enables us for the first time to paint a comparable picture of what happens here. The majority of those interviewed were enjoying levels of wealth unimagined by their parents, and many were doing so in the absence of current membership of a strong faith-based community. They had been brought up in the traditions and expectations of the welfare state, and in a society in which opinion formers appear to have ambivalent attitudes to wealth and wealth creation. The disparity between their wealth and those of their peers was also substantial. It is clear that, aware of these circumstances, many are exploring whether and how best to allocate their surplus assets for the benefit of society. This report has endeavoured to map their questions, searches, experiences and ideas.

In Chapter Fifteen we set out in detail the implications of these findings and recommendations based on them. Equipped with this greater understanding, it is hoped that the public, charities and other non-profit organisations, regulatory authorities, government, financial and legal advisers, the media, and wealthy people themselves will be better positioned to reflect on how individual assets are to be allocated in the service of wise decisions, and the UK can encourage a culture of giving.

15

Implications and recommendations

There are messages for several different audiences arising from the analysis of this research into the attitudes of the wealthy in the UK at the start of the 21st century. Many of those interviewed come from a strong philanthropic and community tradition, and expect to engage in charitable giving as part of how they allocate their discretionary spending. However others, also brought up in a welfare state but with no immediate experience or examples of philanthropic role models, are unclear about their social obligations, uncertain about what might be expected of them and do not move in a society in which such obligations and expectations are explicit.

A number of people want to change that. They want to encourage a social order in which the wealthy see it as part of their role to enhance the cities and communities in which they live, to put something back into the society of which they are part, to invest in talent and creativity, to support the individuals and organisations which sustain the ill, the vulnerable and the disadvantaged and generally to leave the world a better place.

In this chapter we draw on the research to provide some signposts as to how this might be done, and some suggestions for areas of further work. Some issues need to be addressed by more than one group, and these are indicated. We look at each constituency in turn.

Non-profit sector

This covers a diffuse but crucial group of institutions and umbrella bodies including individual charities, community foundations, lobbying groups and membership and training organisations.

Charities

Passion for the cause and relationships with recipients

A constant theme of this research has been that a passion for the cause is the most powerful determinant of major and sustained charitable giving. Donors report consistently and across all sectors their desire to:

◆ Make a difference and be a catalyst for change.
◆ Be appreciated and respected for their support and the expertise which is the source of their wealth.
◆ Be concerned with governance, effective management and accountability.
◆ Have relationships with senior staff in the recipient organisation, including those who deliver the mission, ultimate beneficiaries (where appropriate) and other donors to reinforce the commitment to the cause and make giving enjoyable and fun.

We also noted that badly managed relationships were the main cause of many regretted donations. Interviewees added that while an introduction from someone they respect may influence an initial relatively low level contribution, serious commitment will only develop as a result of the factors above.

(See Chapter Four on the early influence of being well managed, Chapter Five on motivations and Chapter Six on expectations and rewards of well-managed relationships.)

We also learned three other key points about the characteristics of the wealthy.

Disposition of wealth

People are unlikely to leave large legacies to charities with which they have had no relationship. We saw that the 50% of interviewees who have a charitable trust are more likely to leave a charitable legacy to their trust than directly to a charity, but virtually no-one had been asked effectively for a legacy.

There was a range of views about the split between charitable giving in the lifetime of the interviewees and the likely allocation of their wealth on death. In many cases there was concern about the risks of passing too much money to their children. Most interviewees were self-made and appeared to think that their children should also have to strive to achieve a high standard of living, at least to some extent. Advisers were sceptical about the extent to which the new generation of wealthy people would, in the end, disinherit their children. However, this is clearly an area in which, except in the case of family businesses, traditions of retaining money within the family may not be sacrosanct. Many of those interviewed were still in the process of developing their ideas.

(See Chapter Eight on questions of inter-generational wealth transfer and Chapter Twelve for the views of professional advisers.)

Being self-made

The majority of wealthy people (in the surveys on both sides of the Atlantic) derived the bulk of their wealth from their business and professional efforts rather than from inheritance. As Paul Schervish[1] has observed, for such people to transfer the focus of their financial efforts to giving away money, in addition to or in place of accumulation, requires an explicit process of self-reflection and self-education. This is particularly the case for those who do not come from a philanthropic tradition. In the UK this is partly about the attitudes and values of society, and the expectations and responses of decision-makers and opinion-formers to wealth creation and entrepreneurs.

(See Chapter Two on the background of the interviewees, Chapter Ten on perceptions of philanthropy and wealth creation and Chapter Fourteen on the US experience.)

Sensitivity to sound financial management

A feature from the US research is the sensitivity of wealthy people to sound financial management of charitable organisations. Even before the terrorist attacks of September 11th 2001, a considerable group of wealthy people, (40% of the respondents in Paul Schervish's research) were already limiting the amount they contributed to certain charities because of worry about the risks of financial mismanagement and corruption. Since then these concerns have been reinforced in the minds of the general public, based on publicity surrounding the two issues of how those affected by the World Trade Centre bombings were to be compensated, and the role of certain charities in soliciting, managing, and disbursing funds.

[1] In *The Mind of the Millionaire,* January 2002.

Less concern was expressed in the UK research; most people relied on the reputation of the charity and the fact that someone they respected was involved, and had confidence in the underlying regulatory system; if concerned they would check in advance. Although there were reservations about certain generic areas (for example overseas development), knowing that the donation had made a difference was more important.

(See Chapter Six on concerns about financial mismanagement.)

But this does not mean that charities in the UK should be complacent, and the advent of Guidestar UK[2] will mean that donors will be in a position to compare charities in similar fields and at comparable stages of development. With reports issued by organisations such as the charity New Philanthropy Capital, increasing amounts of information will be easily available in the public domain.

There are several implications from these findings.

1. Charities interested in developing and maintaining long-term support from major donors should:

◆ **Be prepared to invest in initiating and managing relationships in a way which addresses the interests and concerns of the donor, involves their partner, if they have one, shows how they have made a difference, is tailored to their wishes and is the responsibility of a single senior person.**

◆ **Consider how to involve high level supporters in a way which demonstrates respect for the expertise which is the source of their wealth, and addresses legitimate concerns about governance and accountability.**

◆ **Involve trustees and senior staff in the cultivation of prospects and donors, including asking them for money, and helping them to develop a real understanding of the issues facing the organisation, supported by an agreed programme of engagement, recognition and feedback.**

◆ **Ensure that those likely to solicit support from potential major donors understand and promote tax-effective giving, and that donors are credited for the gross amount received.**

[2] Based on an American model, this is a computer-based system which from 2005 will provide freely available data on registered charities in a common format.

◆ **Develop and promote a legacy strategy which builds on the personal relationship between donor, charity and its senior staff, and is seen as an extension of an individual programme of engagement.**

Based on the evidence from the research and drawing on my own experience of fundraising over nearly 20 years, there are further implications for charities.

2. In order to achieve long-term support from major donors, charities need to develop a corporate culture in which:

◆ **Fundraising and the development of these relationships are seen as integral to the mission of the organisation; securing long-term financial security should complement the programme activities.**

◆ **Job descriptions, work plans and person specifications at senior level throughout the organisation take account of the need to give effective time to nurturing relationships with potential and actual major donors.**

◆ **Budgets take account of the need for long-term investment in developing relationships, and for detailed prospect research, including the identification of the person best placed to introduce the prospect to the work of the charity.**

◆ **Within the fundraising department there is one "account manager" for each major donor, whether the donor allocates resources from their personal or from corporate assets.**

◆ **Consideration is given to the need for investment in trustee recruitment and training, so that, as with senior and specialist staff, trustees see the fostering of partnerships with donors, and in some case asking them for money, as part of their role.**

◆ **Consideration is given to the place of major donors on a board, and the idea that, as in the US, board members should be expected to give according to their means (whether that is £5 or £5m).**

The question of the tax structure is discussed in the next section. Any advocacy for change should involve charities themselves.

3. Charities should join with others to lobby for tax relief for lifetime gifts and gifts in kind and the simplification of Gift Aid.

Those who are leaders of non-profit organisations – and there are some 1.5 million charity trustees in the UK – and fundraisers themselves can do much to assist potential donors to turn their attention to charity. Such activity will be much more effective if they help potential donors to tap, rather than submerge, the self-determination, desire to be effective, entrepreneurial spirit and intellectual acumen that have characterised their business and investment activities. Their success in achieving this will provide greater personal rewards for donors and encourage larger charitable contributions for their causes.

Community foundations

We have seen the powerful impact of the community foundation in the North East. This is based on the combination of a very solid community feeling and the influence of a strong and committed director and support team. However, throughout the entire interview base we noted the interest in making a difference, in seeing how the money is spent, in supporting talented or disadvantaged individuals and the powerful influence of being part of a community or network. There would appear to be opportunities to attract donors who feel a connection to the local community, when:

◆ They can see how their money is spent.
◆ It can be used to embellish local facilities.
◆ Relatively small sums can make a major difference.
◆ There can be rewarding relationships with beneficiaries, other donors and the staff of the community foundation.
◆ There is minimal administrative bureaucracy.

However, we noted that expressions of feelings of community were minimal in London, although there were a few commitments to individual boroughs.

(See Chapter Three for influences and Chapter Five on motivations.)

4. The Community Foundation Network should encourage further investment in the development of strong local foundations.

As with charities, the role of volunteer leaders who will themselves give and encourage others to do so will be crucial.

5. Community foundations should work with others to develop a framework and provide guidance on appropriate levels of giving.

The Community Foundation Network is growing in strength and coverage. As the experience and effectiveness of the network develops, it should have a positive and exponential impact on philanthropy in the community.

Umbrella and membership organisations

Several organisations have a professional interest in one or more aspects of the work of the charitable sector. Some, such as the Charities Aid Foundation, feature in this report. Others, such as the Institute of Fundraising, have an interest in the effective promotion of fundraising, and assuring adherence to professional standards of fundraising, reporting and benchmarking. The Charity Tax Reform Group and The European Association of Planned Giving has been advocating the introduction of US-style planned giving products. The Giving Campaign has been actively engaged in the promotion of charitable giving.

Without identifying every such entity, it is clear that there would be benefits to the sector as a whole if there were a collaborative approach to and participation in many of the recommendations in this chapter.

In particular these might include:

6. Promotion of changes in the tax system.

7. Participation in a debate on appropriate levels of giving, and how to help people discern their true level of financial security.

8. Collection and publication of better and more informed statistics and benchmarking information.

9. The development and marketing of training courses for leaders and trustees to ensure that they understand the implications of this work for major donor development.

Government

Treasury

Government ministers and others have frequently referred to the desirability of emulating US levels of giving, particularly among the wealthy. As we see in Chapter Fourteen, apart from the different bases of calculation there are many reasons why a different approach has developed. Most are matters of history, values and tradition, and will be slow to change, although many of the recommendations in this chapter attempt to facilitate that process.

However, practices in the US are sustained by a tax regime in which there are four significant differences:

◆ Planned giving of capital in the lifetime of the donor is underpinned by tax mechanisms which permit the donor to make an irrevocable commitment to a gift at a later date, enjoy tax relief at the time of the pledge, and retain or allocate the income on the capital.

◆ This approach is also adapted for works of art; part-ownership can be transferred year-by-year, with tax relief given for the calculated value of the fraction of the gift at current market price.

◆ Gifts in kind at all levels are eligible for tax relief.

◆ Tax benefits are the same for each giving mechanism, including gifts in kind, and go to the donor.

Planned giving and split interest trusts

We have seen that the very wealthy in the US channel about two-thirds of their charitable giving through gift funds, trusts, and foundations. About half of the respondents in the UK research have established charitable trusts.

This may represent a tendency among wealthy people to organise their giving in a way that offers them the opportunity to control the timing, incidence and level of gifts; to vary the recipients over time; to co-ordinate family involvement; and, in the US, to synchronise charitable giving with their changing financial needs. The charitable trust mechanism in the UK is a well tried approach for those who are in a position (financially and psychologically) to make an irrevocable decision to allocate capital and its associated income to charitable causes. No-one interviewed in the UK was using a trust as a device to transfer regular earned income. As we have seen, planned giving in the US is supported by fiscal benefits which provide an opportunity for strategic philanthropy which is simply not available in the UK.

We know that major giving is linked to passionate engagement and involvement. The level of giving to institutions where donors are involved is relatively high. However, whereas in the UK research about a third give 80% or more of their donations to causes where they are directly involved, in similar US research it is double this – about 70%. Of course, there are major issues here related to governance and board development, discussed in relations to charities earlier in this chapter. Nevertheless, the mechanisms available to sustain that giving are also relevant.

(See Chapter Five on motivations and Chapter Fourteen for comparisons with the US.)

As we report in Chapter Nine, several of those interviewed in the UK research would advocate the implementation of US-style planned giving products in the UK. This alone would not change attitudes, but it seems possible that in time it would have a very significant impact on giving by the wealthy, as they become more confident in the knowledge that they can control the timing of the transfer of capital. This is what happened with the introduction of mechanisms such as the charity remainder trust in the US. This gives tax relief for gifts of capital at the time that the irrevocable promise to give is made, even if the date of receipt is some time in the future, for example at the death of the donor.

A number of organisations have been promoting the implementation in the UK of this approach. The mechanisms encourage long-term planning and wealth allocation while addressing donor concerns about security of income. Because the recipient is confident of the gift they nurture the donor in a manner appropriate for a committed major giver. The donor enjoys all the benefits of a relationship with the recipient organisation and other donors, explored in detail in Chapter Six. Well managed, such association may lead to further support, and the wider family will experience the rewards of appreciation and recognition. The beneficiary organisation can develop strategies based on a secure income stream, and borrow against the security of the future gift for capital developments.

It is this kind of model which underpins the endowments of great educational and cultural institutions in the US; it is estimated that over 40% of the value of such endowments is based on planned giving arrangements[3].

10. Mechanisms similar to the US charity remainder trust and other split interest models should be introduced in the UK, with the same fiscal treatment as in the US.

Gifts of works of art

The report of the Goodison Review, published in January 2004, recommended changes in the tax treatment of gifts of works of art. The evidence of this research strongly supports those recommendations.

Wealthy people (and their professional advisers) respond to a mechanism which enables them to make a long-term and strategic plan relating to the disposal of their assets, including non-financial assets. They are informed about the benefits and tax mechanisms, and are far more likely to take a holistic and long-term approach to gifts of capital, including works of art. Many of those who are likely to own and collect significant works of art pursue their interests in several countries. They are aware of what their fellow donors and enthusiasts who are US citizens are able to arrange. Were such changes to be made in the UK tax system, it would also acknowledge that major donors operate in an international marketplace, particularly in the arts.

11. The proposals set out in the Goodison Review relating to the tax treatment of donations of works of art should be implemented[4].

Gifts in kind

US donors of relatively modest objects (such as second-hand clothes, cars and computers) receive a certificate indicating the value of the donation from the recipient charity. This can be used as the basis of a tax claim and inculcates the idea of the benefits of tax-efficient giving at a relatively early age and modest income levels.

It is possible that this approach would be open to abuse. In the US there is current concern[5] that individuals and companies are taking over-generous deductions for gifts of non-cash items. Politicians are looking into limiting such deductions, or establishing systems for obtaining independent valuation and more effective monitoring by the Internal Revenue Service.

[3] See for example paper by Peter Mimpriss in *Update*, Allen and Overy, January 2002.

[4] The comments are limited to the recommendations in the Goodison Review on tax treatment because it is those which are substantiated by this research.

[5] Reported in the *Chronicle of Philanthropy* 1 April 2004.

However, as with works of art, it should be possible to devise mechanisms which restrict the opportunities for fraud. The benefits of such an approach outweigh the disadvantages.

12. Consideration should be given to the introduction of a system in which donations in kind attract tax relief.

Gift Aid

We note in Chapter Seven that although many of those interviewed understand tax mechanisms, they still find them complicated, especially Gift Aid. The same is true of share giving, made more difficult by the lack of consistent advice from Inland Revenue offices. Very few volunteer leaders can explain Gift Aid clearly. Many charities do not understand it, and have not established systems to collect the tax due to them, in some cases because they perceive the necessary investment as too high. Estimates of unclaimed Gift Aid range from about £400m to approaching £1bn. Donors themselves dislike a system in which the amount of tax relief for a donation depends on the giving mechanism, and informed donors resent the cost to charities of the bureaucracy associated with collecting the Gift Aid due to them. There is also some irritation that charities do not always credit the donor for the gross sum received.

Outside the boundaries of this research, it is realised that, as with the use of Gift Aid for entrance tickets to heritage sites and museums which the government is currently reviewing, there is a vested interest in the current complex system. Many charities have invested in systems and training to promote Gift Aid, and fear the loss in income from donors who would not gross up their donation[6]. They cite the experience with corporate donations, when a change in the system directing tax relief to companies did not result in an equivalent rise in corporate support. However, in that case there were different decision-makers: in most cases the tax relief was retained by the finance department for the company as a whole; the community affairs budget was unchanged, at least in relation to any tax relief.

Income might drop slightly in first year or two after any change for those charities who have invested in promoting Gift Aid; this would appear to penalise alert and effective organisations, and perhaps would have to be compensated for in some way over an interim period. The director of fundraising of a major organisation in receipt of a seven-figure sum from Gift Aid, and a member of the reference group for this research, told the

[6] Expressed, for example, in correspondence in *Third Sector* in 2003, and discussions at meetings organised by The Giving Campaign.

author in April 2004 that he would favour a US-style approach, even though he recognises it might take a few years to regain the current income level. This is because he is confident that in the long run the donor response and the administrative cost savings would outweigh the short-term disadvantage and income drop. For charities as a whole it would be much easier to explain, much cheaper to promote – publicity materials and examples would not have to be changed every time tax rates change – and much cheaper to administer.

13. A review should be undertaken of the advantages and disadvantages of retaining the current approach to Gift Aid. As part of the review, consideration could be given to interim arrangements for those organisations currently in receipt of substantial Gift Aid claims.

Tax returns

It has been suggested that the tax relief should be the same irrespective of the donation mechanisms, with all the relief going to the donor. Simple receipts could be provided to the donor, who would report the giving on an annual tax return. The form could prompt the taxpayer to consider whether they had given the maximum for which they could claim a tax allowance.

In the US the practice of completing annual tax returns is both a reminder of the charitable commitments made in the year and an opportunity to consider whether the taxpayer has made the most of the possibility of income tax relief in that tax year.

14. Further steps should be taken to use the occasion of the annual tax return process to alert taxpayers to the opportunities and options for tax relief for charitable giving.

Inland Revenue and Customs & Excise

We have noted complaints about inconsistent treatment of benefits for donors, particularly in the arts and heritage sector. We have also reported the experience of those asking for money, and apparent lack of consistent guidance by tax offices, particularly about gifts of shares.

(See Chapter Six for benefits and special access, and Chapter Eleven on the experience of askers.)

15. The treatment of benefits, the application of VAT regulations and guidance on tax mechanisms should not depend on the individual tax office or Customs & Excise official. There should be clear guidelines which can be applied across the country, to ensure consistency.

Home Office

To the extent that the strength and independence of the charity sector depends on how much money it raises from those with most capacity to give, it is essential that the underlying messages about the motivations of potential major donors, and what they seek in the relationships with the organisations they support, are heard by those seeking funds.

The initiation and maintenance of those relationships require investment. The investment is not only necessary for research and for individual donor management. As we have seen, fundraisers need to strengthen their understanding of giving mechanisms and present them in a way which is not only about a financial transaction, but as a means to philanthropy that is mutually beneficial to donors and recipients[7].

Organisations need to consider how to involve the interested donor. A crucial aspect of this is the question of governance, the role of trustees, and their recruitment and performance. Also of key importance are the concepts of accountability, the process of evaluation and measurement of effectiveness and impact, and a commitment to transparency on these issues.

With the introduction of the new Charities Bill, it is essential that the Charity Commission, which has issued new guidelines on effective charities[8], and other organisations with an interest in the sector, present reliable and clear advice.

The Home Office has a unique perspective on the voluntary sector, and links across a range of government departments and non-profit organisations.

16. The Home Office should help co-ordinate a strategic approach which, among many other objectives, will show those with substantial means that they are needed and will be welcome as partners in the strengthening of civil society.

[7] *The Guide to Giving*, available on the *Philanthropy* UK website and from the Association of Charitable Foundations, provides a comprehensive and clear guide for donors to all the giving mechanisms.
[8] CC60 *The Hallmarks of an Effective Charity*, issued in April 2004.

315

Department of Trade and Industry (DTI)

The importance of workplace experience as an influence on giving is noted in Chapter Four, and the implications for the corporate sector are explored later in this chapter.

17. Consideration should be given to encouraging companies to include in annual reports not only accounts of corporate social responsibility programmes and the allocation of shareholder funds (perhaps as a share of profits) to charitable causes, but also a policy statement about employee giving, the extent of payroll giving, and any expectations of levels of personal giving by directors and senior staff.

Department of Culture, Media and Sport (DCMS)

We have noted that the arts and culture are major beneficiaries of those in our survey, particularly among older donors. (See Chapter Two.) This may have been distorted by the number of lottery-funded arts projects seeking support in the period prior to the research – a phenomenon also observed in the National Audit Office report on funding Museum and Galleries published in January 2004[9]. Nevertheless, the arts are of major interest as a focus of support, including small companies and talented individuals as well as national institutions. Enjoyment of the arts and associated activities such as collecting were among the reported opportunities of being wealthy. (See Chapter Nine.)

It is in this sector where, in the US, the twin influences of planned giving products to underpin endowments and the involvement of major donors as board members are among the strongest. It is also here (among other sectors) where we see the reinforcing power of relationships – with the institution, with the creative artists and experts, and with other donors.

(See Chapter Fourteen for the US experience.)

The National Audit Office report mentioned above highlights the need for a more entrepreneurial approach to income generation, and the requirement for trustees and senior management to understand the need for and support investment in the necessary recruitment and training. The need for development (fundraising) to have appropriate status and resources is also noted.

[9] As reported in Chapter Two.

DCMS is already investing in programmes to encourage individual philanthropy in the arts, through its support of the Maecenas Initiative established by Arts & Business in March 2004.

Recognition of the need for the leaders of arts institutions to have a range of skills beyond those of scholarship and institutional management, and of the lack of widespread availability of a pool of talent from which to draw, has also led to the development of the Clore-Duffield Leadership Programme[10] .

18. Drawing on the experience of that programme, the work funded by the Treasury (the National Audit Office report and the Goodison Review), its own investment in the Maecenas initiative and the findings of this research, DCMS should:

◆ **Give clear guidance to organisations in the arts and heritage sectors about the role and responsibilities of trustees in developing and managing relationships with major donors.**

◆ **Encourage a diverse range of skills and networks on boards, including those conducive to the identification and involvement of potential high level supporters.**

◆ **Working with others such as the Treasury, support the implementation of the recommended changes to and simplification of tax mechanisms, and a consistent approach to advice from the Inland Revenue and others on permissible benefits.**

Department for Education and Skills

Schools

While it is impossible to plan for the religious and family experience of individuals, the importance of the influence of school was mentioned by several people. (See Chapter Four.) Undoubtedly, investing in and supporting effective schools programmes which include volunteering as well as fundraising would have a major impact in the long term. The work of The Giving Campaign in developing *The Giving Nation* is to be commended[11].

19. The development of the citizenship component in the national curriculum should be strongly supported, and opportunities for volunteer activities incorporated into the programme.

[10] Funded by the Clore-Duffield Foundation, this was set up in 2003 and is directed by Chris Smith, former Secretary of State for Culture, Media and Sport.

[11] Building on the new citizenship curriculum, The Giving Campaign developed *The Giving Nation* to help young people understand and participate in giving.

Universities

The research indicates a wide range of views about the extent to which preferential treatment for suitably qualified children should be offered to major benefactors. What is apparent from this and the US research (reported in Chapters Six and Fourteen) is that:

a) In US academic institutions relationships are nurtured from the earliest contact in the expectation that parents and graduates will in due course contribute to the institutions attended, to enhance the facilities, improve opportunities for the next generation of students, provide bursaries for those best able to take advantage of them and strengthen the reputation of the schools and universities to the benefit of all alumni.

b) Much of the support is in the form of commitment to the endowment funds which is made as part of a planned giving programme.

c) In this field as elsewhere donors manifest a range of motivations and requirements for involvement, appreciation, recognition and respect. A model which was mentioned more than once is that of the Chancellor's Court of Benefactors at Oxford University; donors reported their enjoyment of a long-term relationship and the feeling of engagement and appreciation beyond the fact of the financial contribution.

At the time of writing the funding of universities is a major issue. Support from private individuals is only one aspect. Nevertheless, there are points arising from this research which should be highlighted.

20. Institutions of higher education should be encouraged to develop a culture in which:

◆ **Development (fundraising) is part of the leadership responsibilities of vice-chancellors and heads of colleges and departments.**

◆ **Appropriate volunteers and donors are invited to participate in the governance and leadership structures.**

◆ **Development should be given the necessary status and resources.**

21. Working with others such as the Treasury, the implementation of the recommended changes to and simplification of tax mechanisms should be supported, particularly to encourage planned giving.

Charity Commission

The important role of the Charity Commission was recognised, particularly by advisers. But there was criticism of the perceived bureaucracy involved in establishing and managing a charitable trust. This was regarded as regrettable, since those who were thoughtful about this issue pointed out that the creation of a trust is a manifestation of a strategic commitment to philanthropy, an irrevocable allocation of a sum (often substantial) to charitable purposes, the employment of a structure which encourages family involvement and the opportunity to consider a philanthropic legacy for the family. It represents and requires a mature and considered approach.

But the downsides – administration, publicity, openness to applications for support – were also noted. Sometimes these negative views were reinforced by criticisms of the reported focus of donations, albeit to registered charities. The lead critic was regarded as being Luke Fitzherbert of the Directory of Social Change[12].

A perhaps unexpected consequence of the introduction of Gift Aid for any level of gift, and the possible use of this combined with a CAF account for small gifts, is that some people feel that they can enjoy the benefits of the relationship with the beneficiary without the inconveniences of a trust. Some advisers took this view as well. There is a risk that the rate of formation of trusts will decline, as people choose the option (one-off gifts) with the same tax benefits and less external interference, and requiring less time and less commitment.

There was also adverse comment on what were seen as the mixed messages about the desirability or otherwise of the allocation of company shares to a charitable trust, with the risk of pressure to diversify at a later date.

There was very limited discussion about the role of the Commission as it monitors operational charities. However, those involved in asking for money commented on the sometimes conflicting ideas, as they saw it, expressed by trustees but citing the Commission, about the need on the one hand to invest in fundraising, and provide detailed reports and feedback, and on the other to minimise fundraising and administration costs. With the advent of Guidestar UK (see above) more information is likely to be available about other charities in similar sectors.

(See Chapter Seven on the practice of giving and Chapter Twelve on the views of advisers.)

[12] See Appendix Four for his comments.

22. The Charity Commission should:

◆ **Continue its programme of simplification of guidelines and procedures.**

◆ **Promote the simplified form of charitable trust developed with the Association of Charitable Foundations[13].**

◆ **Clarify the position in respect of the encouragement of entrepreneurs to allocate company shares to a foundation, and the possible conflict between this encouragement and later advice to the trustees of such a foundation to diversify investments and therefore to sell some or all of the shares.**

Employers

We have noted the importance of workplace experience in engendering the practice of giving, particularly in American companies. This goes far beyond payroll giving, important though this is for employees at all levels. What is involved is the establishment of a corporate culture, led from the top, in which there is a clear expectation that "corporate social responsibility" extends beyond the allocation of a proportion of shareholders' funds, and includes individual commitment to charitable projects. These could include projects local to the workplace as well as regional or national charities chosen by staff.

It should be recognised that in the US, where this approach is more common, it is seen as the responsibility which goes with, and perhaps sweetens the response by others to, the very high salaries at the most senior level. We observe in the UK media reports of what are seen to be massive pay packages (including bonuses, share options and pensions) being sought and justified for senior executives on the basis of having to compete in a world market, especially the US. But, as we have seen, in the US there are philanthropic expectations from senior executives which are not replicated in the UK. Neither of the chief executives of leading UK companies interviewed for this research said they felt a responsibility or pressure to be a major personal donor, although they are proud of what their businesses do.

We saw that none of those interviewed in the UK were using payroll giving, although with the 10% incentive then in place it was the most tax-efficient mechanism for employees and those receiving a company pension. Some employers, particularly in the City, provided such schemes

[13] Available on the *Philanthropy* UK website www.philanthropyuk. org and in the *Guide to Giving* (see bibliography).

and sometimes added contributions to employee donations. For example, a bank employer of an interviewee in the adviser group promotes Give as You Earn, in a scheme in which employee contributions are matched pound for pound. An amount up to £250,000 goes in to the corporate charitable trust to match up to £200 per month from individual employees. Over the period of the research the tax incentives for payroll giving meant that £100 from a high rate taxpayer could be worth almost £400 a month to the recipient charity. Only 180 out of 1,200 staff, mostly high-earning, participated in the scheme.

Those who advocated internal as well as external corporate league tables included City high earners; they suggested that awareness of individual generosity on the part of senior staff would help to address the antipathy to "fat cats" and the companies which employ them. More than one suggested that a proper component in performance appraisal would be assessment of the employee's contribution to the reputation and respect in which senior staff members are held, internally and externally: factors affected by awareness of effective volunteer activity and financial contributions on the part of the individual.

It is recognised that there are very different attitudes to public statements of generosity in the UK. Nevertheless, there is powerful evidence from this research that UK citizens who have experienced what might be called US-style programmes of senior staff engagement come to see them as a positive factor in developing their approach to philanthropy.

(See Chapter Four on early influences on giving, Chapter Seven on the practice of giving, Chapter Ten on encouraging philanthropy and perceptions of entrepreneurs, Chapter Twelve on the views of advisers on the need for expectations of levels of giving and Chapter Fourteen on the US experience.)

23. Major employers in the City and industry, supported by organisations such as Business in the Community, the CBI and the Institute of Directors, as well as City professional associations, could promote the expectation and practice that senior staff will contribute financially and in other ways to the communities in which they live and work by:

◆ **Encouraging staff earning above a certain level to pledge a percentage of their income, as well as volunteering time, to charitable causes.**

◆ **Raising awareness internally and externally about these exemplary levels of giving by senior management.**

◆ **Backing such encouragement by process facilitation, such as the provision of advice on establishing a simple charitable trust[14], and expert guidance on the various tax-efficient mechanisms[15], including payroll giving, and arranging for appropriate systems to be in place at the time of bonus awards.**

◆ **Introducing and promoting a payroll giving scheme on a continuing basis[16].**

24. Employers could facilitate the process by:

◆ **Making this the responsibility of a senior executive director.**

◆ **Ensuring that directors lead by example, with an internal report on levels of giving.**

◆ **Making a public commitment to this programme, and to reporting on it in the annual report, including the overall amount given by senior staff as a percentage of their income.**

◆ **Leveraging the impact by matching the amount contributed by staff.**

◆ **Working with local community foundations, Business in the Community and other organisations to identify suitable projects and institutions for support.**

◆ **Putting in place practical and workable arrangements for staff to give time.**

[14] For example, the simple short form model approved by the Charity Commission in 2003, with the Crystal Mark of the Plain English Campaign is available from the *Philanthropy* UK website, www.philanthropyuk.org

[15] Freely available in The Guide to Giving, also on the *Philanthropy* UK website.

[16] This has been facilitated by the introduction in the March 2004 budget of a grant to SMEs to enable them to invest in the systems required for payroll giving.

Those concerned with donor guidance and the promotion of philanthropy

Several organisations are exploring and developing approaches to providing guidance to would-be donors. In addition, charities themselves have a major interest in awakening the concern of high net worth individuals. At the same time we have noted various themes, emerging in the US as well as the UK, which are relevant here.

Attitudes to financial security and benchmarking

It has been suggested that helping individuals to assess their real level of financial security would have potentially high rewards for charitable causes. We have seen that the wealthy, even at relatively high levels of net worth, tend not to regard themselves as completely financially secure and therefore not as able or ready to make sizeable financial contributions to charity as might be expected from their net worth. This feeling is stronger in the UK where "new rich" are more recently wealthy than in the US[17]. There is also an absence of tax mechanisms that allow for gifts of capital to be deferred while benefiting from the tax relief at the time that the promise is made to give in the future. At the same time, interviewees report that an increase in their net worth would lead to greater charitable giving. This is a complex issue but clearly there would be significant rewards to the non-profit sector if an approach could be developed which would address this conundrum.

We have also noted that another area of uncertainty concerns the appropriate level at which to contribute. As we report in Chapter Four some with new wealth, not being members of traditional faith communities, were unsure about the suitable level of donation. As we quoted:

> The question was how much to give. The closest I got to advice was the historical tithe. The problem is that the more you have, the bigger the percentage you could give. There are no guidelines – there should be: what do you need and want to keep.

> (See Chapter Five on the idea that "having more money" would increase giving, Chapter Eight on financial security, Chapter Nine for the discussion on tithing and Chapter Twelve on the attitudes and experience of professional advisers.)

Although not commented on in the UK or US research, we also note the development of US-based commercial donor advisory services, such as Fidelity.

A productive strategy would be for those with an interest in this field (including organisations such as the Association of Charitable Foundations, the Community Foundation Network, the Charities Aid Foundation, the Institute for Philanthropy and New Philanthropy Capital) to work together with advisers and wealth managers to develop a process whereby people with substantial assets are helped to understand the actual level of

[17] Particularly in banking and IT; in general wealth was realised on flotations earlier (in the late 80s and early 90s) in the US than in the UK.

financial resources they have available, the amount they feel they need to allocate for themselves and heirs, and the amount remaining that they could give to charity should they wish to do so. We have already referred to the work of Claude Rosenberg in this area. His approach is described in Appendix Two.

Part of the guidance could be about benchmarking levels of giving.

25. Organisations concerned with encouraging philanthropy should give further thought to developing a framework for providing guidance to potential donors, and the formulation of a strategy to promote it.

Professional advisers

As The Giving Campaign has identified[18], financial advisers are reluctant to raise the question of charitable giving. This is less strong among those who advise the wealthy (see Chapter Twelve), since there are major issues of asset management and tax avoidance.

Some identified the need for their clients to receive education and advice on philanthropy, including developing an understanding of their level of wealth, their long-term needs and what they might be able to afford.

Nevertheless, we noted a range of attitudes to the role of the professional adviser. Some, whether lawyers or bankers, took an active part in encouraging their clients to consider charitable giving, and particularly the establishment of a trust, as part of their estate planning and asset management. Others, a minority, took no interest in their clients' philanthropic interests and would not raise the subject.

We also saw that a very small minority of interviewees had been encouraged in the development of a philanthropic strategy by their advisers, although they may have followed technical recommendations about structure once they had decided to set up a trust.

[18] *Advice worth Giving.* The Giving Campaign October 2001.

The Giving Campaign has developed a programme, working with trade bodies, to ensure that advisers generally get the information and training they need, and to develop materials advisers can give to their clients, explaining the options for tax-efficient giving.

It is recognised that those advising the wealthy on matters of major asset management and estate planning (whether accountants, lawyers or bankers) can have a major influence on their clients.

It was also noted that there was an occasional lack of knowledge among advisers about all the mechanisms of giving; there was a range of views about the minimum level of endowment needed to establish a trust, and no-one identified the benefits of a flow-through trust supported by payroll giving, even though this was the most tax-efficient way of giving at the time (because of the additional 10% incentive), and many had clients who were high earners in the City. Such trusts may be established with no endowment at all, and may even attract matched funding from an employer.

26. Professional advisers should encourage the development of family strategies for philanthropy by:

- ◆ **Raising the question of charitable giving with their clients.**

- ◆ **Ensuring that that they have the information, training and materials they need to give to their clients, explaining their options for tax-efficient giving, and also the benefits of developing a strategy for philanthropy.**

- ◆ **Helping clients to understand their actual level of wealth, the amount they want and need to allocate for themselves and heirs, and the amount remaining that they could give to charity should they wish to do so.**

Socially Responsible Investment (SRI)
In Chapter Nine we explore the generally very negative attitudes to SRI. The term is used to cover a wide range of investments and strategies. With one exception, even those who expressed a positive interest have a tiny percentage of their portfolio invested in this way. Nearly all of these are women, as well as a married couple who take a shared interest in their philanthropy, and one is a very committed Quaker. As we saw, most of those interested in SRI are people who are actively engaged in the voluntary sector, and meet people as fellow trustees or directors of a community foundation who are professionally concerned with these issues.

The most likely way to increase the interest in and take-up of SRI is for it to be promoted by investment managers as part of a mainstream portfolio, basing the recommendations on the likely rate of return. It may be that people who are supporting areas of social deprivation with their charitable donations will also gradually become aware of the opportunities and benefits offered by investing in these areas.

Clearly, there are problems of definition. A way needs to be found to distinguish between investing in FTSE companies with good track records and various types of community development investment in deprived areas. The timing of this research means that it was not possible to test attitudes to the availability of the community investment tax relief or Charity Bank[19]. Some advisers have now added these to their portfolio of information.

27. It would be useful to organise a debate among those who have been promoting SRI in the face of this perhaps disappointing evidence. This might reveal a need for generic marketing of the concept.

The wealthy

These implications and recommendations are not aimed at the constituency which is the basis of the research – high net worth individuals themselves. However we note a few points.

Summarising the benefits and opportunities of wealth identified by many interviewees we find three main strands. People wanted:

◆ To be able to do their best for their (extended) family.

◆ To engage in what might be regarded as selfish pleasures.

◆ To have the opportunity to be a catalyst for change – with money or time or both.

---

[19] Information on both these concepts is available from the Charity Bank website at www.charitybank.org.

Some, particularly those building a company or career, were focusing their energies on that entrepreneurial activity; it could be said that their desire to make a difference was directed at their business. However, once they had retired or sold their businesses, many looked for fulfilment in the non-profit sector. Few in this position were younger than their late forties or early fifties.

By the end of the interview, some people realised that in the course of the discussion they had said that they:

◆ Felt reasonably secure (75%).
◆ May have set up or inherited a foundation (about 50%), although relatively few such foundations had major endowments.
◆ Were holding on to most of their assets while not intending to pass them to their children.
◆ Were not currently planning significantly to increase the level of their giving or the size of their foundation.

(See Chapter Two for levels of wealth and number of foundations, Chapter Eight for financial security and the discussion on passing money to children and Chapter Nine for gifts to charities.)

Their own awareness of the inherent contradictions in their position produced an introspective exploration of the discrepancy in their approaches, reinforcing the point that in this area, as elsewhere, ideas are fluid and inconsistent.

Some had advisers who are in a position to guide them, including how to involve their children and how to think about how much they can afford. There are many commercial organisations with an interest in addressing these issues. However, several interviewees had identified an absence of guidance on how much they might afford and how much they "should" give. Some were unclear as to the best way to develop a philanthropic strategy.

The Guide to Giving was developed in 2003[20] by *Philanthropy* UK in reaction to the perceived need for and absence of a comprehensive and independent guide for would-be donors of means to all aspects of developing a strategy for philanthropy, and the range of mechanisms available in the UK.

28. *The Guide to Giving* is recommended as a useful introduction and reference book to those who would like to explore matters for themselves.

The media

We have reported the shared perception that the media in general do not contribute to a positive understanding of and encouragement of significant philanthropy. Whether based on antipathy to wealth creation or cynicism

[20] Available free on the *Philanthropy* UK website www.philanthropyuk. org and from the Association of Charitable Foundations.

about motives, negative reporting is seen as a real deterrent. If this continues unabated it risks undermining other efforts to embed the values and practices of giving among the "mass affluent" and wealthy. It is not proposed that accurate investigative reporting be diluted, but that the media, particularly newspapers and magazines, could help to promote role models and celebrate philanthropy.

(See Chapter Ten on perceptions of philanthropy and Chapter Fourteen on the US experience.)

29. The media could do far more to promote a giving ethos by:

♦ **Accurately reporting of major gifts and imaginative volunteering.**

♦ **Promoting and celebrating of role models from a range of backgrounds.**

♦ **Providing more objective information about wealth creation and creators.**

♦ **Developing an informed understanding of the tax regime as it relates to charitable giving.**

♦ **Accurately and consistently reporting giving in relation to wealth.**

♦ **Including people's charitable interests and commitments as part of any general profile, whether in the *FT* or *OK!***

Further research

Some of the questions in this research deliberately echoed those posed in US research. In Chapter Fourteen differences in traditions, practices and motivations between the US and the UK are explored, but there is not a detailed comparison of more qualitative data concerning the nature and extent of causes supported, the approach to involvement, attitudes to financial security and passing money to children. Notwithstanding the fact that the US research by Paul Schervish and John Havens was published in January 2002, it might be interesting to explore this area further.

A more strategic approach would be to plan to align the composition and timing of future research, to make comparison and mutual learning more robust. This could not only be extended to other countries, particularly within the EU, but could form the basis of a planned cohort analysis over time (say every three or five years), with the purpose of monitoring trends within and between countries.

Conclusion

What we have learned is that there are several ways in which a more widespread culture of giving and involvement by the wealthy could be developed and reinforced. They require committed and sustained investment by a number of players – the government, employers, umbrella bodies, community foundations, professional advisers, the media. Some are relatively minor; others will require radical transformation.

We note that there are courses of action which are within the control of charities themselves – those who have the greatest immediate and long-term interest in attracting the support of the wealthy. As we see in Chapter Five, apart from perceived capacity, the single factor which is the most important trigger to increased giving is being moved by a cause. There is much more that charities themselves could do, in all sectors, to make people aware of an issue or opportunity, to produce a reaction of anger, amazement, passion, enthusiasm – and the response that something should and could be done, and that the individual can make a difference.

However, many of the proposals will only achieve maximum impact if reinforced by the activities of other people. If each individual constituency were to implement the proposals within their control or influence, there would be some progress. But for a sustained improvement there have to be real changes in the practices, attitudes and values of a range of decision- makers and opinion-formers. If all, or most, of the recommendations were to be put into practice there would, over the years, be a radical improvement in the exercise of elite philanthropy, and the development of a stronger culture of giving in the UK.

Appendix One (a) – Donor questionnaire

Getting involved

1. People become involved in giving money away in different ways. How did you first become interested?

Prompt if necessary:

◆ Was asked by someone I know/like/respect/wanted to impress.
◆ Was moved/excited by a particular cause/relationships to the community.
◆ Set up a foundation as part of financial planning strategy/family estate planning.
◆ Set up a foundation or CAF account as a result of a major bonus/windfall.
◆ It's always been something that we have done in my family.
◆ It's expected among the people in my community/with whom I mix.
◆ Other.

Influences

2. Some people come from a family with a tradition of philanthropy. Is that so in the case of yourself or your [spouse/partner]? [explore further]

3. Are there any particular attitudes to philanthropy passed on to you by your family? Were there any attitudes you rejected?

If yes to either: What were these?

4. Which of your philanthropic interests, if any, would you attribute to your family traditions or upbringing?

5. How important, if at all, was religion in your family while you were growing up?

Not very important/fairly important/very important/other.

6. How important would you say it is in your life now?
Not very important/fairly important/ very important/other.

If important, what is your current religious affiliation? ....

7. Do you attend a particular place of worship? Which is that? About how often do you attend services?

8. How, if at all, do your religious beliefs influence your giving? Do they lead you to support particular types of institutions? Or to give more?

9. From where would you say you developed your ideas about the obligations of wealth?

Family/religion/friends/experiences/ethical beliefs/business associates/other.

10. To what extent has social pressure influenced your philanthropy?

Relationships with recipients, giving time, rewards of giving

11. In general, how do you see the relationship with the organisations you support?

[What do you expect from them if you give a large sum of money? How do you expect them to involve you? Should you have a say/more of a say in how the money is spent? Prompt about board/committee membership.]

12. Are you currently serving on the boards or committee of any non-profit institution?
        If yes: which ones?

13. Do you undertake (other) volunteer activities? If yes, what do you do?

14. In the last year, how much time have you contributed for charitable causes?

….. hours per week or month

15. What are the main reasons for serving on the non-profit boards of which you are a member? How did you first join?

16. (If has a partner.) During the past year, did your partner volunteer any

time to a charitable organisation? If yes, what kind? Which organisation?

17. In general, why do you continue to give? What are the satisfactions you get from giving?

18. Do you expect some kind of recognition? Does it vary for different causes? For different levels of support?

19. Do you think that supporting causes should give you special access to the services they offer?

Networks

20. Do you know other significant contributors to the causes to which you give major support? How do you meet them?

[Prompt: know them anyway/through business/place of worship/meet at events organised by the charity/sit on same board/other.]

21. Are there certain organisations or types of organisation which you feel under particularly strong pressure to support? If yes, where does this pressure come from?

22. In general, do you enjoy the social aspects of philanthropy, such as attending galas, dinners, private views and other special events, or is this something you prefer not to get involved in?

What was the last such event you attended and why?

23. Do you think there is a "club" or network of givers? What do you think about that? [Prompt: inclusive or exclusive? Do you want to be part of it?]

Criteria for choosing specific causes

24. When you consider the requests you receive do you have certain criteria in mind about what you want to fund and why? If yes, what type of criteria do you use?

25. Do you review all requests on an individual basis?

26. Some people make a distinction between supporting organisations from which they have or expect to benefit (such as educational or cultural

institutions) and those with which they have no personal links (such as environmental or political disasters overseas, medical research, inner city playgrounds, the homeless). What do you think about this? Do you make a distinction?

27. Leading on from that, some people have a view about those aspects of life which the state should pay for, from tax revenue. What do you think about that? Which causes do you think should receive more or less public money?

28. Do you have a different attitude to causes which receive significant sums of public money? Do you know (roughly) how much public money the main causes you support receive?

Attitudes to philanthropy and wealth

29. Thinking generally about philanthropy, some people are critical of philanthropy and philanthropists, with suggestions that it encourages dependency or is associated with social snobbery. What is your reaction to these sorts of criticisms, and what are your views?

30. What do you think about the way major gifts are reported in the media? What do you think about the media attitude to giving generally?

31. What do you think about the status of philanthropy in the UK?

32. Have you ever made a donation that provoked criticism or debate? If yes, how did you feel? What was your response?

33. What is your response to the view that for wealthier members of society, philanthropy is not only a matter of personal choice but is an obligation?

Strongly agree/agree/disagree/strongly disagree/other (explain/specify).

34. What do you think about the concept of allocating a proportion of your income to charitable causes?

35. Suppose there is a range of attitudes towards wealth, from feeling free to enjoy it as one wishes to feeling responsibilities and obligations about its use. Where would you place yourself on such a spectrum?

36. If you feel you do have such responsibilities, to whom do you feel you have these responsibilities?

37. From time to time there are debates about how much wealth the law should allow people to pass on. What are your views about inheritance tax? Should people be allowed to decide what will happen to most of their wealth after death?

38. Do you think that inheritance has negative or positive economic consequences for society?

39. People have differing attitudes about the amount of wealth they should leave to their children. What are your views about this?

40. Have you tried to educate your children during their formative years about your family's relative affluence? If yes, how do you approach it? At what age do you think it is appropriate to do this?

41. Have you done anything to help educate your children about giving, volunteering or otherwise helping others? If yes, please give examples

42. On a scale of 0 to 10, how financially secure do you feel?
(0 = not at all secure, 10 = extremely secure)

43. What is the minimum level of net worth you would need for a rating of 10 on this scale? £………..………………

44. How confident are you that the next generation of your family will be as financially secure as you are now?

45. Having financial resources provides wealthy people with opportunities that others may not have. Are you, your partner or your dependents involved in any of the following?

   a) The start-up or running of one or more businesses.

   b) Financial support of politically related activities or causes.

   c) Management of a family charitable foundation.

46. Are there other activities for your personal development or enjoyment you can think of for which wealth provides a special opportunity for you,

your partner or other members of your family? If yes, please give examples.

47. Some donors do most of their giving in their lifetime while others give primarily through legacies. Have you decided to do your own giving in mainly one way or the other? Why is that?

48. If 100% represents the money that you expect to leave in your will, approximately what proportion do you plan to bequeath to charities?

49. Do you intend to leave it to charities you've supported in the past, or to others, or are you planning to create your own charitable trust?

50. There is increasing interest in socially responsible investment (SRI). Socially responsible investments are designed to have a positive financial return, but also have explicit social and/or environmental goals. Is this an idea you find attractive? If yes, give one or two examples of investments you think of as socially responsible.

51. What would be your best guess of the % of assets you and your partner and children control which is devoted to socially responsible investing?

52. How likely are any of the following changes to get you to increase the amount of socially responsible investing that you do?

	Very likely	Likely	Not very likely	Not at all likely
a) Large financial institutions begin supporting	☐	☐	☐	☐
b) Investment returns become competitive	☐	☐	☐	☐
c) SRI becomes more diverse in terms of causes covered	☐	☐	☐	☐
d) There is increased documentation and validation of the good done by social investing	☐	☐	☐	☐
e) You receive a positive recommendation from your investment adviser	☐	☐	☐	☐

f) A trusted friend becomes involved and recommends SRI ☐ ☐ ☐ ☐

53. Would you describe yourself as someone who didn't inherit any wealth from your family, who inherited

Less than £^{1}/4m/between £^{1}/2m and £1m/>£1m/>£5m/>£10m.

What about your partner?

54. Do others share in your giving decisions? Explain.

To whom have you given, how much, which mechanisms

55. What organisations or causes have you supported over the past three years/do you now support?

Organisation.................................... Amount given............................

56. Would you provide a list of your donations?

57. Thinking about your giving last year, what is the % split between the giving you do about which you feel passionate, and the giving that you feel less passionate about.

.... passionate
.... less passionate
‾‾‾‾
100%

58. Please estimate what % of your giving went to organisations which you, your partner or children are or have been directly involved in as volunteers, members, participants or trustee.

.... involved
.... others
‾‾‾‾
100%

59. To whom you made your last three gifts of £1,000 or less? (Organisation and amount.)

60. What were the main reasons for making these donations?

61. Were any of the gifts you have made over the past year given in

association with others? With whom? Is there a difference about the type of gift you give like this?

62. When you consider the donations you have made, which are the one or two about which you feel particularly pleased? Why is that?

63. Have you ever regretted giving money to any organisation? If so, please explain.

64. Are there any links between the sources of your education or wealth and your giving? If yes, what are they?

65. Have you ever made an anonymous gift to a charitable institution? If yes, please explain to whom and why?

66. On a scale of 0 to 10, how satisfied are you with the current effectiveness of your donations?

67. Is there anything specific you would like to do differently with respect to the giving you do? If yes, what would that be?

68. Which of the following changes would be likely to increase the overall amount you give to charitable causes?

	Very likely	Likely	Not very likely	Not at all likely
a) Your net worth increases	☐	☐	☐	☐
b) You have better information about the tax benefits of giving to charitable causes	☐	☐	☐	☐
c) Tax incentives for you are increased	☐	☐	☐	☐
d) You get more time to think about your philanthropy	☐	☐	☐	☐
e) You find a new cause about which you care passionately	☐	☐	☐	☐
f) You get better information than you now do that your current donations are making a real difference	☐	☐	☐	☐

69. Does worry about the risk of financial mismanagement in some charities affect the amount or nature of your giving?

70. Thinking about giving mechanisms, how do you give/have you given recently? Prompt.

Through a charitable trust
Through a CAF account
Through GiftAid
Through payroll giving
Giving shares
Other

71. Why did you choose that particular mechanism? What do you think about this mechanism or structure?

72. If you have set up a trust or foundation, what were the main reasons for doing so? Would you do it again? Please explain.

73. How would you like to see this develop after your death? Who would you like to run it in the future?

74. Have you changed the mechanisms or the amount you give because of the recent tax changes?

75. Have those changes had any other impact on your philanthropy?
Do you anticipate that they will in the future?

76. What do you/would you feel about your money leveraging tax benefits for you? For the charity?

77. There are many different views about how much money people can or might give away. This is sometimes expressed as a proportion of total income, and sometimes people will say that they need £x to live on, and money to be given away will come out of the balance.
How do you look at it?

78. What proportion of your annual income do you think you give away/roughly how much is your annual giving?

79. What is it about philanthropy that has been and is most important to you?

Asking others for money

80. Have you ever asked people for money for causes you support? What did you think about the response?

81. Do you know people of substantial means who make few or no donations to charity? If yes, does the fact that they don't contribute affect your attitude to them in any way?

Personal information

82. Age.

83. Marital or partner status (past and present).

84. Annual household income.
Less than £100k ☐
£100,000 to £250,000 ☐
£250,000 to £500,000 ☐
£500,000 to £1m ☐
£1m to £2m ☐
£2m to £5m ☐
£5m to £10m ☐
£10m to £20m ☐
Over £20m ☐

85. In which category would you place your immediate family in terms of assets?
Less than £1m ☐
£1m to £5m ☐
£5m to £10m ☐
£10 to £20m ☐
£20m to £50m ☐
£50m to £100m ☐
£100 to £200m ☐
£200m to £500m ☐
Over £500m ☐

86. Education.

      School/university/postgraduate/professional/other.
      Has there been a family tie to any of these?

86. Current (or former, if retired) occupation?

87. Where do/did you work?

88. Does your partner work? Occupation? Place of work?

89. What is the primary source of your wealth?

90. Where do you currently live? For how long? Before?

91. Do you have any children? How many?

92. Which clubs do you belong to, if any?

93. Would you identify yourself as Labour/Conservative/Liberal Democrat/other? ....

Do you have any other comments?

Is there anyone else you think I should speak to?

Thank you so much for your time.

Time taken for interview ....

Appendix One (b) – Asker questionnaire

For those who solicit support from the wealthy

Getting involved, focus of activity

1. I'm talking to you because of your experience in soliciting support from the wealthy. Why do you do this? How did you become involved?

Probe: Concern for cause
        Was asked by a particular person
        Felt it was something I could do
        Other

2. How do you see the balance between directing the strategy for the fundraising and actually cultivating prospects and asking for money?

3. How much time do you think you have spent on this in each of the last three years? How was this allocated?

4. How do you see the relationship with the organisations you support in this way? What do you expect from them if you give a significant amount of time? How do you expect them to involve you?

[Probe about board/committee membership.]

5. Do you think your perceived status in an organisation is important for effective fundraising?

6. Are you currently serving on the boards or committee of any non-profit institution? If yes, which one(s)?

7. Do you undertake (other) volunteer activities? If yes, what do you do?

8. If you could only make time for one of the organisations to which you give time, which would it be, and why?

9. (If has a partner.) During the past year, did your partner volunteer any time to a charitable organisation? If yes, what kind? Which organisation?

10. What satisfaction do you get from giving time and expertise? Why do you continue to do so?

11. What kind of recognition do you expect? Does it vary for different causes?

Influences

12. Some donors and major fundraisers come from a family with a tradition of philanthropy? Is that so in the case of yourself or your spouse/partner?

Asking for money

13. What, in your view, are the key factors which will determine whether someone will support the cause for which you are seeking support?

14. Does it matter whether or not you have made a financial contribution?

15. Do you think there is a "club" or network of givers? What do you think about that? [Probe: inclusive or exclusive?]

16. If you believe there is such a network, what kind of people want to be part of it?

17. To what extent, and in what circumstances, does social pressure influence philanthropy?

18. In general, what do you think about the social aspects of philanthropy, such as attending galas, dinners, private views and other special events? How important is this for major prospects and donors? Does this vary for different causes?

19. Coming on to recognition, to what extent do you think this is important for the donor? Does it vary for different causes?

20. Do you think that supporting causes should give donors special access to the services they offer? To what extent is that an important factor for prospective donors?

21. Have you ever solicited an anonymous gift to a charitable institution? If yes, please explain what happened and why?

22. Some people make a distinction between supporting organisations from which they have or expect to benefit (such as educational or cultural institutions) and those with which they have no personal links (such as environmental or political disasters overseas, medical research, inner city playgrounds, the homeless). What is your experience of this? Does your approach vary with the causes for which you are seeking support?

23. Leading on from that, some people have a view about those aspects of life which the state should pay for, from tax revenue. Is this a point raised by those from whom you have sought support?

24. Do you think that people have a different attitude to causes which receive significant sums of public money?

25. How do you identify the prospects from whom you expect to solicit support?

26. What do you think is the most important success factor in asking for money?

27. Have you ever been very surprised or disappointed at a response? Please explain.

28. What is your experience in asking for support from less established givers, such as younger age groups and celebrities?

Attitudes to philanthropy and wealth

29. What do you think about the way major gifts are reported in the media? What do you think about the media attitude to giving generally?

30. Do you think philanthropy has a high status in the UK?

31. Have you ever solicited a donation that provoked criticism or debate? If yes, how did you feel? What was your response? What do you think was the reaction of the donor?

32. What is your own response to the view that for wealthier members of society, philanthropy is not only a matter of personal choice but is an obligation?

Strongly agree/agree/disagree/strongly disagree/other (explain/specify).

33. Some donors do most of their giving in their lifetime while others give primarily through legacies. Have you been involved in asking people for legacies? What was your experience?

34. Thinking about the attitudes to philanthropy and wealth which we just discussed, how do you use them in your approach to raising money?

35. Do you also contribute financially to the causes which you serve by helping to raise money? What are the reasons for your response?

36. Do you contribute to other causes? Explain.

Money and mechanisms

37. For whom have you been involved in raising money over the last five years? How much do you think has been raised for each of these organisations through your efforts?

Organisation	Amount
………...……	……….
………...…	……….
………...……	……….

38. When you have been raising money, what was the focus of the donation? [Prompt: capital(construction)/endowment, core funding(revenue support)/specific programme or project/unspecified.]

39. What do you think were the main reasons that people made major gifts to these organisations?

40. Why do think they made the contribution to [organisation name] as opposed to another [organisation type (e.g. hospital, children's charity, opera house)]?

41. Thinking about giving mechanisms, do you know the mechanisms used by those from whom you obtain support?
Prompt
Through a charitable trust
Through a CAF account
Through GiftAid
Through payroll giving
Giving shares
Other

42. Why do you think they chose that particular mechanism?

43. What are your views about the relative merits of those mechanisms?

44. How do you think those from whom you solicit support feel about their money leveraging tax benefits for them? For the charity? Do you use this when asking for money?

45. Do you know people of substantial means who make few or no donations to charity? If yes, does the fact that they don't contribute affect your attitude to them in any way?

46. Is there anything else you would like to say about your experience of asking for money from the wealthy?

Personal information

47. Age.

48. Marital or partner status (past and present).

49. Current (or former, if retired) occupation?

50. Where do/did you work?

51. Does your partner work? Occupation? Place of work?

52. Where do you currently live? For how long? Before?

53. Do you have any children? How many?

54. Which clubs do you belong to, if any?

55. Would you identify yourself as Labour/Conservative/Liberal Democrat/other? ....

Do you have any other comments?

Is there anyone else you think I should speak to?

Thank you so much for your time.
Time taken for interview ....

Appendix One (c) – Adviser questionnaire

For those who provide professional advice to the wealthy

1. I'm talking to you because of your experience in advising those with substantial means about the disposition of their assets. What has been your experience in this field? What level of wealth do they represent, in terms of income and assets (range)?

Annual household income of your client base?

Less than £100k	☐
£100,000 to £250,000	☐
£250,000 to £500,000	☐
£500,000 to £1m	☐
£1m to £2m	☐
£2m to £5m	☐
£5m to £10m	☐
£10m to £20m	☐
Over £20m	☐

In which category would you place your clients in terms of assets?

Less than £1m	☐
£1m to £5m	☐
£5m to £10m	☐
£10 to £20m	☐
£20m to £50m	☐
£50m to £100m	☐
£100 to £200m	☐
£200m to £500m	☐
Over £500m	☐

2. What are the main concerns of those whom you advise?

3. In discussion, what proportion of your clients suggest charitable giving, establishing a foundation or some other form of philanthropy as part of their asset management?

4. Does this vary with different types of client?
Prompt: age/gender/religion/ethnic origin/source of wealth/other

5. In what circumstances do you suggest that charitable giving might form part of their wealth disposition? What form does your advice take? What structures do you suggest?

6. What is the reaction to your suggestions?

7. Does this vary with different types of client?
Prompt: age/gender/religion/ethnic origin/source of wealth/other

8. What proportion of your clients, do you think, share a view that for wealthier members of society, philanthropy is not only a matter of personal choice but is an obligation?

Do you think this has changed over the last five to 10 years?

9. From time to time there are debates about how much wealth the law should allow people to pass on. Do your clients express views about inheritance tax? To what extent do they think that people should be allowed to decide what will happen to most of their wealth after death?

10. People have differing attitudes about the amount of wealth they should leave to their children. What is your experience of this?

11. Some donors do most of their giving in their lifetime while others give primarily through legacies. What is your experience?

12. If 100% represents the money that people expect to leave in their will, approximately what proportion do your clients plan to bequeath to charities?

13. I am asking donors how financially secure they feel? (0 = not at all secure, 10 = extremely secure). What would you expect the answer to be for most of your clients?

14. What do you think is the minimum level of net worth your clients would need for a rating of 10 on this scale? £...............

15. How confident do you think they are that the next generation of their family will be as financially secure as they are now?
Very confident/moderately confident/not very confident/ not confident at all.

16. There is increasing interest in socially responsible investment. Socially responsible investments are designed to have a positive financial return,

but also have explicit social and/or environmental goals. Is this an idea any of your clients find attractive?

If yes, give one or two examples of investments they think of as socially responsible.

17. What would be your best guess of the % of assets your clients control which is devoted to socially responsible investment?

18. Some donors come from a family with a tradition of philanthropy. What is your experience? What are your views about this?

19. From where would you say your clients develop their ideas about the obligations of wealth?

Family/religion/friends/experiences/ethical beliefs/business associates/other.

20. Do their views vary with different types of client?

Prompt: age/gender/religion/ethnic origin/source of wealth/other.

21. To what extent does social pressure influence philanthropy?

22. Do you have any other comments?

Is there anyone else you think I should speak to?

Thank you so much for your time.

Time taken for interview ....

Appendix Two

Extract from *Wealthy and Wise* by Claude Rosenberg, Jr., October 1998

Philanthropy also enriches donors' lives

As an investment manager for over 40 years, I have observed that too many people, including many of those with considerable wealth, find their money more a source of worry than pleasure. Many needlessly deprive themselves of personal amenities. Others wish to invest in their community and help address its needs and problems, yet they unnecessarily deprive themselves of this pleasure too.

But there is a solution to all these problems: by adopting a more generous approach to charitable giving, donors can experience an exceptional sense of personal satisfaction and fulfilment while improving society. This is certainly true of myself and my wife. Other than our love of one another and our family, philanthropic activities have represented the high point of our lives. The same is true for countless individuals I know personally, from varying levels of wealth. I have also seen how planned giving strategies can strengthen family bonds, while conveying essential values and social responsibility to children and young adults.

Further, charitable involvement can prove extremely stimulating and simply be a tremendous amount of fun. In sum, philanthropy can truly add joy to your life and to others around you. *Wealthy and Wise* and its newtithing approach has already helped make positive changes in the lives of many donors and recipients. The door is wide open for many more donors to duplicate such achievements.

How to begin: meet your personal needs first

Throughout my career, I have seen at first hand the understandable fears and concerns that plague people about their finances. We all want to live comfortably, right through our senior years; we want to protect ourselves against catastrophic illness that could threaten our prosperity; we want to plan our estate well, provide the best education for our children, and enhance our family's way of life; we want to prudently nurture our investment assets, and not jeopardise the income they produce.

Given these desires, my strategy first requires that you do some basic financial planning to cover such essentials as housing, health coverage, income needs in retirement, and estate plans. This is crucial for determining how much philanthropy you can undertake. Only after you have addressed these issues can you gauge your disposable income and the abundance of your investment assets.

Know the current value of donations past and present

Our perceptions of the value of money become easily outdated. We often fail to acknowledge the shrinking purchasing power of money and the growth rate of our own investment assets. This misperception may distort into ineffectively low sums how much we think we can spend, or how much we think we can give to charity.

When I was young, a pack of chewing gum sold for a nickel. The same pack costs 50 cents today. Does this mean that gum is now expensive? Of course not.

Our incomes and other assets have likely grown along with inflation. In fact over the long term, they probably have even exceeded it.

For example, the stock market for the past 20 years has risen at far more than three times the inflation rate over that time. So as donors, it's important to adjust our thinking to the passage of time. For example, when someone asks us today to donate $1,000 we may be taken aback. We may only relate to what $1,000 used to buy, making the request seem audacious in what it asks us to forego. In truth, assuming the $1,000 is more like what $100 was in my childhood, the request probably isn't that bold at all.

Similarly, if you give consistently to charity, remember that donating the same dollar amount year after year actually means you are contributing increasingly less money in terms of buying power, while the value of your own investment assets may well be rising.

Table 1, *The effects of inflation*, depicts the declining buying power of $1,000 over the past 23 years. If you already give to charity, are satisfied with your recipients' accomplishments, and have seen your own assets beat inflation and meet your obligations, the "ravages of inflation" documented here may give you good reason to adjust your giving upward.

Table 1 The effects of inflation

If you donated...	in....	an equivalent donation in 1998* would require...
$1,000	1997	$1,030
$1,000	1990	$1,246
$1,000	1985	$1,525
$1,000	1980	$1,933
$1,000	1975	$3,003

OR...

If in 1998 you donate..	it is equivalent to a donation of...	back in...
$1,000	$971	1997
$1,000	$803	1990
$1,000	$656	1985
$1,000	$517	1980
$1,000	$333	1975

*For 1998, a conservative 3% inflation forecast was used. For any further updated figures, see www.newtithing.org

The advantage of *newtithing* – a modern, reliable formula to determine prudent giving levels

Affordability is the single biggest issue for most individuals as they explore charitable giving. Ironically, people's assessments of how much they can afford to donate is often significantly flawed. First, people typically misjudge their affordable giving capacity by forgetting to consider the tax deductions that reduce the actual cost of a gift. For example, if you are in the 30% tax bracket, a gift of $1,000 doesn't actually cost you $1,000. After the charitable deduction, it really costs you just $700. If you are in the 50% bracket, the net cost is only $500. And if you donate an appreciated security rather than first convert that security into cash, the capital gains tax savings further lowers your cost by perhaps another $100 to $250.

Second, throughout history, the typical approach to charitable giving has been to base donation amounts on gross income alone. Consider the custom of "tithing", normally defined as donating 10% of one's yearly income. Although tithing constructively encourages philanthropy, its financial "formula" is actually outmoded in two significant ways:

♦ **Tithing does not distinguish between *gross income* and the far more important sum "surplus income[1]"**, i.e. the income available after you have paid taxes and met living expenses.

♦ **Focusing exclusively on income, tithing ignores a significant portion of most people's financial wherewithal: their *investment assets*** – the savings accounts, money market funds, bonds, stocks, real estate and other investments that may generate additional income or capital appreciation[2]. Clearly, we need to change our attitudes about our money and its usage. We need a more realistic gauge of our surplus funds.

How to employ *newtithing*

How secure you feel about your level of investment assets significantly influences how much you are comfortable spending or donating, a decision also influenced by your annual income, financial obligations, and capital gains or losses. You can make your financial assessment retrospectively by surveying your standing over the past year, or by projecting into the coming year.

Assume you want to know what a comfortably affordable donation would be for an individual or household with an annual reported salary income of $100,000 and with $500,000 of investment assets yielding an additional income of $30,000. The following five steps of newtithing enable you to track your net worth and gauge how much you can comfortably afford to spend or donate now or in the future.

1. **Determine your "surplus income"** – *your income minus living expenses and income taxes*. To determine your surplus income, subtract from your total income of $130,000 (salary plus investment income) your living expenses (estimated at $75,000) and income taxes (estimated at $30,000). This leaves surplus income of $25,000, which will likely land in an investment vehicle, thus adding to your investment assets.

2. **Determine your "discretionary funds"** – *your surplus income plus the amount of change during a year in your investment assets*. To conservatively estimate your discretionary funds, we have assumed

[1] i.e "disposable income".
[2] Investment assets do not include one's home or related possessions that do not produce income and that normally should be considered "untouchable" during one's lifetime.

352

the following average results that produce new end-of-year investment asset totals: a) fixed income investments (savings accounts, money market funds, bonds, etc…), representing 30% of capital, will not appreciate at all in price; and b) equity investments (stocks, as well as real estate, private investments, etc…) representing the other 70% of your portfolio, will at least appreciate enough over the long-term to exceed inflation. Regarding these equity investments, we have assumed annual 7% gains in value, leading to a conservative 5% increase over your start-of-year $500,000 in investment assets, for an increase of $25,000 in surplus income plus $25,000 in expected capital appreciation. Eureka! An increase of $50,000 over your start-of-year investment assets.

3. **Determine your "total available assets"** – *your discretionary fund plus start-of-year investment assets.* Combine your $50,000 in discretionary funds with your $500,000 in start-of-year investment assets, for a total of $550,000 of total available assets.

4. **Calculate the true cost of your potential donation(s)** – *your potential donation minus its tax savings.* Determine an appropriate donation level for the year (to illustrate, say $10,000). Assuming that you make your donations in appreciated securities, factor in the resulting tax savings from your contemplated donation. In the 30% marginal tax bracket, the savings on a $10,000 charitable donation is $3,000, making the next cost of your donation only $7,000.

5. **Determine how much better (or worse) off you are after your donation** – *your total available assets minus your after-tax donation.* A $10,000 gift costing you only $7,000 would reduce your $550,000 in total available assets to $543,000. This sum amounts to an 8.6% increase over your start-of-year investment wealth, well ahead of expected inflation and allowing for additional expenditures. Compounding your investment assets at 8.6% for the next five years would raise your asset wealth to $820,000 in half a decade. Not a bad outcome for a generous soul.

What if disaster strikes? Won't I regret donating anything?

If you were to sustain a drastic financial loss – say 90% of your earning assets – I can't guarantee that you won't be sorry about many things. But your charitable contributions probably won't be one of them.

To illustrate this, compare two individuals with initially identical financial profiles: (See Table 2). One of them, the "donor", makes a charitable gift that costs $50,000 after the tax deduction, while the other, the "non-donor", gives nothing.

Table 2 Charitable contributions and drastic financial loss – $

	Donor	Non-donor
Original investment assets	1m	1m
Less donation after tax saving	50,000	0
Investment assets before loss	950,000	1 million
Less 90 percent loss	(855,000)	(900,000)
Remaining investment assets	95,000	100,000

Source: Newtithing Group, San Francisco

Note the tiny difference in remaining investment assets between the donor and non-donor after the loss – just $5,000, a miniscule $1/2$ of 1% original investment assets and approximately 5% of the remaining sum after the loss. Clearly the charitable gift is neither the culprit of financial loss nor the straw that breaks the camel's back.

Newtithing guidelines

To suggest possible giving levels for various taxpayer groups, we examined IRS categories of adjusted gross income, and conservatively projected disposable income and investment assets for each taxpayer level. A distilled version of suggested levels appears in Table 3, Possible affordable donation levels.

[3] Securities, real estate, and private investments using 1995 IRS income data extrapolated through year-end 1997. To produce conservative estimates, values of personal housing, IRAs, 401Ks, etc, were omitted, as were increases in values of real estate and private investments from 1995-1997.

To create conservative calculations for preserving your financial security, our findings purposely underestimated investment assets[3] and potential growth figures, and overestimated personal expenses.

While we do not suggest donation increases for the two lowest IRS taxpayer categories, the average individual in the next five higher taxpayer categories can afford to give substantially more to charity. Certainly, the higher the taxpayer category, the far greater is the potential for increased charitable giving. Around two-thirds (or nearly $100bn) of increased donations could come from the top taxpayer bracket alone. In *Wealthy and Wise*, I offer specific suggested donation amounts for more than 130 different financial profiles of adjusted gross income and investment assets. Further, our website (www.newtithing.org) offers a calculator which allows you to enter and analyse your financial standing, in order to determine your suggested donation amount.

Our suggestions strive to account for the respective needs of each taxpayer group. For the groups represented by the four lowest levels of income ($94,400 of average reported salary or less) and investment assets shown in Table 3 (below), the donations suggestions assume that individuals need their investment assets to grow as much as is realistically possible. For the next two higher levels, however, the suggestions emphasise more moderate asset growth. And for the top level, suggested donations are recommended (simply for illustrative purposes) so as to maintain asset wealth roughly even with inflation. Not surprisingly, people in the top taxpayer category are the very ones who should be considering far more generous deployment of their wealth. Their abundant investment assets qualify them as excellent candidates for "capital reduction" through substantially increased charitable donations during their lifetime.

Table 3 Possible affordable donation levels – $

Average reported salary[4]	Average investment assets[5]	Discretionary funds[6]	Average actual donations[7]	Possible affordable donations[8]	Cost of possible affordable donations[9]
29,910	55,820	2,000	660	660	555
50,090	104,290	9,300	1,250	1,250	883
69,060	182,210	18,800	1,970	2,900	2,018
94,400	474,160	44,100	3,010	8,800	5,386
173,310	1,548,530	129,300	7,460	33,800	17,846
337,520	4,449,400	350,400	17,190	140,000	73,640
811,990	19,945,880	1,495,700	101,700	1,337,000	869,127

Source: Newtithing group, San Francisco

4 From year-end 1995-1997; conservatively estimated since it excludes income growth of 11.8% (Table B-27, Economic Report of President, 1998).
5 See footnote 3 opposite.
6 Composed of: surplus income and current-year capital gains for each asset group (for commons stocks, a 20-year annualised total return was assumed 9.29%).
7 The average of: IRS itemised donations and Giving USA's estimate of donations made by non-itemising filers.
8 Based on "average investment assets" and "discretionary funds".
9 Assumes donations of appreciated securities. Assumes the wealthiest group's donations exceed the maximum level for allowable tax deductions, thereby reducing their average tax deduction rate to 33%.

Appendix Three – Bibliography

Edwards, Laura (2002) *A bit rich? What The Wealthy Think About Giving.* London: The Institute for Public Policy Research

Goodison, Nicholas (2004) *Securing the Best for our Museums: Private Giving and Government Support* HM Treasury

Goldberg, Jacqueline and Kosmin, Barry A (1998) *Patterns of charitable giving among British Jews* London: Institute for Jewish Policy Research

Hudson, Mike (2003) *Managing at the Leading Edge: New Challenges in Managing Nonprofit Organisations.* London: Directory of Social Change

Hurd, Howard & Lattimer, Mark (1994) *The Millionaire Givers: Wealth & Philanthropy in Britain.* London: Directory of Social Change

Lloyd, Theresa (2003) *A Guide to Giving.* London: The Association of Charitable Foundations

Ostrower, Francie (1995) *Why the Wealthy Give: The Culture of Elite Philanthropy.* Princeton, NJ: Princeton University Press

Passey A, Hems L & Jas P (2000) *The UK Voluntary Sector Almanac.* NCVO

Pharoah, Cathy & Walker, Catherine (2002) *A Lot of Give.* Charities Aid Foundation

Ritchie, J & Lewis, J (ed.) (2003) *Qualitative Research Practice: A Guide for Social Science Students and Researchers.* London: Sage Publications Ltd

Rosenberg, Jr., Claude (1998) *Wealthy and Wise: How You and America Can Get The Most Out Of Your Giving Through "Newtithing".* (Synopsis of the book Wealthy and Wise.) Newtithing Group, San Francisco

Schervish, P & Havens, J (2002) *The Mind of the Millionaire.* Social Welfare Research Institute, Boston College

The Giving Campaign has produced a number of guides and research reports on a range of related topics including *A Fundraiser's Guide to Tax-Effective Giving* and a report on attitudes of financial advisers. They can be obtained from The Giving Campaign website at www.givingcampaign.org.uk.

Appendix Four – Criticism of trusts and foundations

In Chapter Seven there was reference to Luke Fitzherbert of the Directory of Social Change and his criticisms of certain practices by some charitable trusts. We decided to offer him the opportunity to comment. This is his response.

At the Directory of Social Change (DSC) we are used to being attacked for our editorial criticisms of the work of some charitable trusts – our more frequent expressions of praise or admiration naturally arouse no corresponding response.

Our critics generally fall into one of two groups; donors who fail to fully realise that when they have given money to a charitable trust it is no longer "theirs" but belongs to a public institution; and their lawyers (who feature prominently again in the comments given to Theresa Lloyd).

We have some sympathy with the donors, who may not have fully realised the consequences of their decision to hand over the money to a trust. They could, of course, keep both total privacy and full tax effectiveness by simply giving the money anonymously to existing charities of their choice. However, the attraction of putting it into a trust is considerable; you get the promise of "perpetuity" that will bring credit to your generosity – and to your name if you like – indefinitely into the future.

However, a consequence of endowing a charitable trust is public accountability. We exist to support the development of a strong, respected and effective voluntary sector and – as one Chief Charity Commissioner pointed out to one of the complainants – this is helped rather than hindered by "the beneficial light of public scrutiny".

Indeed, our support from the Commission has been consistent. The present Chief Commissioner, John Stoker[1], personally launched a recent DSC guide whose promise of independent comment on major charities had been publicly and powerfully deplored in advance of publication.

With the lawyers we sometimes have less sympathy. Their letters can verge on the unseemly and we have found it necessary from time to time to threaten a complaint to the Law Society about the making of improper legal threats – so far, a rather successful tactic.

[1] Geraldine Peacock CBE has been appointed Chair of the Charity Commission from July 2004.

What do we criticise? Mainly a lack of transparency, as unfortunately there are still trusts that do not meet even the most basic factual reporting requirements of the Charity Commission. In particular, it has been a long fight to get all trusts to reveal who gets their grants, though now there are only a small minority of offenders. Even now, the grants lists, and the accompanying annual reports if they exist, may not give enough information to form a fair view of their work – an entry in a grants lists such as "St Johns: £1,000,000", for example, does not take one much further.

We do not normally criticise individual grants, except as illustrations of some more general issue. For example, we do not like it if a trust funds medical research without either using the established process of peer review, or explaining what it does instead – we believe that some trusts are at risk of being blinded by plausible applicants from specialist fields which they do not fully understand.

Generally, we simply look to see evidence of careful grant-making – or even, at best, of unusual and imaginative funding. Ideally, we will know about this from the trust's own reports. Whether or not we would personally like the results is neither here nor there. Some programmes that we have repeatedly praised for their energy and enterprise would certainly not be to my personal taste; an example is the success of Carnegie UK in making standard practice the "interpretation" that is now to be found attached to heritage locations almost everywhere. I don't like it, but it was a remarkable achievement in the use of modest funds to achieve lasting social change.

We do comment on particular grant-making policies. For example, it seems to us that there was already an over-emphasis on three-year grants even before the lottery and then the government weighed in with ever greater tranches of such funding on top of what trusts already provided. We think trusts should at least have considered looking for alternative approaches. But, as far is reported, the few that have, like the Baring Foundation, are the exception rather than the rule.

There are also several practices which are perfectly legal in themselves but which we believe work to the disadvantage of charities generally and which we would like to help discourage. They include:

◆ Payments for professional services to trustees or to those connected with them (unless, to quote the Charity Commission, "there is no realistic alternative").

◆ The making of charitable grants to expensive fee-charging public schools and charitable hospitals – an issue expected to be addressed at last in the forthcoming Charities Act[2].

◆ A failure to diversify the investments of a trust (unless not doing so is authorised in the trust deed). There have been a number of huge losses of charitable funds as a result of trustees failing to do this – the Nuffield Foundation and the Ronson trusts are two names that come to mind.

◆ More generally, and along with the Charity Commission, we regret the absence in a trust of any clear policies by trusts about what they are trying to achieve with their grants.

This list is not exhaustive and there may be new issues in the future, especially as the Charity Commission is becoming more energetic in calling for effective annual reports from all charities. But the point remains the same. The Directory of Social Change will continue to describe the work of these charities as fully and as fairly as it can. To repeat, they are public institutions and not private ones. The dangers to philanthropy, if both the best and the worst of trust practices are not kept before the public eye, can be clearly seen not so far away. So bad is the public reputation of the many smaller endowed trusts and foundations in the US that the Attorney General of New York has formally proposed that the freedom to create such charities be extinguished. We at DSC believe it is useful for us to try to promote the best in philanthropy and to deter practices that damage its reputation.

[2] The draft Charities Bill was published in May 2004 and this issue is under review.

Index

Altruism
    and giving   101
Anonymous giving   154
Appreciation   85, 114, 311
Asian   193
    importance of family   188
    sense of community   57
    social networks   54
    the immigrant experience   58, 289
Asking for money   127, 243
    anonymity   253
    being a donor as well   128
    donors
        attitudes to responses   131
        awakening an interest   129
        offering public recognition   130
        styles of asking   128
        support from the recipient   130
        targeting and timing   129
    effectiveness   248
    fashionable causes   251-252
    importance of in-house team   246
    key factors   249
    origins of fundraising activity   244
    recognition   253
    rejections   247, 256
    role of the fundraiser   246
    social pressure   252
    special access   252
    tax mechanisms   254
Association of Charitable Foundations   34, 320, 323
Attitude of government   238

Beacon Awards   241
Being a catalyst for change   81
Belief in the cause   78
Benefits of inheritance   190
Board membership   296
    and obligation   295

attending events   94
comparisons with the US   295
time given   107

CAF accounts   144, 157, 167, 168-169 173, 319
Cathy Pharoah   28-29, 275
Causes supported
    arts and culture   42
    education   44
    environment   45
    health and medical research   44
    overseas development   45
    religion   45
    social welfare   43
Causes supported in the US   300
    political parties   301
Changing attitudes   238
Charitable trusts   46, 48, 71-73, 85, 99, 105 109, 115, 126, 133, 135-136, 139, 140, 144, 153, 155, 157, 159-165, 167-169, 180, 182, 187, 190, 193, 196, 198-199, 203, 214, 216-217, 219-220, 255, 266-267, 270, 276, 278, 282, 293, 298-299, 304, 310, 319-322, 324-325
    development after death   219
    disadvantages of   163-165
Charities Aid Foundation   28, 34, 48, 139, 157, 275, 309, 323
Charities as pioneers   229
Charity Commission   34, 158, 163, 315, 319-320
Charity remainder trusts   292, 298, 311-312
Christian
    tithing   207
Claude Rosenberg   208, 274, 324
Communal responsibility   228
Community foundations   96, 158, 167-168, 293, 308-309, 322, 325, 329
    Tyne & Wear   69

Community Foundation Network 34, 308-309, 323
Comparisons with the US
    altruism and philanthropy 284
    attitudes of the wealthy 282
    attitudes to the state 282
    board membership 295
    characteristic of the elite 283
    community responsibility 282
    factors likely to increase giving 297
    financial security 296
    focus of giving 299
    gifts in kind 294
    gifts of works of art 293
    giving as a norm 284
    immigrant society 288
    satisfaction with giving 297
    tax structures 291
    the workplace experience 284
    values 282
    welfare state 287, 289
Conscience 81
    role of 87, 89

Department of Culture, Media and Sport 316-317
Department for Education and Skills 317
Developing a philanthropic strategy 71
Directory of Social Change 164, 319
Donation as membership 99
Donor management 115
Donor-beneficiary relationship
    essential features of 112

Early experiences of giving 63
    a personal response 73
    school and university 63
    the realisation of wealth 66
    workplace initiatives 65
Estate planning 217
Events
    attending 92
    role of 93

Factors likely to increase giving
    UK 104-105
    US 297
Family businesses 189
Financial mismanagement 104, 122, 305
Financial security 175
    advisers' views of 259, 274
    and age 179
    and family businesses 178
    and gender 180
    and level of wealth 177
    and source of wealth 178
    attitudes to 323
    feelings of 176
    inconsistency of perception 180
    US 296

Gift Aid 157, 165,167
    advisers suggesting 271
    complaints and 255
    tax incentives and 172
Gifts in kind 47, 276, 294, 312
Gifts of shares 157, 169-171, 255, 271, 299
Gifts of works of art 293
Giving
    altruism and 101
    an obligation to the less fortunate 87
    and advocacy 229
    anonymously 154
    appreciation 85
    appreciation and recognition 114
    arts and culture 42
    being a catalyst for change 81
    belief in a cause 78
    CAF accounts 168
    causes supported 42
    changes which might increase overall level of 104
    commitment 147
    community foundations 167
    consultation and influence 119
    control over how money is spent 85
    defining a place in history 85

Giving (cont)
    developing a strategy for   71
    developing with experience   70
    direct involvement   146
    early experiences of   63
    education   44, 65
    emotional response   73
    encouraging children   143
    environment   45
    feeling passionate about   147
    governance   120
    health and medical research   44
    history of family giving   55
    in lifetime   218, 265
    influence of faith   51
    influence of school and university   63
    involvement   146
    levels of   46
    linking expertise, time and money   84
    mechanisms   156
    most satisfying donations   147
    motivations for   49
    networks   91
    new learning opportunities   86
    obligations   303
    overseas development   45
    payroll giving   171
    personal involvement   74
    planned   41
    political   199
    posthumous   217
    putting something back into society   88
    regional context   46
    regretted donations   151
    religion   45
    response to personal experience   86
    satisfaction with   150
    self-actualisation   83
    shares   169, 255
    sharing the decision   145
    sharing with a partner   92
    small gifts   142
    social   142

    social engagement   91
    social opportunities and aspirations   94
    social welfare   43
    special access   97
    tax incentives   172
    the donor network   91
    the moral dimension   87
    the nature of the cause   138
    through private company   171
    time   52, 106, 108, 279
    tithing   207
    total by UK population   276
    why people give   78
Giving and advocacy   229
Giving circles   95
Giving in the UK context
    by individuals   276
    by mass affluent   277
    by the wealthy   277
    causes supported   278
    charitable trust donations   276
    corporate gifts   276
    estimating value of   275
    levels of participation   279
    tax efficiency   278
Goodison Review   191, 294, 312, 317

Hindu   264, 273
Home Office   315

Importance of the family   188
    delaying the decision   189
    expectations   189
    family businesses   189
Influences
    community   55
    contribution to society   57
    faith and religious tradition   51
    family values   54
    inter-locking   79
    of family discounted   59
    the immigrant experience   58

Inheritance tax   191, 262
    benefits of   196
    double taxation   191
    impact on families   192
    ineffectual mechanism   193
    largely avoidable   194
Inland Revenue and Customs & Excise   314
Institute of Jewish Policy Research   289,
    300
Interview times   42
Interviewees
    age   38
    annual household income   37
    asking for money   127, 243
    attitudes to financial security   323
    attitudes to tithing   207
    board membership   296
    causes supported   42
    charity remainder trusts   292
    developing a philanthropic strategy   71
    disposition of wealth   304
    early experiences of giving   62
    education   39
    extent of passionate commitment   147
    family businesses   189
    feelings of financial security   176
    foundations   167
    gender   39
    geographical origins   41
    giving shares   170
    giving time   108
    government responsibilities   225
    leaving money to charity   216
    marriage and children   39
    most satisfying donations   147
    net worth   36, 177
    payroll giving   172
    political giving   234
    private company giving   171
    reducing state support   290
    regretted donations   151
    religious backgrounds   41
    sample and data   35
    security and age   179
    security and gender   180
    security and source of wealth   177
    setting up trusts   159
    small donations   141
    social obligations of wealth   201
    source of wealth   39-40, 177-178
    support from recipient charity   130
    the immigrant experience   58
    trusts and other charitable activity   199
    unsolicited requests   136

Jane Tewson   74
Jewish   155
    community   63, 92, 129
    community ties   46
    importance of family   188
    insecurities   180
    network   251
    positive response   271
    sense of community   57
    social networks   54
    the immigrant experience   58, 289
    tithing   207

League tables   239
Learning   86
Leaving money to charity   216
Lifetime giving   265
Linking expertise, time and money   84
Luke Fitzherbert   319

Major gifts   124, 126, 129, 138
Making a difference   105, 133, 298
Margaret Thatcher   62, 69, 111
Mass affluent   277
Mechanisms for giving   156
    attitudes to   159
    CAF accounts   157, 168-169
    charitable trusts   157, 159-165
    community foundations   158, 167-168
    description   156
    Gift Aid   157, 165-167
    gifts of shares   169-171
    payroll giving   171-172

Index

Mechanisms for giving (cont)
    private company giving   171
    tax incentives   172-173
Media   327-32
    role of   232
Moral dimension   87
Motivations   77
    being a catalyst for change   81
    belief in the cause   78
    creating a better society   81
    having an impact   81
    obligation to the less fortunate   87
    psychic benefits   83
    relationships   89
    self-actualisation   83
    the moral dimension   87
Muslim   46
    tithing   207
National pride   82
Nature of the cause   138
Network for Social Change   95
Networks   54, 91, 95, 231, 251
NHS   151, 230, 243, 289
Non-domiciled   115, 173, 192

Obligations   46, 53-54, 56-57, 201, 245
    board membership and   295
    of state   225
    philanthropic   202
    social   263
    to the less fortunate   87
    where they lie   205
Opportunities provided by wealth   198
    charitable activities   199
    other interests   200
    political activities   199
    setting up businesses   199
    support of family members   200
    the arts   200
    time and money   201
Ostrower, Francie   30, 281-283, 295, 300
Oxford University Court of Benefactors   84, 115, 318

Passing money to children   186, 261
    a 'moderate' amount   187
    source of wealth   261
    traditions of family inheritance   186
    too much   187
Passing values to children   180
    awareness of wealth   183
    effectiveness   185
    family and school   182
    professional advisers   184
    self-reliance   184
    skipping a generation   185
    starting young   181
Payroll giving   157, 171-172, 208, 274, 316, 320-322, 325
    interviewees and   41
Personal approach
    importance of   136
Personal experience
    response to   86
Philanthropy definition   27
Place in history   85
Planned giving   310
Private company giving   171
Professional advisers   31-32, 34, 184, 258, 324-325
    advice on structuring philanthropy   268
    charitable trusts   269
    client concerns   266
    estate planning   264
    Gift Aid   271
    gifts of shares   271
    response to advice   271
Putting something back   88

Quaker   46, 203
    tithing   207

Recognition   115-118
Reciprocity   86, 110, 145
Recommendations
    charities   304
    Charity Commission   319
    charity remainder trusts   312